SECOND EDITION

The Writer's Guide to
Queries, Pitches & Proposals

by Moira Anderson Allen

ALLWORTH PRESS
NEW YORK

Published by Allworth Press, an imprint of Allworth Communications, Inc., 10 East 23rd Street, New York, NY 10010.

Cover and interior design by Mary Belibasakis

Page composition/typography by Integra Software Services, Pvt., Ltd., Pondicherry, India

ISBN: 978-1-58115-743-7

Library of Congress Cataloging-in-Publication Data

Anderson Allen, Moira.
The writer's guide to queries, pitches & proposals / by Moira Anderson Allen. 2nd ed.
    p. cm.
Includes bibliographical references and index.
ISBN 978-1-58115-743-7 (pbk. : alk. paper)
1. Authorship–Marketing. I. Title.

  PN161.A55 2010
  070.5'2—dc22

                    2010020928

Printed in Canada

Contents

Acknowledgements

A great many people helped with the development of this book. My thanks go out to all the contributors who have provided chapters, sidebars, or just incredibly useful quotes (yep, you're all in the "bios" section)—and to the many writers who have offered their queries, book proposals, and other "pitch" letters to this updated edition. Thanks also to Tad Crawford of Allworth Press, for his guidance on the first edition of this book and his interest in bringing forth a second edition. And a special thanks to my very patient husband, Patrick, who only twitches slightly when I shove a manuscript in front of him to review...

Introduction

When I wrote the first edition of this book in 2001, the publishing world was a tough place for writers. Competition was fierce and breaking in to new markets was a perpetual challenge.

Eight years later, the only thing that has truly changed is that the marketplace is tougher. During those eight years, a host of Internet publications and "webzines" have arisen—and a great many of them have folded. Writers hoping for a new and ever-expanding online marketplace have been disappointed; paying Web-based markets have become scarce and quite a few have crashed and burned without paying their writers. A great many print publications have also folded (ironically, often citing "Internet competition") as the reason for their failure.

As a result, today more writers than ever are competing for a shrinking number of "slots" for their articles, stories, columns, and books. A tightening economy has only added to the challenges writers face.

That's why it's more important than ever to understand how to make a good "first impression." You may be able to write a brilliant article, story, or novel, but if you don't know how to get your foot in the door and convince an editor of this, that brilliant work will remain forever nestled in your sock drawer. Because, you see, an editor doesn't want you to send in that brilliant work. An editor wants you to explain *why* you should be permitted to send in your work. In short, to get your foot in the door, you need to know how to "pitch."

This book will help you do just that. Whether you're seeking to break into a new magazine with a dynamic article, launch a column, sell your first book, get started as a business or commercial writer, or find a grant or funding to support your writing efforts, this book will give you tips on how to succeed, along with real-world examples of pitches that *have* succeeded. Whether you're a newbie trying to crack your first markets or an experienced writer hoping to reach bigger and better markets or branch out in a new direction altogether, this book will help.

Why try to cover so many different topics in a single volume? A better question might be—in today's economy, why buy eight different reference books for your shelf when one can do the job? The goal of this book is to do that job. To accomplish that goal, I've turned to a wide range of experts to provide their knowledge and advice. These writers remind us that where they have gone, you, too, can go—and they tell us how.

If there's a particular type of market you've been hoping to break into, chances are that you'll find the tools you need to get started within these pages. This book can be read in two ways: from cover to cover, or by selecting the specific topics or types of markets you want to learn more about. Each section is designed to stand alone, so you don't need to read the section on "article queries" if you're just interested in how to write a novel synopsis. (I do recommend, however, that everyone take a quick look at the "basics" outlined in chapter 1!) So dig in—and happy pitching!

Moira Allen

editors@writing-world.com

1

The Perfect Pitch: Ten Steps
to a Winning Proposal

The life of the professional writer is getting tougher. Good markets are becoming harder to find and to break into. Other markets vanish overnight without a trace—or change the rules without warning, imposing rights-grabbing contracts while offering little in return. Editors are flooded with inappropriate manuscripts and queries—often to the point that they no longer bother with rejection letters, but simply ignore material they don't want. Publications that were once friendly to freelancers are now closing their doors to unsolicited submissions, making it harder than ever to make a sale.

As a writer, however, your toughest challenge isn't cold-hearted editors or grabby contracts. It's the competition. Each year, more and more writers enter the marketplace. Many don't have a clue as to how to proceed, which accounts for the overwhelming number of badly written manuscripts and queries editors receive every day. Others, however, are good—and that's the problem: There are always more good writers than there are markets for those writers.

To compete with the thousands of "good" writers in the marketplace, you have to be able to develop queries and proposals that are more than simply "good." They have to be great. They have to rise *above* the competition. They have to stand out in every respect: Content, preparation, and presentation. They have to be as nearly perfect as you can make them.

The chapters that follow will discuss ways to craft "the perfect pitch" for a variety of markets. This chapter, however, will discuss essential steps and requirements that are basic to every proposal. Following these steps will give you the best possible chance of beating the competition—and making a sale.

Step 1: Research the Market

Proposals and queries aren't generic; there's no such thing as a "one-size-fits-all" pitch. Editors prefer proposals that are tailored for their publication and their audience—and they can tell when a writer has never seen their publication. Before you draft a query or proposal, therefore, you need to familiarize yourself with your target market. This usually means taking several steps:

READ THE GUIDELINES

One of the most commonly cited reasons for rejection is that the writer did not pay attention to a publication's guidelines, sending in a piece that was too long, too short, or totally unsuited to the publication. Today we have a profound advantage over writers a decade ago: We no longer have to send out self-addressed, stamped envelopes (SASEs) and wait weeks for a publication to send us its contributor's guidelines. Nor do we have to rely on outdated, inadequate market listings in printed guides. Today, most publications post their guidelines online, and if they don't, we can request them by e-mail. So there's absolutely no excuse *not* to review a publication's guidelines before sending a query.

This is your first and most important avenue of research. With luck, you may be able to determine exactly what a publication does and doesn't want. Guidelines generally specify the preferred word count for submissions, whether unsolicited submissions are accepted or whether a writer must query first, and how to submit (e.g., by surface mail, e-mail, with or without attachments, etc.). Often, they offer tips on style and presentation—e.g., "no first person accounts." They may even provide insight into the publication's target audience (e.g., "upscale travelers between twenty and forty-five, with incomes of $100,000 or higher...").

Unfortunately, not every publication offers detailed guidelines. Some may leave you wondering just what, exactly, an editor means by a statement like, "We're looking for crisp, exciting writing," or, "send us your best work!" (I've yet to see a publication that asks one to send their worst work...) And many publications still provide no guidelines at all. Which leads to the next step:

REVIEW THE PUBLICATION/PUBLISHER

Again, writers today have an advantage: Many periodicals now post sample material online. Many will post either articles from their current edition or archived articles from back issues—and many also will post the table of contents from their most recent edition. Book publishers may post sample chapters of new releases, which is a good way to determine the style and subject matter the publisher is currently seeking.

It's still a good idea to go beyond the Internet when researching a publication or publisher, however. If you're planning to query a print periodical, try to find a copy at the library or at the local bookstore or newsstand. Many periodicals offer free sample copies to writers, and most offer free copies to potential advertisers.

Never assume that magazines on the same general topic are, in fact, the same. I once examined two publications on "country lifestyles" and noted that while one featured ads for high-end furniture and expensive works of art, the second offered ads for such things as collectible frogs. And while there are several pet magazines on the market, each has a very different focus. In the world of dog magazines, the *American Kennel Club Gazette* focuses entirely on the world of purebreds and is aimed at breeders and exhibitors, while *Dog Fancy* targets the average pet owner and will consider articles on mixed-breed pets. *Bark!* tends to aim more toward the upscale pet owner and is more likely to display dogs in rhinestone collars or living in penthouses. And while many *Dog Fancy* readers loathe the idea of hunting, that's what *Gun Dog* is all about. These differences often aren't apparent in the brief listings available in *The Writer's Market*, and not all of these publications post guidelines online.

Examining a publication can also help you decide whether you want to *be* in that publication—or whether you belong in it. Do you really want your thoughtful article on women's health to be surrounded by ads for horoscopes and sex aids? Will your piece on "baking for the kids during the holidays" find a home in that magazine for young, single working women?

If you're researching a book publisher, again, don't rely on guidelines alone to help you choose. Check the publisher's online catalog to see what titles and authors it publishes. This will help you avoid the "rookie" error of sending your gritty police procedural to a publisher of cozy mysteries with recipes. In the nonfiction field, it will tell you whether a publisher accepts work by relatively unknown authors, or whether it only publishes material by "big names" or by authors with a string of degrees in the field.

Check your bookstore for more details about a potential publisher. Pick up a few of its books and look through them. Do you like what you see? Does the cover attract your attention, or make you want to put the back on the shelf—face down? Do you like the interior design, font, paper quality, and artwork, if there is any? Would you want to see your own title produced the same way? If not, keep looking.

The Internet offers yet another way to research book publishers: by looking up the Web sites of their authors. Even if the publishers themselves don't offer sample chapters, the authors may, and this will again give you a chance to review what the publisher offers without having to buy a bunch of books. If the author invites e-mail correspondence, you might also politely enquire as to the author's experience with a publisher.

This can also work for magazines; recently, a publication accepted an article query, but asked me to tell them what I "wanted" for the piece. Since the publication did not post its pay rates and I had no idea what their standard range might be, I contacted an author friend who had worked with this magazine in the past and asked his advice. He was able to suggest a fee range that was actually several hundred dollars more than I might otherwise have asked for—so never underestimate the value of networking in researching a market!

CHECK THE TERMS

Another question to consider before submitting a query or proposal is what your target market offers—and what it expects from you in return.

Your first question will undoubtedly be about money. How much does the market pay? Does it pay on acceptance or publication—and how soon after either? If you're pitching a book, what royalties does the publisher offer, and what sort of advance can you expect? Are those royalties paid on the cover price or net sales? A publisher that offers 7 percent royalties on the cover price will actually pay you more than one that offers 15 percent of net (the amount the publisher receives after bookstore and distributor discounts).

Money, however, is only the first question to ask. Another vital issue is the rights you'll be asked to grant to the publisher. More and more magazines are asking writers to give up huge chunks of rights, including all rights, with no increase in pay. Some require the right to resell or distribute your article to other markets, without passing a penny back to you. Fortunately, many magazines that request all rights are now adding terms that license reprint rights back to the author after a certain period, which means that we're no longer being asked (or being asked quite so often) to give up any chance of ever reselling a piece.

While some writers believe that one should never, under any circumstances, give up all rights to your work, others believe that at times the payoff may justify the sacrifice. If a market is particularly prestigious and will be a serious boost to your publications list, and/or if the pay is excellent, selling all rights may make sense, especially if you can negotiate the right to resell the piece later. However, I've seen demands for "all rights" from tiny publications with minimal circulation, and for as little as $25 in return. The bottom line is simple: Before pitching to any publication, decide whether they are offering something you want badly enough to justify what you may have to give up in return.

Step 2: Research the Competition

One of the key questions you'll need to ask before submitting a query or proposal is: "Has it already been done?" Has a similar article been published by that magazine (or by one of its competitors)? Is a similar column already available in syndication? Has the publisher already produced a book on your topic, or on something very close to your topic?

Researching the competition is vital when pitching a book proposal. If, for example, the publisher you're targeting has just issued a book about shape-shifting dragons who play rock music in New York, don't expect them (or, quite probably, any other publisher) to want another manuscript on the same theme. If you're pitching a nonfiction title, you'll be expected to discuss exactly how your book compares to the competition—which means that you'll need to know what else is available on the topic.

Fortunately, you can conduct much of this research during Step 1. By reviewing the titles on the shelves, or in a publisher's online catalog, you'll be able to determine whether that publisher has recently produced any titles similar to yours—or whether a title produced years ago is still a popular seller. You'll also be able to determine what competing publishers are producing, which can work to your advantage in your proposal. (A publisher may be more willing to accept a book that could compete favorably with a title issued by another publisher.)

Checking the competition for a magazine article can be a little more difficult. The primary question you will want to answer is whether the magazine has published a similar article (or even one on a topic close to yours) within the past year or two.

Fortunately, many periodicals now list their back-issue index online. This will give you a list of titles of previously published articles, even if you can't review their contents. Also, many magazines issue an annual index at the end of the year so if you want to request a sample copy, try to request the December issue.

For online publications, this research is generally even easier because most online publications archive their materials forever. However, this also means that the "two-year" rule no longer applies; if an online publication has *ever* published something on a particular topic and it's still available on their Web site, they are unlikely to be interested in another piece on the same theme. Conversely, by reviewing the pieces an online publication already has in a particular area, and then proposing something that augments their current inventory, you may be well on your way toward making a sale.

Step 3: Follow the Guidelines

This is one of the easiest and most important steps to follow when pitching a query or proposal—yet it is one of the most often ignored. Many amateur writers suppose that *their* article, story, or proposal will be the "rule-breaker"—the one that is so good that the publisher will just have to accept it, even if it breaks every "do" or "don't" in the publisher's guidelines. In reality, it just doesn't happen; again, editors cite "failing to meet our guidelines" as the most common reason for rejecting submissions.

On the bright side, this means that you can instantly elevate your proposal above the slush pile by simply *following* a publisher's guidelines. So before you send that pitch, be sure that you:

- **Send it to the right person.** Nothing says "I haven't read your guidelines" like mailing a query to an editor who left the company two years ago. Generally, a publication's guidelines will give you the name of the editor you should contact. In some cases, you may have to choose between multiple editors—e.g., one for feature articles, one for departments. Be sure you've chosen the right person! If in doubt, call the publication and ask.

- **Observe the limits on word-count.** Don't bother asking a magazine to consider a query for a 3,000-word article if they accept nothing longer than 1,800 words. Similarly, don't propose a 200,000-word book to a publisher who doesn't publish anything longer than 100,000 words. In some cases, you may also need to observe the minimum word-count: If a publication says that it publishes articles "between 750 and 1,500 words," don't try to sell them something that's only 500 words.

- **Stick to the rules.** If a publisher says "no first-person accounts," don't send a first-person account. If it says, "no stories told from the pet's point of view," don't send a manuscript allegedly written by your poodle. If it says "no humor or poetry," don't send humor or poetry. This may sound simplistic—yet it's the rule most often broken by new writers.

- **Understand the audience.** Often, a publisher's guidelines will describe the target audience in terms of age, gender, occupation, interests, and even income. Make sure that your proposal fits into the parameters of that audience. For example, if a magazine targets younger women, an article on retirement communities won't sell—but you might be able to pitch a piece on how to start planning for retirement at twenty-five.

- **Prepare your manuscript correctly.** Most publishers expect writers to understand the basics of manuscript format: double-spaced, wide margins, readable font, etc. Some, however, have specific guidelines. For example, while most editors don't care what font you use as long as it is readable, there are some who want manuscripts to be submitted in courier. Many publications have specific guidelines regarding how to submit materials electronically. Pay special attention to guidelines about how to query by e-mail: If the publisher says "no attachments," never send an attachment. Again, following this simple rule will cause your query to stand out over the dozens that not only ignore the publisher's guidelines, but are also prepared by writers who have not learned the basics of manuscript format.

- **Send what the publisher asks for.** If the publisher requests clips, send clips (presuming you have them); don't just refer the editor to your Web site. If the publisher asks for three sample chapters, send three sample chapters and no more. If the publisher asks for a certain number of pages of your novel (regardless of how many chapters that may be), send that number of pages. If the publisher wants a copy of your resume or CV, send it. Don't, however, send anything the publisher has not requested (e.g., unwanted clips or samples, letters of recommendation, reviews, etc.). Never assume that you can improve your case by sending something that the publisher doesn't want.

Step 4: Prepare Your Manuscript Properly

When editors are asked for advice on how to "beat the odds," the very first piece of advice they always give is "proofread, spell-check, and format your manuscript properly." Editors are deluged with improperly formatted submissions and submissions riddled with spelling and grammatical errors.

While good spelling and punctuation aren't enough to sell your idea, they *will* set your proposal apart from the majority of the slush pile. Proper format and a "clean" manuscript send the message that you are a professional—even if you've never sold anything in your life. And this is exactly the message you want to send.

Before you send out a query or proposal, therefore, be sure that you have not only run it through your computer's spellchecker, but that you have also proofread it visually. Remember that a spellchecker won't catch errors in word usage—"there" for "their," or "half" for "have." Errors like these are a dead giveaway that you haven't bothered to proofread your work.

If you have any doubts about grammar and punctuation, be sure that the grammar-checking function of your word-processor is turned on while you spell-check. This can be a handy tool for catching incomplete phrases, faulty punctuation, etc. Grammar-checkers can give faulty results when it comes to style, however, so don't rely on them to actually improve the quality of your writing itself.

If you aren't sure how to format a manuscript properly, find out before mailing anything to an editor. Writer's Digest Books offers an excellent book on manuscript format, and you can also find information on this subject online. Note that different types of proposals may require different formats—for example, a fiction synopsis may be either single- or double-spaced—so check with the publisher or agent for their preferences before submitting.

Step 5: Send a SASE

If you actually want a response to your proposal, be sure to include a SASE (unless, of course, you're submitting via e-mail). Now that we no longer have to type or photocopy our manuscripts each time we send them out, it has become customary to assume that submissions are "disposable"—i.e., not only does the publisher assume that you don't want your actual article back, there's no need for you to *have* it back. (You wouldn't actually send the same folded, rumpled submission to anyone else!)

If you *are* submitting materials that should be returned (such as photos), be sure to include a SASE with enough postage to cover their return. Remember that items weighing more than 13 ounces can no longer be shipped back to you in a stamped envelope, but must either be sent via metered mail or taken to a post office.

If you are querying a publisher outside your country, be sure to include at least two IRCs (international reply coupons) for a response. If you can obtain correct postage for that country, that's even better. If you live outside the U.S. and are submitting material to a U.S. publisher, you can purchase U.S. postage online at *www.usps.com.*

If you would like confirmation that an editor or agent received your query or proposal, include a self-addressed, stamped postcard for an immediate response. Just type a line on the back that reads something like:

Dear Author,

We have received your manuscript, "title," on

(Date): _____.

We hope to be able to respond to your manuscript by

(Date): _____.

(Signed): _____

The second line is optional, but useful if you'd like an estimate of when you can expect to hear from the editor or agent.

Unfortunately, it is becoming more and more common for editors to simply discard materials they do not want, without bothering with the courtesy of a rejection. This is a difficult situation for writers, but as yet does not mean that we can afford to discard the "rules" and submit queries or proposals without an appropriate SASE. However, as more and more publishers are choosing to accept electronic queries and proposals, writers today actually may find they have to spend very little on stamps, return postage, or even on paper and envelopes!

Step 6: Follow Up Appropriately

The question that plagues every writer when submitting a query or proposal is "how long do I wait for a response?" The first and most obvious answer is "as long as the guidelines tell you to wait."

Most publishers provide an estimate of how long it takes them to reply to a query or proposal. Wait until that amount of time has elapsed before following up, even if you've submitted by e-mail. (E-mail submissions are often answered more quickly than surface mail, but don't assume you can get an instant response to your query just because it's physically possible.) I also prefer to wait at least an additional two weeks before sending a polite inquiry—usually by the same medium as the original proposal (e.g., if a query was sent by e-mail, follow up by e-mail; if it was sent by surface mail, follow up by surface mail). See chapter 2 for more details on following up on an article query, and other chapters for specifics on following up on various other types of proposals.

Never be afraid to follow up on a submission. Many new writers fear that they will anger an editor or agent and incur a rejection by following up.

This is not true. Editors and agents are familiar with the standard courtesies and protocols, and will not think you are "over-eager" or unprofessional for following up. Quite often, they may simply be so busy that your material has gotten lost in the shuffle, and a follow-up is just what is needed to bring it back to their attention.

On a less positive note, following up can also help you determine whether *you* are dealing with a professional organization. If, for example, you have submitted your material to an agent, and have been assured repeatedly that it will be reviewed "in the next month," but never is, this is a good indication that you need to look elsewhere.

Step 7: Be Professional

This really isn't a step; it's a state of mind. It isn't a matter of how many works you've sold, or how well known you are in your field—it's a matter of how you conduct yourself. A new writer without a credit to his or her name can appear every bit as professional as a writer who has published a dozen novels.

It is remarkably easy to appear professional (so easy, in fact, that it's a wonder that so many writers fail to do so). All you have to do is the following:

- **Learn the basics.** Understand how business is conducted in this industry and act accordingly. Dozens of books have been published on the basics of the writing profession; you can also find this information for free on dozens, if not hundreds, of writing Web sites.
- **Be courteous.** No matter how tempted you are to send a nasty letter to an editor who has taken months to respond to your query, control yourself. This is especially true today, as editors are more in touch with one another via the Internet than ever before—which means that word can quickly spread about "problem" writers. The good news is that word also spreads about *good* writers. If you make a positive impression on editors, even when they reject your material, you're likely to make a good name for yourself.
- **Don't reveal your amateur standing**. If you've never published anything before, don't say you have. Don't describe yourself as a mother of three, or someone who has always yearned for publication, or a writing student, etc. Don't tell a publisher that your family, friends, or instructors all think you're wonderful. Instead, behave as if writing, and submitting material, is the most natural thing in the world to you—and publishers are likely to believe you!
- **Don't argue and don't complain.** When you begin to send out work, you *will* be rejected. Sometimes, it may seem that you are rejected for no good reason. Sometimes you'll get a letter that makes you wonder if the editor even read your query or proposal, as the reasons given for rejection seem to bear no relation to what

you actually wrote. When such things happen (and they will), you will not accomplish anything by asking the editor to reconsider—and you certainly won't accomplish anything by sending a nasty letter to the editor questioning his or her ability to read above the second-grade level. In short, even when editors and agents don't behave professionally toward *you*, it is still in your best interest to behave courteously toward *them*.

Step 8: Expect and Accept Rejection

Rejection happens. It happens a lot. It happens to everyone—to experienced pros as well as beginners. Often, your work will be rejected for reasons that have nothing to do with quality. Some common reasons for rejection include:

- **Not enough space.** If a magazine can only publish ten articles per month and receives five hundred, 490 of those articles will be rejected—even if they are excellent. Most magazines also have a standard "mix" of articles each month. Thus, if a magazine publishes one medical article every month and it receives three high-quality pieces, two will be rejected.

- **Something similar is already on file.** When you come up with the "perfect" idea for an article or book, don't assume that you're the only person to have thought of it. Often, your proposal will be rejected because a similar piece is already on file but hasn't been published yet, or because something similar has been assigned to another writer. Never assume, by the way, that if your query is rejected and you subsequently see something on a similar topic from that publisher, that someone "stole" your idea. It is very common for editors to receive multiple queries on very similar topics—because, presumably, if several writers study the same magazine, they're going to reach similar conclusions about its needs.

- **Something similar was recently published.** "Recently," in the print world, usually means "within the past two years." It's just not possible for a writer to obtain *every* back issue of a publication (unless you're a subscriber), so you often can't determine whether your topic has been covered or not.

- **Something similar was recently published by the competition.** Often, editors don't want to try to compete with another high-quality book or article that is already on the market. Thus, if a book on your topic already dominates the market, you may have a tough time convincing an editor to accept yours, no matter how good it is.

- **The timing is wrong**. "Timing" is one of those subtle, intangible concepts: "I might have bought this a year ago, but I just don't feel like buying it now." Editors' tastes change, and so do the tastes and interests of readers. As editors are usually buying well in advance of publication (as much as six to twelve months for magazines, and as much as two to three years for books), editors aren't just thinking about what is selling *today*, but about what they believe will sell *tomorrow*. So even though your topic may be "hot" right now, it may still be rejected because the editor doesn't think it will be hot in two years.

- **Indefinable issues of taste.** Sometimes your proposal won't appeal to an editor simply because your writing doesn't match that editor's taste. That doesn't mean your writing is bad; it simply means that it isn't for everyone. Since that's true of every writer—*no* writer has 100 percent worldwide appeal—it's nothing to fret over. Eventually, you'll find the right match.

Step 9: Hone Your Skills

Of course, there is always the possibility that your work *is* being rejected on the basis of quality. No one who writes articles or books about writing likes to come out and say, "Hey, you know, it's possible that your writing needs *work*!" But it *is* possible, and you need to be able to accept that possibility—especially if you are experiencing rejection after rejection. Good writers are those who know there is always room for improvement.

There's a little-known secret in the editing business: The worse a writer's work, the less an editor will say about it. This may sound harsh, but look at it from an editor's perspective: Editors are not in the business of trying to train or educate unskilled writers. They are in the business of locating *skilled* writers who can contribute quality material. If an editor feels that a writer's work isn't even *close* to measuring up to that publication's standards, that editor will generally send nothing more than a form rejection. However, the closer a writer is to being publishable, the more likely an editor is to add a personal note to a rejection, perhaps encouraging the writer to try again, perhaps offering a specific comment on areas that need improvement. If an editor suggests a single area for change or improvement, this often means that very little is standing between you and publication.

However, this certainly doesn't mean that every time you receive a form rejection, the editor thought your work was abysmal. The majority of editors *never* make personal comments on rejections, no matter how good a writer's work may be. You can't assume, therefore, that if you're not getting personal rejections, you're no good. However, you *can* assume that if you *are* getting personal notes on your rejections, you're impressing editors, even if you aren't selling your work—*yet*.

It's also important to watch for patterns in your rejections. If five editors reject your stories for five different reasons, this doesn't give you much information. If, however, five editors all say you need to improve your grammar, you need to spell-check more carefully, or your work needs to be more organized or less "chatty," this is a good indication of a problem area that needs work. Keep in mind that you are never obligated to follow another person's advice on how to write. If your goal is to sell your writing, however, seeking out and following *good* advice is often a wise idea.

If you are starting to feel that you could paper your walls with rejection slips, and you're beginning to wonder whether the problem lies in your writing, find out. Join a critique group that focuses on your type of writing—or join several—and see what type of feedback you receive. Sign up for an online writing course. Do whatever you can to improve your skills. And finally—

Step 10: Keep Trying

Rejection is inevitable. Success is not. However, failure *is* guaranteed to anyone who gives up after the first rejection, or the third, or the tenth. It isn't hard to find accounts of well-known writers who experienced dozens of rejections before going on to become millionaires.

The true secret of "the perfect pitch" is to find the perfect match—and that may not happen on your first try, or your second, or your tenth. You may have to go back and retool your proposal; you may have to run your material by a critique group; you may have to take some courses to improve your skills. But no matter what you do, the only way to sell your work is to keep trying—and trying, and trying, and trying.

SECTION 1
Querying Periodicals

2

Writing the (Almost) Perfect Query

Perhaps the most common form of writing "pitch" is the query letter. This is the first, and often only, opportunity you have to convince an editor that you have something worthwhile to offer. Hence, the query can be the "make-or-break" point of your writing career. Nearly every other type of proposal or pitch in this book involves some type of query, so mastering this skill is vital.

Why Query?

Many writers wonder why editors would rather see a query than a finished article. How can a one-page letter demonstrate the quality and content of a 2,000-word piece? Wouldn't an editor be able to make a more informed decision if he or she could read the entire article?

Queries also add an extra delay: You have to wait for a response to your query before you can receive a response to the article itself. Wouldn't eliminating the query cut the waiting time in half? In addition, most of us prefer to write about a topic when it is fresh in our minds, but by the time we receive a response to a query, we've usually gone on to other things. Isn't it more logical to write the article at once?

These are all valid concerns. However, the primary issue is not whether a query is "better" than an article. The issue is that in most cases, writers don't have a choice. Editors are inundated with badly written, inappropriate manuscripts. In response, many have simply closed their doors to unsolicited submissions. The better-paying or more prestigious the market, the more likely it is to insist on queries. Some publications also pay less for unsolicited material than assigned material, which means that querying first can increase your income—in some cases by hundreds of dollars. In short, queries aren't optional; they may be your only chance of making a sale.

Benefits for All

Queries benefit writers *and* editors. Perhaps the most obvious benefit to an editor is length: it's easier to review a one-page letter than a ten-page manuscript. Queries enable an editor to determine, almost at a glance, whether a writer:

- Can write effectively
- Has a coherent, well thought-out idea
- Has a basic grasp of grammar and spelling
- Has read the publication
- Has an idea that fits into the publication's content
- Has the expertise or credentials to write the article
- Approaches markets in a professional manner

Queries also save time for the writer. Writing a single-page query is a much smaller investment in time and effort than writing an entire article, particularly if your article will require extensive research or interviews. By querying first, you avoid wasting time on an article that may be rejected— perhaps because the editor already has a similar article on file or has run something like it in the past, or for any of a dozen other reasons that have nothing to do with the actual quality of your work.

A query also gives the editor a chance to give you feedback on your idea before you write the article, enabling you to tailor that article precisely to the needs of that market and audience. An editor might want a longer article than you proposed, or a shorter one. The editor might want you to include interviews with certain experts, or to provide specific information in a side-bar. Querying saves you from having to make time-consuming revisions to your material after you've written it, and ensure that the editor receives exactly what he or she desires.

Sometimes, a query can result in a completely different assignment. If an editor is impressed by your credentials and writing style, but can't use the idea you've proposed, he or she may approach you with an alternate suggestion. When this happens, it often opens the door to a long and productive relationship.

Finally, it's much easier to set up interviews when you have a firm go-ahead from an editor. Experts are far more willing to talk to you if you have an actual assignment and can explain exactly where the material will be published. It also prevents you from wasting an interviewee's time when you don't know whether you'll be able to find a market for your article or not.

Essentials of an Effective Query

Take another look at the list of things an editor can determine from your query. Your goal is to make a positive impression in each of those areas. If you miss even one, you risk rejection. It may seem impossible to cover all those bases in a single page, but it can be done. All you need is five basic components:

- The hook
- The pitch (or offer)
- The body
- The credentials
- The close

Each component is vital, but none is especially difficult. Most involve little more than common sense and the ability to write effectively.

THE HOOK

Like an article, a query should grab an editor's attention from the very first line. Indeed, many writers use the first line of their proposed article to open their query. That first line, the "hook," should demonstrate your ability to write effectively and interestingly—and it should also demonstrate that you are familiar with the publication you are targeting.

A hook can be a single sentence or a brief paragraph. Hooks come in all forms; here are some of the most effective:

The "Problem/Solution" Hook

This hook demonstrates exactly how the information in your article will benefit the reader by defining a problem common to many of the publication's readers—and then proposing an article that will help solve that problem.

Don't just state what your article is about. Show how the topic relates to the reader—*why* it is a problem. For example, if you are writing about cancer in pets, don't just say, "I want to send you an article about cancer in pets." Instead, demonstrate the significance of this topic to the reader: "No diagnosis is so dreaded by pet owners as the word 'cancer'" (defining the "problem"). Then, explain how your article can help: "Fortunately, if an owner knows how to spot the signs of cancer early, this diagnosis doesn't have to mean the end of hope."

Following are examples of some successful problem/solution hooks:

- The pet magazine market is an ideal place for newer writers to "break in." However, it is constantly flooded with inappropriate submissions. To break in, one must understand what these magazines want, and what they won't accept. ("Writing for Pet Magazines," sold to *Byline*[1])
- For anyone who enjoys decorating with antique or delicate quilts, care is a vital concern. Most of us realize that we can't just pop Granny's handmade quilt into the washing machine or douse it

---

[1] Read this article online at *http://www.writing-world.com/freelance/pets.shtml*

with bleach, but what are the alternatives? How can we protect fine fabrics from further dirt and damage? ("Caring for Quilts: How to Preserve a Perishable Heirloom," sold to *Traditional Quiltworks*)

- Writing is a solitary endeavor. Day after day, night after night, freelance writers make time with computers, often to the detriment of human contact. We forget that "solitary" does not mean "isolation." ("Networking: The Key to Balance in a Writer's Life," by Terri Mrosko, sold to *Inklings*)

Be sure that your problem actually does affect (or at least interest) a large percentage of the publication's audience! By doing so, and by offering a solution appropriate to that audience, you provide solid evidence of your familiarity with the publication.

The Informative Hook

This type of hook generally presents two or three lines of useful or intriguing information (such as facts or statistics), followed by an explanation of how it relates to the target audience.

To open a query on cancer in pets, for example, you might say, "Every year, XX percent of America's pets will be diagnosed with cancer. Of those, XX percent will die within the first year. But you can beat those odds, by taking advantage of new treatments and technologies that significantly prolong a pet's life..."

Here's an example of an information hook:

> Thanks to a translation glitch, Microsoft was forced to pull its entire Chinese edition of Windows 95 from the marketplace. Microsoft recovered—but that's the sort of mistake few small businesses can afford! ("How to Localize Your Web site," sold to *Entrepreneur's Home Office*)

For this type of hook to work, your information must be genuinely interesting (and relevant)! Your goal is to intrigue the editor with information that may not be commonly known, not to bore the reader with a host of statistics.

The Question Hook

A problem/solution hook or information hook can also be posed as a question, such as:

- Did you know...?
- What would you do if...?
- Have you ever wondered...?

Your goal is to capture the editor's attention with an intriguing question to which (presumably) he or she may not know the answer. However, such a hook also poses an inherent risk: If the answer to "Did you know?" is "Yes," or if the answer to "Have you ever wondered?" is "No," your hook may fail. Save this hook for unusual items; don't use it for obvious questions.

The Personal Experience/Anecdote

A personal experience hook can be used to demonstrate that you have actually solved the problem or lived through the experience you intend to write about. This hook is effective when querying publications that commonly use first-person articles, articles with lots of anecdotes, or articles that have a more informal or personal tone.

Here are some ways to work your experiences into a query:

- Last summer, our beloved 15-year-old cat succumbed to cancer. Along the way, we learned a great deal about this disease and how it affects cats. ("Answers to Cancer," sold to *Cats Magazine*)
- As a full-time freelancer, I also teach writing classes. During a recent query letter critique, one of my students raised her hand. "I feel like I know how to write a good query," she said hesitantly. "But I keep worrying about sending them out. What will I do if I actually get an assignment?" She seemed surprised that I could relate to her fear... ("Conquering Writers' Anxiety," by Kelly James-Enger, sold to *Inklings*)
- Forget-me-nots. I love their wistful name. I love their tiny blue flowers. And yes, I love that growing them is as simple as pie. ("Forget-me-nots: Simply Unforgettable Spring Flowers," by Mary Rose, sold to *Fine Gardening*)

Don't use this type of hook for markets that do not use personal experience articles, first-person articles, or anecdotal material.

The Attention-Grabber

The purpose of this type of hook is to make an editor sit up and take notice—hopefully long enough to read the rest of your query. It can range from a snippet of dialogue to an evocative declaration:

As I fell from the top of Yosemite's El Capitan, I wondered if my life would truly flash before my eyes—or if I would stop screaming long enough to notice.

Such a hook must be truly "grabby." It must also lead to an appropriate article. If your "El Capitan" hook leads to an article about illegal parachuting in Yosemite, it might lead to a sale; if it was just a bad dream brought on by indigestion (and you're actually pitching an article about foods to avoid before bedtime), you might want to try something else.

Hooks to Avoid

Certain hooks scream "amateur" and are guaranteed to speed your query to the rejection pile. These include:

- **The personal introduction.** Never begin with a line like "Hello, my name is John Smith, and I'd like to write an article about..." Don't give the editor irrelevant personal information, such as "I have been a writer for seven years, and I'd like to offer you a piece on..." or "I am a housewife and mother of three lovely children, and have recently decided to pursue my lifelong dream of writing..." Unless your hook actually calls for a personal experience, keep yourself out of it.

- **The "suck–up" hook.** Don't bother telling editors how much you enjoy their publication; prove it by offering an appropriate query. Editors aren't impressed by queries that proclaim, "I've been a subscriber to your magazine for twenty years, and I have the perfect story for you..."
- **The "bid-for-sympathy" hook.** Never tell an editor that this is your first attempt to get published, or that you need to sell this article to put food on the table. A query that begins "I am an unpublished mother of three" simply alerts the editor to the fact that you don't know what you're doing.
- **The "I'm perfect for you" hook.** Don't sing your praises ("I am a highly experienced professional and will be an asset to your magazine") or those of your article ("I know your readers will love this piece"). Don't tell an editor that your article is "good" or "informative" or whatever. Your query is a sales tool; it's not a press release. If you can't demonstrate the value of your article (or your writing ability) in the query itself, no amount of hype will help.
- **The "I'm an amateur" hook.** Never announce that you haven't been published before, or that you're not sure how to write a query. Proclaiming your amateur status will not cause an editor to treat you more kindly or "cut you some slack." Also, never tell an editor that your writing teacher suggested that you submit a piece for publication, or that your friends all think you're the next Erma Bombeck. Be professional, even if you haven't sold anything before.
- **The "I hope you're smarter than they are" hook.** Never tell an editor that other publications have already rejected the article you're proposing. Such queries try to imply that while *other* editors were dumb, you're hoping *this* editor will be smart enough to recognize a good thing. In reality, editors trust the judgment of other editors: If you reveal that your work has already been rejected several times, an editor will suspect that there may be a good reason for this.

Finally, make sure you choose a hook that matches the style of your target publication. If the publication never uses personal experiences or first-person accounts, don't use the personal-experience hook. If a market never publishes statistical information, don't load your hook with facts and figures. If the publication uses a conservative style, don't offer an overly dramatic "attention-grabber." Use your hook to demonstrate that you are familiar with the publication's style and tone—and that you know how to write for that particular audience.

THE PITCH

Once you've "hooked" the editor, it's time to move on to the pitch. This usually appears in the next paragraph, though it may sometimes appear in the same paragraph as your hook.

Your "pitch" describes what you are offering. Often, you'll start by explaining how your article will solve the problem or answer the question posed in your hook. It's also the place to offer a working title for your article and a suggested word-count. (Though a title isn't necessary, it can help the editor get a better sense of your concept.)

Here are some of the pitches that followed the hooks listed above:

- I'd like to offer you a 1,500-word article titled "Internationalizing Your Online Market." The article would discuss how small businesses can take advantage of "localizing" agents to tailor their products and market strategies to the international marketplace."("How to Localize Your Web site")
- "Forget-Me-Nots: Simply Unforgettable Spring Flowers" is an exuberant thousand-word profile detailing... ("Forget-me-nots: Simply Unforgettable Spring Flowers")
- Cancer is not an immediate death-sentence for a cat; some forms of cancer can be managed medically to prolong a cat's life with little or no discomfort. However, it is vital to recognize the presence of cancer early, and discuss options and treatments with a veterinarian as soon as possible. To help your readers do just that, I propose a 2,500-word article on "Cancer in Cats." ("Answers to Cancer")

Including the word count in your pitch is a good way to let the editor know that you've reviewed the publication's guidelines and also that you understand how many words are necessary to cover a particular topic. But be careful; a good way to sink your proposal is to suggest an article on a wide-ranging topic (e.g., "how to publish a book") that you imagine you can cover in a ridiculously short space (e.g., 1000 words).

THE BODY

An editor wants to know exactly what your article will cover. That means you must know the answers to the questions you plan to address—and have a working outline of your article in mind. This will constitute the body of your query—the section with the greatest power to make or break a sale. It is usually one to four paragraphs in length and presents the details of the article you are proposing.

A good way to summarize your proposed article is to divide it into logical subtopics. The longer the article, the more subtopics you are likely to include. For example, if you are writing about cancer in pets, a 700-word article would probably cover only one topic (e.g., "the warning signs of cancer"). A 2,000-word article, however, might cover three to five subtopics (e.g., "common types of cancer," "warning signs," and "treatments"). If you have too many subtopics, your article will appear too generalized, without enough information in each area. If you have too few, your word count may seem inflated. One way to determine if you have the right balance is to divide the word count by the number of topics: A 2,000-word article with five subtopics gives you 400 words per topic.

List those topics, with a brief description of each, in the body of your query. Here's how I outlined my "Cancer in Cats" article:

My article will cover:

- The types of cancers most common in cats (including mammary tumors and cancers of the mouth, lips, and gums—some of which are preventable!).
- How to recognize the signs of cancer early (what is that lump?).
- The symptoms and progression of various types of cancer (weight loss, diminished appetite, coughing, and wheezing can all be signs of cancer).
- The types of treatments available, pros and cons of different treatments, how treatments can affect a cat's life expectancy and quality of life, and how to find treatment (not every city has an animal cancer clinic).

Some writers like to use bullet points to set off their subtopics. Others use plain paragraphs. In some cases, the entire body of your query may fit into a single paragraph, like the following:

The article covers techniques of hand-cleaning delicate quilts to avoid damaging fragile fabrics and prevent fading and staining. It discusses ways to remove spot stains (including blood spots and rust stains from needles and other metal contact). It also discusses ways to mend damaged quilts without destroying the integrity of an heirloom piece. Finally, it discusses the best ways to store or display quilts in order to preserve and protect them. ("Caring for Heirloom Quilts")

There is no rule as to the best presentation style. You don't want an editor to become bogged down in a twenty-line paragraph, however, so try to make your letter visually appealing as well as informative. Make sure that the editor can determine what you are offering quickly and easily.

Body Mistakes to Avoid

Since the body of a query is a writer's only opportunity to describe the article, writers make two common mistakes: not saying enough, and saying too much. Here's how to avoid these errors:

- **Don't use your query as a "fishing expedition."** Don't write a query when you don't actually have an article in mind, but simply want to discover whether an editor has an interest in a particular topic or subject area. Also, don't query simply to let an editor know that you are available for assignments, unless you have already worked with the editor before. Impress the editor with your ideas and material first; then, after you've sold two or three articles, you can ask for assignments.

- **Don't "tease."** Don't tell an editor that he will have to read your article to find the answer to the questions you've posed. Answer those questions in the query itself. Editors will want to know exactly what you have to say on a topic before asking to see your article.

- **Don't raise questions to which you don't have the answers.** A common error is to promise that, once you have been given the assignment, you will "find out" the answers to the questions you pose in your query. This, however, shows that you don't already have those answers. Don't say "I will interview experts to try to find out the best solution for Problem X." If you can't provide details about the solution, an editor will not be able to determine whether the results of your research will be useful.

- **Don't clutter your query with data.** An editor wants to know the *type* of information your article will cover—but not necessarily the facts and figures themselves. If you're covering cancer treatments, for example, explain that you will cover specific therapies and name them—but don't go into detail about how they work. Save that for the article.

- **Don't over-describe your article.** Some writers try to cram chunks of their article into the query. Avoid this temptation! Your query is not a condensed version of your final article; it is a summary of that article. Think of it as a description, an overview. (If you have trouble summarizing what your article is about without using portions of the article itself, try explaining the article out loud to another person without actually looking at the text.)

THE CREDENTIALS

Besides wanting to know what your article is about, editors also want to know why *you* are the best person to write it. For new writers, this section can be the most terrifying: "How can I convince an editor to buy my article if I don't have any writing credits?"

Fortunately, credentials do not necessarily have to include writing credits. Often, other credentials (such as professional experience) are more important. You should also check the publication's guidelines, and bylines of other authors in the publication, to determine what credentials are most valued by that publication. Relevant credentials are most likely to include:

- **Professional experience.** If you work (or have experience) in the field about which you are writing, this is often the best credential of all. Many editors would rather work with experts, even if they are mediocre writers, than with writers who may not have an in-depth knowledge of the subject. For example, Mary Rose sold her article on forget-me-nots on the basis of being an experienced gardener (which she demonstrated by submitting photos of her garden); it was her first article sale. Some publications, in fact, will accept material *only* from experts.

- **Academic degrees or training.** If you have a degree or specialized training in a field, that is often enough to convince an editor that you can write about it. Some types of publications (including academic and scientific journals) accept material only from writers who have the necessary academic credentials.

- **Teaching experience.** If you teach about the subject you're proposing, you can probably convince an editor that you have the ability to communicate effectively about that subject.

- **Personal experience.** If your article is about personal experiences or personal self-help topics, you may be able to sell it on the basis of your own experience. For example, if you're writing about finding a retirement home for an elderly relative, you may be able to "pitch" that article on the basis of having gone through this experience yourself. However, your experience needs to somehow go beyond that of the ordinary person or ordinary reader. For example, if you're writing an article on child-rearing techniques, the mere fact that you are a parent isn't going to be enough to convince an editor to buy the piece. Keep in mind as well that personal experience will not substitute for professional credentials in publications that prefer articles written by "experts."

- **Writing experience.** Different publications place different levels of value on previous writing experience. Some insist upon it; others don't care. Some editors are only interested in whether you have written on relevant topics; for example, a history publication may not be impressed by the fact that you've sold several articles to gardening magazines. If you have written only fiction, that may not help you sell a nonfiction article (unless it is *about* writing fiction), and vice versa. Also, the less professional your writing experience, the less it will help you. Being "published" in arenas that are considered equivalent to "self-publishing" (such as having posted articles on your topic on your Web site or blog) won't help you at all. Being published in certain types of nonprofit (nonpaying) venues, such as your church newsletter, is also unlikely to impress an editor.

- **Interviews.** If you don't have the right credentials yourself, one way to sell your article is to interview other experts who *do* have the necessary credentials. This is often the ideal solution when you can't demonstrate relevant expertise.

The best place to list your credentials is usually in the last, or next-to-last, paragraph of your query, right after the body. Here are some examples:

- As Webmaster of MusicPhotographer.com, it has been my job to connect music writers and photographers with the markets that need their work. This is the only site devoted to music journalism on the Web. I'm also writing the first guide on the topic. Reviews for my last book, *The Van Halen Encyclopedia*, are available at Amazon.com. ("How to Write for the Music Market," by C.J. Chilvers, sold to Inkspot)
- I currently have over 75 articles published in *The West Life*, *The Plain Dealer*, and *The News Sun* newspapers; magazines including *Women as Managers* and *Asthma Magazine*; and e-zines such as *Inscriptions* and *The Writing Parent*. I specialize in career and business management articles. ("Networking: The Key to Balance in the Writer's Life," by Terri Mrosko, sold to *Inklings*)
- My husband and I spent 15 months in England, and became adept at photographing inside dimly lit cathedrals and similar buildings. I have been a freelance writer for more than 30 years, and am the host/editor of the popular writing site Writing-World.com (which attracts over one million visitors per year) and the British travel site TimeTravel-Britain.com. ("The Chichester Cathedral Flower Festival," by Moira Allen, sold to *British Heritage)*
- I am qualified to write this article from a mum's perspective as I have been living with egg allergy for the past two years and I have meticulously researched every aspect of egg allergy in order to make my life, and the lives of those who care for my daughter, including the helpers at our church mother and toddler group easier. It is this information I want to share with your readers. ("Eggs—The Unusual Suspect," by Dawn Copeman, sold to UK's *Home and Family* magazine)

THE CLOSE
Use your final paragraph to thank the editor for taking the time to consider your proposal and make a final "offer" to help close the deal. I usually use this paragraph to provide an estimate of when the article can be delivered:

If you'd like to see the article, I can have it in your hands within thirty days of your go-ahead. Thanks for your time and attention; I look forward to hearing from you.

The close can also encourage the editor to follow up with questions, or for clarification:

> Interested in this topic for *Inklings*? As a self-employed writer who often struggles with writing-related anxiety, I believe I can bring a unique perspective to this piece. Let me know if you have any questions about this story idea, and thank you for your time. ("Conquering Writers' Anxiety," by Kelly James-Enger)

Closes like these show professionalism and courtesy—two factors that always appeal to overworked, under appreciated editors!

FORMAT

Since there are still many editors who prefer traditional "paper" queries to e-mail queries, understanding proper letter format is still important. (The format of e-mail queries will be discussed in the next chapter.) A badly formatted letter, such as a query typed on erasable bond with a faded ribbon and smudged with corrections, will not inspire an editor to read further. It's no use arguing that appearances shouldn't matter and that content is all that counts; editors assume that if you can't handle the basics, you won't be able to handle the important stuff either.

A well-formatted query includes the following elements:

- **A decent letterhead.** You can design a basic letterhead on your computer simply by printing your name and address at the top of the page in an attractive, but not excessively fancy, font. You can also design a letterhead online at places like iPrint.com or have it done at your local print shop. However, these days it's far simpler (and cheaper) to do it yourself and simply pick up some high-quality paper to use for queries.

- **A business-style body.** If you aren't familiar with terms like "block" or "modified block," don't worry. Just follow the format of the examples at the end of this section. Always include a blank line between paragraphs, and don't indent more than five spaces (if you indent at all).

- **Contact information.** Your letterhead should include complete contact information, including your full name (or pen name), address, telephone number, fax number (if any), and e-mail address. It isn't necessary to include your URL; include that in your credentials section if you wish to refer an editor to your Web site.

- **A formal salutation.** Unless you know the editor personally, don't use first names. If you're not sure whether the editor is male or female, use the editor's title (Dear Editor Johnson:).

- **Clean, spell-checked copy.** A query riddled with typos won't lead to a sale. Don't rely solely on your computer spell-checker; visually proofread your query as well.

- **Quality paper.** Always use a paper that is at least 20-lb bond. Some writers use fancy textured bonds or colored papers for queries, on the theory that this will help them stand out from all the plain white paper on an editor's desk. Don't get too fancy, however; stick with subtle colors (such as ivory, gray or parchment). Never use colored inks, and avoid papers with pretty borders or decorative designs. Never use erasable paper (if it even exists today!). If you live outside the United States and aren't sure what "20-lb bond" is, look for a paper that is relatively heavy; a good test is whether you can read text from another sheet of paper through the page, or read text that has been printed on the reverse side of the page.
- **A SASE (self-addressed stamped envelope).** Don't use a #9 (insert) envelope for your SASE; use a full-size business envelope (#10), folded in thirds. Be sure it has adequate postage. (If you are submitting to a publication in another country, include International Reply Coupons [IRCs]. One IRC is usually sufficient for postage between the United States and Canada; two are advisable for correspondence between other countries.)

Clips

Many editors request clips, which are copies of previously published materials. The key word here is "published"—never send unpublished or self-published material as a clip!

It is always best to send clips that are relevant to your target market, if you have them. If you're pitching to a gardening market, send gardening clips. If, however, you don't have relevant clips, send the very best clips you have (e.g., from the most prestigious publications). A clip from *Smithsonian Magazine* will probably still impress a gardening editor, even if it's on a completely different subject.

It is not a copyright violation to photocopy your own articles (even if you've sold all rights) for use as clips. You are not trying to "publish" that material; you're simply using them as examples of your writing ability. Don't bother making color copies unless the clips also include examples of your own photography. Another option is to scan your clips and store them as PDF files, and then print them out whenever you wish to send copies.

Many writers struggle with the question of how to present "electronic" clips. A printout of an article published online doesn't always look the same as a printed page. Such work is every bit as valid, however, if it comes from a reputable publication. Be sure that your printout includes the name and URL of the online publication, if possible.

Writers whose work appears primarily online are often tempted to refer editors to the location of that material. This is becoming increasingly acceptable, but use caution. If an editor asks for clips, send at least one hardcopy, and then refer the editor to the URLs of other work.

Don't send clips of unpublished work or work that has only appeared on your own Web site, blog, or a "self-publishing" Web site. No matter how good these materials are, they are not considered "published" by current editorial standards. It's also better to avoid sending clips from amateur publications, such as office or nonprofit newsletters, unless they directly relate to your proposal or support your credentials. Don't send copies of "letters to the editor"; this is not considered a publication. Remember, a bad clip is worse than no clip at all!

And what if you *have* no clips at all? Don't despair. Most editors will consider the merits of your query first, and your samples second. (To be honest, many editors don't have time to read clips, even though they request them.) If your query is strong enough and you can offer appropriate credentials, the lack of clips won't necessarily ruin your chances, unless the publication specifies that it works *only* with published writers.

Response Time

How long should you wait before following up on a query? The easy answer is "as long as the publication's guidelines indicate." I usually allow another two weeks over the published response time before following up on a query. Then, it's time for a polite inquiry regarding the status of your proposal. Usually, this should be sent via the same medium as your original query. If you queried by e-mail, use e-mail; if you queried by surface mail, use surface mail. Your first follow-up inquiry should simply ask whether your query or proposal was received, and if it was, when you might anticipate a response. Send a copy of the original query, so that the editor won't have to dig it up out of the file; this will also encourage a more immediate reply.

If you still do not receive a response after another two to three weeks, you may wish to send a more urgent follow-up—e.g., "I would like to know whether this query is still under consideration, so that I may send it on to other markets if it is not." If this produces no response, it's not out of line to call the editor or agent, and ask (*very* politely) whether your proposal has been received and whether it is being reviewed or considered for acceptance.

Sadly, more and more writers are reporting that they no longer receive any response from editors who don't intend to use their material. Many editors are no longer bothering to send out rejection letters, even when you enclose a SASE. Besides being discourteous, this is profoundly frustrating for writers, who have no sure way of determining the status of their material. Editors often don't seem to realize that a rejection is not simply "bad news"—it also lets writers know that they are now free to submit their material elsewhere.

If you receive no response to your second or third inquiry, your best bet is usually to assume that your material is *not* being considered. It is then advisable to send a final letter to the editor, formally withdrawing your material from consideration. This letter can be phrased very simply:

Dear (Editor):

As I have not received a response from your office regarding my query for (article title) that was submitted on (date), I am assuming that you are not considering this material for publication and am hereby withdrawing the material from consideration. Thank you for your time and assistance.

This withdrawal letter is important, as it protects you from the appearance of having submitted material to two publications simultaneously. If the first editor or agent *does* finally respond to your query after you've sent it somewhere else, the second editor won't feel that you've violated publishing protocol.

The ability to write a good query is one of the most important skills a writer can develop. A good query shows that you can write and that you are a professional—qualities that may result in an assignment even if the editor can't use your original proposal. Think of a query as your letter of introduction: If you make a good impression, you are likely to be invited back. If you make a bad impression, you may find that door forever closed.

And if the door doesn't open, don't panic. Re-polish your query, tailor it for another market, and send it out again. It can often take two or three tries before you find the right article for a particular market—or the right market for a particular article. Eventually, if you are persistent and professional, your work *will* find a home.

3

Beyond the Basic Query

The tried-and-true approach to queries outlined in the previous chapter is the best way to approach editors whom you have never dealt with before. However, there may be times when you wish to handle things just a bit differently—for example, when sending an e-mail query, when querying an editor with whom you have worked in the past, or when dealing with international publications.

E-mail Queries

Today, e-mail is rapidly becoming the preferred method of approaching editors. Among electronic publications, that preference is nearly universal; many electronic publications don't even post a mailing address.

Both editors and writers find that e-mail queries save time and money. The writer doesn't have to spring for paper, ink, and stamps—and when you hit the "send" button, you know your query will reach the editor in seconds rather than days. Since the editor doesn't need to draft a formal response on official letterhead, you may also receive a reply more quickly.

Don't assume, however, that just because nearly instantaneous communication is possible, you *will* hear from an editor immediately. One common complaint amongst editors is that writers now start "following up" within hours of sending their original query, rather than weeks. Regardless of how a query is sent, a publication's posted response times still apply—and if that response time is "three months," don't start nagging an editor in three hours!

Another editorial complaint is that the instantaneous nature of e-mail queries seems to encourage many writers (particularly amateur writers) to spend less time actually *composing* those queries. Many e-mail queries seem to be dashed off with little attention to style or presentation—as if the speed of the medium inspires haste in the writer. Many are not proofread carefully (and not all e-mail programs offer spell-checkers). Editors also find that e-mail queries often tend to be less formal, more chatty (and sometimes even "cutesy"), than traditional queries—qualities that are rarely endearing in a query in any form. Just because a query can be transmitted instantaneously, that doesn't mean a writer should consider this an invitation to "dash off a quick note" to an editor and hit "send."

While e-mail queries contain many of the same elements described in the previous chapter, none of the format rules that are so essential to hardcopy queries apply. Instead, e-mail queries have their own format issues, which one ignores at one's peril. E-mail queries also contain unique elements that need special attention. Understanding these elements can mean the difference between an assignment and a very fast rejection.

ELEMENTS OF THE E-MAIL QUERY

The Header

With e-mail, you can't impress an editor with nice paper or a snappy letterhead. Instead, you must rely on a few lines within your header to provide vital information about yourself and your query. Your header is your "first impression;" make sure it's a good one by putting the right information in each of these sections:

- **To:** As with a surface-mail query, it's important to address your query to the right person at the right address. Try to locate the exact e-mail address of the editor you wish to contact. Some publications may have a specific address for submissions, such as "submissions@"—check the guidelines to be sure.
- **From:** You probably wouldn't think of signing a traditional query with a name like "Crystal Windsinger" or "Rafe Moondragon." If you use such a nickname to communicate online, make sure it doesn't slip into your professional correspondence. Similarly, if your personal e-mail address is something like "*2hot2trot@ wowser.com*," consider setting up something a little more professional for editorial correspondence. (A simple first and last name typically works best; editors have seen too many variations on "WriterLady" or "PenWoman"!)
- **Subject:** Include the word "Query" in your subject line, along with a brief (two- to three-word) description of your proposal—e.g., "Query: Cancer in Cats" or "Query: Writing for Pet Magazines." Never leave this line blank. Avoid cuteness or excessive informality. A subject line like "May I have a moment of your time?" looks too much like spam and could cause your query to be deleted. (Granted, one writer did send me a query with the subject line "Of Confetti and Green Sunsets" and got published anyway—but not until her second try!) Never use words like "urgent" or "important" or "read right away"—these will certainly get your query booted to the spam folder.

The Text

The safest way to handle the text of an e-mail query is to treat it just like a traditional query, with all the "essentials" (hook, pitch, body, credentials, and close) described in chapter 2. Such an approach will rarely go wrong.

However, one of the advantages of e-mail is its ability to save time—and many editors find that they prefer e-mail queries to be shorter and more concise than surface-mail queries. One reason for this is that an editor likes to be able to read an entire letter without having to scroll through a long "page." The less scrolling an editor must do to read your query, the better.

Consequently, many writers are turning to brief, one- to three-paragraph e-mail queries. The hook is often eliminated entirely; writers often begin directly with the pitch, followed by a single paragraph of description, and closing with a summary of the writer's credentials. Here's an example of a short but successful query to the UK women's magazine *My Weekly*. The author, Abby Williams, notes that this was her first successful pitch—and that she went on to write fifteen more articles for this publication!

> Dear (editor name)
>
> I am currently researching the growing environmental nuisance of plastic bags. I wondered whether you might be interested in an article about this, firstly advising readers of the global problem, its effect on our natural world, what alternatives readers can use (including photos) plus useful contacts, and if governments/supermarkets are actually doing anything about this problem. I was interested to learn that turtles often mistake upturned plastic bags in the ocean for jelly fish which they eat, causing either a blocked digestive tract, or worse!
>
> I look forward to hearing from you if you feel an article of this type might be of interest to your readers.

When crafting an e-mail query, therefore, give serious thought to ways that you can "condense" your information into a compact summary that the editor can view within a single screen. Just be sure that your summary actually covers all the points that you wish to make!

Credentials and Clips

It's perfectly acceptable to list your credentials in an e-mail query just as you would in a traditional query. Many writers, however, also use this opportunity to provide a link to a Web site where editors can learn more about the writer's qualifications, or perhaps view writing samples. Others list that information after their signature, or in their signature block (see below). You can't be certain, however, that an editor will actually check the sites you list, so it's wise to state your credentials explicitly, and offer Web sites as a source of additional information.

One frustration many authors feel with electronic queries is the impossibility of including "clips." (Never send copies of your published articles as attachments to an e-mail query!) Once again, URLs are usually the best answer. If you haven't developed an author Web site yet, consider doing so, if only to post samples of your published work where they can be viewed by editors who are considering your proposals.

The Address Block

In a traditional query, your name, address, and other contact information would go at the top of the page (or be incorporated into your letterhead). In an e-mail query, it should go at the bottom, below your typed signature:

> Jane Smith
> 1042 Gloriana Lane
> Whippet, IL 60606
> (555)123-4567
> (555) 123-4568 (fax)
> *janesmith@isp.com*

By the way, do not assume that you no longer have to include this information on your submission itself! As an editor, I receive far too many e-mail submissions with no contact information (sometimes the author even omits a byline), necessitating a back-tracking through e-mails to locate that information. Your contact information needs to be included not only on your query but also on *anything* that you submit.

The Signature Block

You may wish to use a standard "signature block" to include your Web site and any special credentials you'd like to list. This is a good place, for example, to list a book title that you've published. It's not a good idea, however, to include your mailing address and other contact information in a signature block, as you don't want that information to accidentally be transmitted or forwarded in other types of e-mails.

Avoid overly cute signature blocks or blocks that involve graphic elements. Save the cats, dancing weasels, and emoticons for personal correspondence.

Format

There is little you can do to improve the standard, boring format of an e-mail query. What you can do, however, is ensure that your attempts at "style" don't make an e-mail query even harder to read! If, for example, you type your query into a word-processing program (like MS Word) and use certain types of characters (e.g., long dashes, "smart" or "curly" quotes) that you would use in a normal (nonelectronic) query or submission, your text may come across looking like this:

> Yet I,m not alone every writer I know struggles with "writer's anxiety‰. "First you're anxious if you don't have work, but then when you do, you're anxious about making it the best you can,‰ says fulltime St. Louis freelancer Kris Rattini, who's written for Family Money, Family Circle, and Boy's Life. "If it's a new editor, it's just intensified because you want to make a good impression and get more assignments.‰

To avoid this type of gobbledygook, be sure to observe these basic guidelines:

- Single-space your text.
- Double-space between paragraphs; don't indent.
- Avoid long blocks of text. Use short to medium-length paragraphs.
- Don't use bullets; they rarely show up as bullets on the receiving end.
- Don't insert any "format" commands (such as bold, italics, or underlining). Use asterisks to indicate *boldface*, and underscores to indicate _italics_ or _underlining_. (In a query, there should be little need for either.)
- Go into the "AutoFormat" menu and turn off smart quotes, m-dashes (—) and any other special formatting in both the "AutoFormat" section and the "AutoFormat as you type" section. If your text already includes smart quotes, you can then do a search-and-replace by simply typing in a quote-mark and/or apostrophe in both the "find" and "replace" boxes and doing a "replace all." (For users of Word 2007, check the "Help" index to find out how to add the AutoFormat icon to your Quick Access toolbar, at the top left of your screen, as this function is no longer included in the regular drop-down menus.) Replace m-dashes with a pair of hyphens (--).
- Don't use any other special character keys—including accents, tildes, etc.
- Avoid emoticons, such as :) or <g>. Save these for personal correspondence.
- Never use HTML or other special types of formatting. Don't insert graphics. Don't use colors (either in your fonts or your background.)
- Use a readable font—at least 10pt. or, preferably, 12pt. Arial and Courier are good fonts for e-mail queries. Make sure your font size is set to "normal." If you're not sure how your font looks to others, e-mail a test message to a friend and ask for an evaluation.

- If you're copying and pasting text from Word into an e-mail program, mail a copy of the message to yourself first. I've often noticed that Word text, when pasted into an e-mail, may mysteriously lose line breaks, causing paragraphs to run together. By mailing it to yourself first, you can catch any inadvertent glitches before sending it off.

Attachments

In a word, don't. Many editors will simply delete unsolicited attachments unread—and with the number of viruses circulating on the Internet, attachments are becoming more unwelcome than ever. Your query should be contained entirely within the body of the e-mail itself. The same applies to submissions; never send an attachment unless you have cleared it with the editor first, and determined what type of file to send. Also, turn off any functions in your e-mail program that generate automatic attachments. (It's also a good idea to periodically check your e-mail program for viruses, so that you don't inadvertently pass along unwanted problems with your queries.)

Online Submissions

Some publications don't provide an e-mail address; instead, they require queries (and sometimes even complete manuscripts) to be submitted via an online submission form. This requires you to either type your query directly into the box or copy and paste it from another application. If copying and pasting, the rules about "no special characters" still apply. When using this type of form, it's not a bad idea to create a duplicate of the information and e-mail it to yourself, so that you'll have a dated record of the submission and also be able to duplicate it if you need to follow up later.

Queries to Editors You Know

Once you have worked with an editor on two or three assignments, you no longer need to sell yourself as you would in a query to a new market. Your editor should already be familiar with your credentials and your writing ability. Consequently, your pitches to "regular" editors can focus more on the content of the proposed article rather than on convincing an editor that you can do the job.

In time, you may be able to "pitch" articles with much less detail than you would use in a typical query. You may start to use very short "quick pitches" to suggest article ideas—or even submit a "multiple-pitch" query that proposes several article ideas at once.

QUICK-PITCH QUERIES

A quick-pitch query allows you to bounce an idea off an editor to see whether there is any interest, without investing a great deal of time in the query itself. Again, this generally works only with editors who already know your work and know that you can deliver whatever you promise (though some may ask you to submit a more detailed query if they are interested in the idea).

Here are some examples of quick pitches I've received and accepted:

- Something for nothing, in the current economic climate? Sounds impossible, but it's not. My article considers the potential of free-ware—free software you can download from the Internet—as a viable alternative to mainstream products, which may be beyond the financial reach of many of us, at this time. The programs discussed are of a standard comparable to that of popular retail brands. Special emphasis is given to packages for writers and screenwriters. The article, "There's No Such Thing as a Free Lunch. But..." is 1,185 words long.

- I have another article that I think your readers would be interested in. The title is "Researching That Agent—Online," and it's approximately 1,260 words. It's an informative piece that deals with successfully researching a prospective agent's career, track record, and biographical information and then using that information to your benefit in a strong query letter. The piece suggests great reference sites and unheard-of-but-better-than-the-rest search engines as well as association sites, and makes five suggestions for using the gleaned information in a query letter without stepping over the line.

- Whether it's local, regional, or national or low-paying, medium, or high-paying, knowing the appropriate market to target and when to move on is an important step in a freelance writer's career. Are you interested in a 1,000-word article that outlines steps to moving up levels within the different market ranks? The article will include advice from writers at different levels in their careers and how they target the appropriate market.

And here's an example of a quick-pitch query I sent to *The Writer* that resulted in a two-part article sale:

I have recently developed a class on how to prepare a nonfiction book proposal. Would you be interested in an article on this topic? (Ideally, I'd love to offer you a two-part article—one on all the steps you need to take BEFORE writing the proposal, including market research, and one on writing the proposal itself.)

All of these queries were submitted by e-mail, which is the ideal mechanism for quick-pitch queries. Many of the pitches I receive from regular contributors run no more than three to five lines. However, note that each still contains all the necessary information an editor needs to make a decision—provided the editor *already* knows that the writer is capable of delivering what he or she promises. Since such queries are easy to read and reply to, quick pitches are likely to receive quick responses.

MULTIPLE-PITCH QUERIES

A multiple-pitch query offers an editor a selection of several article ideas rather than just one. Such a query usually suggests from two to ten topics, with a paragraph of detail apiece.

This type of query is, by definition, a fishing expedition—and as I mentioned in chapter 2, fishing expeditions are usually *not* appropriate when you are making contact with an editor for the first time. This type of query should only be used with an editor with whom you have already worked—preferably several times. The editor needs to know, without question, that you are capable of fleshing out any of the suggested topics, even when the query itself doesn't provide nearly the level of detail of a traditional query. This type of query enables the editor to pick and choose from a selection, and such a query can often result in more than one assignment. (Rarely, however, will an editor accept every idea on your list.)

Here's an example of a multiple-pitch query I submitted to the online publication *Inkspot*:

> Dear Debbie,
>
> We've talked about several articles recently, and I wanted to find out whether you are interested in any/all of these:
>
> 1. Author chats—are they useful? I've talked to several authors who have given "chats" online. This article would discuss whether an author chat is worthwhile and how to make the best of one.
> 2. Teaching writing classes offline. This piece would discuss how to teach a writing class in a "real world" environment.
> 3. Teaching writing classes online. The follow-up to the previous article would discuss how to teach a successful online writing class.
> 4. Giving a talk—this would fall under the category of "promotion." I'd like to include information on how to prepare for a talk, and also information on the technical side—how do you give a good presentation? What will your listeners want to hear? What about handouts, outlines, charts, etc.? I think this would be most effective as a longer article on *Inkspot* (rather than an *Inklings* piece)—and it could be broken into two parts, one on technical presentation and one on personal preparation.
> 5. How to obtain a teaching job—this might make a good *Inklings* piece, on how to find (and land) a job at a community college or similar organization. It wouldn't discuss "how to teach," but rather, how to locate places to teach, submit a proposal, etc. (This and #2 might make a good two-part series.)
> 6. What if your work is stolen? I would like to talk to the National Writers Union and other sources to find out what recourses you actually have if your work turns up somewhere else. What steps should you take? What rights do you have?

7. How to develop a "business plan." Since I've just done this for 2000 (and found it an amazingly "focusing" process), I thought it might make an interesting article, perhaps for January.
8. International copyright—someone recently wrote to me and wanted to know about copyright protection when sending his manuscript to a publisher in another country. Would this be worth researching for *Inklings/Inkspot*?

Four of these eight topics were accepted—and topic #5 is now part of this book!

In many cases, an editor will respond to a multiple-pitch query with a request to flesh out one or more of your pitches into a full-fledged query. In this case, you won't need to worry about a hook or credentials (assuming the latter have been established); instead, concentrate on the body of the query, explaining exactly what will be covered and how the article will be organized.

International Queries

International publications can be an excellent way to expand your network of markets. If you live in the United States, consider targeting the host of English-language publications that can be found in Canada, Great Britain and Ireland, Australia, New Zealand, India, South Africa, Singapore, and other regions. If you live outside the United States and write in English, you have the option of expanding to United States markets. And if you speak and/or write fluently in another language, your market options expand even further, as there is a great demand for good translations of materials that have been previously published in English.

Unfortunately, it's not as easy to locate international markets on the Web as it is to find markets based in the United States. While most U.S. publications have Web sites that make it easy to find an editor's e-mail, this is not always true abroad. In many countries, Internet use is not as well established as in the United States, sometimes due to language issues, sometimes due to the fact that it's not always easy to obtain high-speed connections in rural areas. Hence, a great many non-U.S. publications have, at best, a "consumer" Web site aimed solely at potential subscribers (and often offering very little substantive information) or no Web site at all.

A variety of market guides exist to help you track down markets in English-speaking countries. For Great Britain and Ireland, you can choose from *Writer's Market UK and Ireland, The Writers' and Artists' Yearbook, The Writer's Handbook,* or the *Children's Writers' and Artists' Yearbook.* Australian markets can be found in the *Australian Writers' Marketplace*; Canadian markets are listed in the *Canadian Writers' Market.* For markets in other parts of the world, visit Worldwide Freelance Writer at *www.worldwidefreelance.com*; this site offers a weekly e-mail newsletter with market listings from around the world and extensive compendiums of international markets.

Since so many international publications do *not* have a Web presence or, necessarily, an easily available contact e-mail for an editor, contacting such publications must often be done the "old-fashioned" way, with a query sent by mail. When querying international editors, all the rules set forth in the preceding chapter apply—and apply even more strictly than when dealing with U.S. editors. In the United States, a certain degree of informality is often acceptable; however, what passes for "casual" in the States may be considered "discourteous" abroad. When in doubt, err on the side of formality, extra courtesy, and unwavering professionalism.

It's also important to know *what* to pitch overseas. Obviously, topics of limited local or regional appeal will rarely find a market elsewhere. (However, local "color" pieces can often be converted into useful international travel articles.) Even articles of a more general nature, such as pieces on health or how-to articles, should be examined with care. An article on healthcare, for example, won't be useful overseas if the methods, treatments, or medications are not available in the other country. Articles that rely on an understanding of American culture, society, idiom, humor, or jargon are also rarely marketable outside the country. You may also need to make a convincing case for why an editor of a non-U.S. publication should buy from *you* rather than from a writer in their own country.

In both your query *and* your article, you should avoid American slang, idiomatic phrases, or humor that may not "translate" well, even if your article is going to another English-language publication. It's less important, however, to worry about international spelling, punctuation, or usages such as the way of indicating dates, times, numbers, currencies, and so forth; the editor of the publication will generally be able to resolve those minor issues. If you *do* know these international usages, so much the better—but if you don't, don't let that stop you from sending out a query.

Your query should be very clear and specific. Don't assume that an editor will "know what you're talking about." If you need to refer to recent events, news items, or articles, provide specific references (Web references are best). If you plan to interview an expert, spell out that expert's credentials. When it comes to your own credentials, determine whether you can provide anything that indicates an understanding of your target publication's audience.

The good news is that once you've made contact with a formal query, you will probably be able to conduct the rest of your correspondence by e-mail. Most non-U.S. editors *do* have e-mail; they're just less likely to make it publicly available. This means that most likely, you won't need to include a self-addressed envelope with IRCs (international reply coupons); few editors actually want to have to make a trip to their local post office to redeem them. Even publications that insist on doing business by surface mail in their own country are generally willing to make an exception for international correspondence.

Another issue to be aware of when dealing with international publications is that many are far less concerned about lengthy, formal contracts than

U.S. publications. Don't be surprised if all you ever receive is a letter (or e-mail) of acceptance. You may also find it difficult to convince an editor to "keep in touch" and let you know when your article is scheduled for publication, so follow up regularly (and politely). Be sure to request a contributor's copy when the article *is* published.

Payment issues can also be difficult; many international publishers will wish to simply issue a check in their own currency. Since this can cost you anywhere from $15 to $25 (or more) to deposit in a U.S. bank account, depending on your bank's charges for (a) international currency exchange and (b) a non-U.S. check, keep this in mind when doing your market research. If an international publication only pays, say, the equivalent of $35 to $50 for an article, and you're likely to lose more than half of that in exchange and check-cashing fees, it may not be worth the effort. Fortunately, more and more international publications are turning to PayPal as a means of paying writers in other countries; while this, too, will involve some fees, they are typically much lower than what your bank will charge. Some larger international publications also maintain accounts with a U.S.-based bank and can issue checks in U.S. currency.

While dealing with publications outside your own country can take some getting used to, the benefits can be extensive. International publications may be open to topics that you can't sell "at home," and they can also be excellent places to sell reprints of material you've already marketed in your own country. And, again, if you write fluently in a language other than English, your potential market area will be even greater. If you can write a great pitch, the world is your oyster!

Two Sample International Queries

Here's a pitch from a writer based in India to the U.S. publication *India Currents*:

> Dear Vandana,
>
> Words from around the world have been adopted into the international language, English—learned and passed on by ancient travelers, conquerors, missionaries; like seeds dispersed, far and wide they traveled with the wind and took root in different countries.
>
> Some of the oldest languages (Tamil, Pali, Prakrit, Sanskrit) are rooted in the country that is now called India. It is natural that words from these ancient tongues contributed to the English we speak today. Latin, which is the oldest European language alongside Greek, is said to have been much influenced by Sanskrit and has many words taken from it.
>
> While most people are aware that India gave words like guru, karma and curry to English, do they know about such taken-for-granted words as ginger, cot, and jungle?

I would like to write an article, about 850-1000 words, on Indian words in present-day English for India Currents. I am familiar with your Web site and have read your contributors' guidelines but I can't think of the right slot for such a piece. Do let me know if you would be interested in seeing this article for possible use.

I'm a freelance writer based in Bangalore, India, who loves the different aspects of language (writing, crosswords, word origins, expression, linguistics...). I have had more than a hundred articles published so far in India and other countries. If you would like to see samples of my work, do let me know.

I look forward to hearing from you!

Sincerely,
Hasmita Chander

Here's an example of an e-mail query that I accepted for Writing-World. com. Before accepting this query, I asked the writer whether she would be able to cover the family history market in the United States as well as the United Kingdom; she agreed to do so, and clinched the sale!

Dear Ms. Allen,

Would you be interested in an article on the opportunities for family historians to be published in family history magazines? We have a number of these in the UK and I am sure there are plenty more in the US and other countries. I have been published a number of times in these magazines although I am not an expert, simply a keen amateur.

I appreciate that you wrote an article on the subject of family history for the 8:03 Newsletter, but mine would be rather different. In it I would explain the type of article that the magazines require which could be written be non-experts, and also give advice on writing them. The level of knowledge of the subject which is required varies from magazine to magazine, and intriguing stories involving ancestors (which have been verified) are very popular. But not all the content has to be based on personal stories or histories. For example, for several years I have written a regular column for one magazine which simply required historical research.

Because family history is now such a popular hobby, there are also openings in other magazines, such as retirement and general interest ones. I have had a piece on the pit-falls of family history research published in the retirement magazine of the civil service for which I used to work.

Looking forward to hearing from you,
Rosemary Bennett

4

Approaching Trade Magazines with Letters of Introduction

by Denene Brox

Many writers think that in order to write for magazines you have to write great query letters outlining a catchy idea. But if you want to land assignments without having to query, using letters of introduction (LOI) is something that you can easily add to your marketing plan today. So what exactly is a LOI and how can writers use it to land assignments with magazines? A LOI is a simple letter introducing yourself, your expertise, and your writing availability to editors. Now, before you get overly excited about sending your LOI to an editor at a top glossy publication like *Glamour* or *The New Yorker*, I must point out that LOIs work best with industry trade publications (publications targeted to readers in certain industries). Perhaps there are a few writers who have broken into the majors without querying the editor with a specific idea, but those cases are just as rare as winning the lottery. The competition is too steep, and those editors are bombarded with too many query letters to throw assignments to writers who submit LOIs.

I realize that trade pubs aren't as glamorous as the glossies. But, if you're looking to build clips and make money, they are great in many ways. A lot of trades offer decent pay and don't require as much legwork on your part. I once sent an e-mail LOI to an editor at a trade, and a couple of weeks later she offered me two assignments with her publication, each paying several hundred dollars. Not bad for a writer who didn't have any major credits, and up until then had made a whopping $25 per article! I took the assignments and collected my first big check.

On the flip side, I once spent many hours crafting the perfect query letter for a nutrition article for a major newsstand glossy. The editor expressed interest in the pitch, but wanted some revisions to the idea. I was so excited to have the attention of a New York City editor that I went to work perfecting the query. I spent hours revising it to meet her specifications and sent it off to her, certain that I'd land the assignment. You can imagine my disappointment when she ultimately rejected the pitch. What did I get for the hours I spent working on that pitch? Nothing, zero, nada! (To make for a happier ending, I eventually sold the idea to another newsstand magazine, so all wasn't wasted. But my story does illustrate the relative ease that a LOI can bring a writer.)

When I first started with trades, I focused on industries where I had relevant work experience. Since I only had a couple of clips from my college reporting days to show to trade editors, I relied on my experience in the workforce to get my foot in the door. The logical place for me to start was with trades that focused on financial services. Having worked in the retail banking industry for five years, I played up my experience in banking—and landed a few assignments.

Below is an example of how I used a LOI to break into financial publications:

Date:

To: *Editor@trademagazine.com*

From: Denene Brox
Subject: Writing for Financial Trade Magazine

Dear Mr. Editor (Remember to always find out the editor's name),

My name is Denene Brox and I'm a freelance writer based in the Kansas City area. I am writing to inquire about freelance writing opportunities with *Financial Trade Magazine*. I've written for numerous publications including *Kansas City Magazine and Transitions Abroad*. I am available for work-for-hire assignments, and I'd also be happy to come up with a few article ideas if you prefer to receive pitches from writers.

In addition to my writing experience, I have five years of experience working in the retail banking industry.

Can I e-mail you some clips? I'd be happy to send you PDF attachments of my work.

Mr. Editor, I look forward to working with you. Thank you for your consideration.

Sincerely,
Denene Brox

Notice how I said that I've written for "numerous" publications. I didn't mention the fact that I only had a few clips. I also played up my industry experience to show that I have background knowledge in banking. I got several editor responses to this e-mail and eventually landed assignments with a banking trade publication.

You can use a similar approach to break into trades. What industries do you have work experience in? You can play up everything from working in fast food to manufacturing. What was your major in college? Whether you majored in engineering, business, or basket weaving, there are trade magazines that focus on just about every industry. Mine your life and get creative. If you have no clips, don't mention clips at all. Just state your relevant work or other experience.

My experience in banking ultimately helped me launch my writing business! If you don't have any clips, don't worry. Remember to play up your related experience. If you're pitching a trade devoted to elementary school teachers, for example, be sure to mention your work with your child's PTA.

Here are some tips and resources for locating and contacting editors at trade publications:

- **Buy or check out a copy of the latest *Writer's Market*.** This thick resource book provides market information on all aspects of the publishing industry—from book agents and publishers to trade and consumer magazines. There is a section especially for trades that's organized by industry. Read the guidelines for the publications you'd like to pitch, and pay extra attention to those that state "work-for-hire." This means that the editor(s) assign stories to freelancers without the writer having to pitch story ideas.
- **Pitch ideas.** Just because a lot of trade publications don't require you to query with an idea doesn't mean you shouldn't come up with any. Feel free to approach the editor with a well-written query if you do have a good idea that fits the publication.
- **Locate trade publications** by visiting TradePub.com. There you will find dozens of trade publications you can potentially write for.
- **Use your *Writer's Market* and the Internet to locate contact information for editors.** *Writer's Market* is a good start, but be sure to double check by going to the publication's Web site or calling the publication. I have found that the editors' names and e-mail addresses are easy to locate online.
- **E-mail your LOI to trade editors.** I have received quick responses from my LOIs. Most of the editors say they will keep my information on file (in which case I follow up several months later to remind them about me), and other times they have written back with assignments. That's gold!

- **Keep records of which editors you approach.** You don't want to send an editor your LOI more than once because you didn't remember that you already approached him/her.
- **Personalize your LOIs (and queries).** Use the editor's name and play up your experience that relates to the publication's focus.

Sending LOIs can help you get a steady roster of clients for your writing business while you focus on sending queries to editors at the majors.

5

Newspaper Queries

by Amy Chavez

Newspapers publish letters to the editor, travel stories, features, op–ed pieces, and more. In addition to regular staff members and reporters, newspapers use freelancers to help fill their papers with fresh new material every day. Many newspapers also have a Sunday magazine, inserted into the regular Sunday edition, with local features about the city and its goings-on. The Sunday magazine will have a separate staff from the newspaper and should be queried accordingly.

Although print newspapers are considered a dying breed by some, online newspapers will likely be around for a long, long time. Query an online newspaper as you would a print newspaper.

You can query multiple print newspapers simultaneously, as long as the readership of the papers doesn't overlap. (You can be pretty safe by using the 100-mile rule: If two newspapers are within 100 miles of each other, query only one at a time.) Most newspapers will not care if the piece has already been published in a newspaper outside of their 100-mile radius, since their readers will most likely not have seen it.

This means you can make money over and over for the same piece. Newspapers can also be a great reprint market for articles that previously appeared in other mediums such as newsletters, magazines, or books, as long as the content is appropriate for that particular newspaper's readership.

How to Read the Masthead

Print newspapers rarely publish guidelines, but you can quickly find out who is in charge by reading the masthead. The masthead is the section of the paper that lists the managing editor, the editor-in-chief, the editors, and other staff members. Larger newspapers will have a different editor for each section, such as a news editor, sports editor, features editor, etc. If an editor is listed for the section to which you wish to submit, send your query to the appropriate editor. Full contact information for editors, including e-mail and at least one phone number, should be available online.

Smaller papers may list only the editor-in-chief or the managing editor. In that case, send your query to one of them or call the paper to find out who would be most appropriate to query for your article idea. While you're on the phone, ask if you might be able to speak with the person to run your idea past him or her first.

The annual *Editor & Publisher International Year Book* (available at most libraries) lists addresses and editors of U.S. and Canadian daily newspapers, as well as alternative newspapers and specialty newspapers covering topics such as parenting, seniors, ethnic groups, and real estate. *The E&P Year Book* also gives you valuable information on how often the newspaper is published (daily, weekly, bimonthly), its circulation figures, whether the paper has a Sunday magazine, and a list of the paper's weekly sections and special editions.

Weekly sections focus on subjects like food, entertainment, business, education, church, etc. For example, the weekly food section may be on Mondays, the entertainment section on Tuesdays, etc. Weekly sections often have their own editors. Special editions are published at specific times of the year and have seasonal or popular themes. Example titles of special editions include spring, bridal, back-to-school, health care, baby, home improvement, and holidays.

Knowing what weekly sections and special editions a paper offers will enable you to time your query and target your audience so that you'll have a better chance of acceptance. If you have an article idea that you think would fit into a paper's special edition, call the newspaper and ask them what month the special edition appears, so you can get your query in about six weeks before the publication date. Also, be sure to ask for the name of the editor in charge of that edition.

Making Contact

With the exception of some travel articles or ongoing series of articles, newspaper items are usually short enough (roughly 500–1,500 words) that most editors prefer you send the article, either by snail-mail or e-mail, along with your query. (To put it another way, your query also serves as your cover letter.) Newspaper editors are very busy and work with daily deadlines, so the shorter and more to the point your query is (about half a page is enough), the better your chances of making a sale. Your query letter should briefly state why you think the article is relevant to the readers of that particular paper.

Don't bother sending clips with your query, as most editors are too busy to look through them. However, you should note in your query letter if you have been published before, and where. You can include an SASE if you wish, but many editors don't have time to respond unless they actually want to accept your article. Don't expect the editor to send a rejection for unwanted material; in most cases, it will simply be trashed.

Most newspapers don't encourage telephone inquiries. However, if you feel strongly that you need to talk to an editor before you query, especially if the query is about something timely such as pressing news, go ahead and call. You may also be able to call the editor of a smaller, local paper in your area. If you do call, however, do your best to make it worth the editor's time to talk to you. Don't waste time with idle chit-chat.

Most newspapers accept e-mail queries. Check the newspaper's home page for a list of e-mail addresses of the editors of the print edition.

Op-Ed, Travel, and Feature Articles

The newspaper sections most open to freelancers are the op-eds, travel articles, and feature articles (including profiles). Although newspapers don't all call their feature section by the same title, look for this type of article in sections with names like Living, Weekend, or Style. Regular features such as book or restaurant reviews, music, and theater are usually assigned to staff or reporters.

The easiest area to break into newspapers is through the op-ed pages. The op-ed page showcases opinions of about 400-800 words and is open to a wide variety of subjects and styles. With op-ed pieces, you must send the completed article. Along with the article, send a short cover letter explaining why you wrote the piece. The cover letter is also a good place to cite any credentials you may have that would give credibility to your piece. If you write an opinion piece about a current issue on the education ballot, your piece will have more weight if you happen to have a background in public policy. If you write an opinion piece on the Israeli-Palestine conflict, it will help the editor to know if you lived in Israel for several years. However, if you have no special background related to the piece, that's OK too. Also, don't limit yourself to newsy items. The op-ed section is a good place to submit humor and satire. You can even submit a section from your published book here. In the op-ed section, anything goes!

Features and travel articles require a little more expertise. You'll be expected to demonstrate more knowledge of your subject matter, and more professionalism in your query.

Three Ways to Make Your Query Irresistible

1. **Give it a local slant.** Unless you're querying a national newspaper such as the *New York Times, USA Today,* or the *Wall Street Journal,* your story will have a much better chance of being accepted if it has a local slant. This can be hard to do if you're writing from another state, but there are things you can do to give an otherwise generic story a local slant. For example, if your story is about a small town in the United States, then perhaps your story would have relevancy to readers of other small-town newspapers. Or, if you wrote a feature story about the Amish

in Ohio, you could do a little research and tell readers where they can buy Amish goods in their town. Or, perhaps you may be able to find an Amish person living near that town that you could highlight in a sidebar to your article. Your sidebar would be different for each paper, focusing on a different person. Mention any local slants in your query letter.

2. **Look for tie-ins to newsworthy events**. Travel sections require some type of tie-in to current news or local events. Even international travel can be relevant if you can think of a proper tie-in. If you want to write about your recent trip to Poland, for example, and you find out that your town is having an international food festival next month, you could write about Poland and inform readers that they can see traditional Polish costumes and sample the delicacies you describe in your article by attending the International Food Festival. Do a little extra research and find out if there are any other events such as Polish dancing or a Polish crafts booth at the festival. In your query, tell the editor how beautifully your piece will fit in with the articles that his/her staff will be writing about the International Food Festival.

   Vietnam is just starting to open up to tourism, which makes Vietnam newsworthy and a good possible candidate for a travel article. If, after doing some research, you find that cheap flights and bargain seaside accommodations abound, tell the editor in your query that you'd like to tip off readers to this undiscovered paradise.

   Editors are also always looking for local travel articles. Look for travel trends, such as the recent surge in adventure travel, and write an article about local places to go for adventure. In your query letter, tell the editor that your article highlights places locals can go for thrills without leaving the state.

3. **Offer photos.** If you have decent photos to go along with the article, this will help sell your story. Some newspapers pay extra for photos; others do not.

If you're just starting out and don't have the confidence to query newspapers, you'll be glad to know that there is a way to get published without having to write a polished query letter. Many papers have a section that openly solicits readers' stories. These sections pay very little, if at all, but are easier to break into, and do not require a query letter. Read your newspaper carefully for a column or section that is devoted to reader essays on a special topic (such as women's issues, traveling, parenting, or anything people share in common). At the bottom of the story, you will find a note inviting readers to send their stories. You may find this the perfect way to break into newspapers and to start a relationship with a newspaper editor.

Most freelance newspaper writers start by publishing in their local newspapers. Since bigger newspapers are inundated with submissions, you're much more likely to find a place for your work in your local paper. Furthermore, your local paper will be more open to your ideas and opinions and is a great place to start making contacts. After you've found success at home, you can query bigger, more prestigious papers with a polished query letter that includes mention of your previously published articles.

6

Sample Queries

This chapter offers a selection of sample queries that worked; every query shown here resulted in an acceptance and a publication. As an indication of how things have changed in the past few years, our original "sample query" section included primarily surface-mail queries. In this edition, the vast majority of the queries I received in response to a call for "queries that worked" had been submitted via e-mail.

Noelle Sterne, Ph.D.
(address)
(city/state/zip)
(phone/fax)

September 8, 20—

Loren Mosko, Editor
Novel and Short Story Writer's Market
4700 East Galbraith Road
Cincinnati, OH 45236

Dear Ms. Mosko:

Writers have often been taught that a short story must be small in scale—
a single event, an individual character's evolution, a sole interaction.
From such instruction, writers may feel restricted in subject or setting
and discard potentially powerful ideas.

But many stories demonstrate that the scope can be broad or grand and
still produce the gemlike characteristic short story quality. My proposed
2,000-word article "The Sweep of the Story" shows how writers can
incorporate sweep into their stories without losing the genre's essence.
With examples from such masters as D. H. Lawrence (recapping a
mother's lifetime), Shirley Jackson (covering an annual event), and Ray
Bradbury (traveling light years), as well as lesser-known writers, in four
vital points I advise writers how to integrate and "manage" the sweep of
their stories:

1. Establish Your Sweep

Don't be afraid of the sweep. Like a movie camera "panning" a grand
view, it can set a compelling scene, give the reader many clues about the
story, and irresistibly arouse curiosity. Then you can "zoom in" to the
smaller incident, character, or relationship that is the story's focus.

2. Make Your Sweep Relate

To use sweep successfully, it should not be simply your version of a
lush description of, say, war-torn years, à la Gone With the Wind. Your
sweep must relate precisely to the heart of your story. Otherwise it will
seem self-indulgent, and readers will likely lose interest before they even
get to the "real" story.

3. Decide How Long to Make Your Sweep

When you've established your sweep and tied it closely to the story, decide how long you want to stay in the larger scene. Here you can "test" the sweep, expanding it or reining it in.

4. Measure Your Sweep

Once you have a draft down, go back and gauge the sweep you've decided on. Simply count the words or pages that treat the larger scene and compare them to the total length. If your sweep is too long, readers not only lose patience but become confused about your point. If the sweep is too scant, readers may miss its importance.

This article frees writers from thinking that they must always limit their short stories to small and narrow subjects. As your readers observe how other writers use the sweep and experiment with their own, they won't rule out any subject as too "big" for great short stories.

My fiction has appeared in *Alternatives, Philadelphia Review and Columbia* (university alumni monthly), among other magazines. More recently, I have concentrated on writing for writers. Current credits include articles this fall in *Writer's Journal* and the children's writer's magazine *Once Upon A Time.* For several years I have known Maria Witte, former editor of *Writer's Forum,* presently Managing Editor of *Writer's Digest* and Executive Editor of two *Writer's Digest* special interest publications (SIPs). She has published or accepted five pieces for *Writer's Forum, Writing Basics, and You Can Write for Children.*

Further, Brian Klems, Associate Editor of *Writer's Digest* and Executive Editor of the *Writer's Digest* SIP *Spiritual Writing,* will publish two of my articles in this magazine, to appear in October 2005.

Sincerely,

Noelle Sterne, Ph.D.
Enc/SASE

Noelle Sterne
(address/city/state/zip/phone)

December 17, 20—

Ron Kovach, Senior Editor
The Writer
21027 Crossroads Circle
Waukesha, WI 53187

Hello, Ron—

Many children's authors may not recognize that they can draw on more publicity opportunities for their works than can mainstream authors. I became aware of this fact through the publication and extensive publicity, much of which I initiated, for my children's book *Tyrannosaurus Wrecks: A Book of Dinosaur Riddles* (HarperCollins).

The book was in print for eighteen years, has been widely used in schools, and was featured on the first dinosaur show of the award-winning PBS-TV series for children, *Reading Rainbow.* This episode continues to be aired nationwide on public and cable television networks.

Using illustrations from my experience with *Wrecks,* my proposed 2500-3000-word article "Let Them See Your Title! Publicizing Your Children's Book" describes over fifteen avenues children's authors can use to broadcast their names and titles and extend the lives of their books. These methods apply equally to commercially- or self-published authors.

The following venues will be discussed:

1. Schools, teachers' groups, PTA groups
2. Public libraries, malls, bookstores
3. Church and synagogue children's groups
4. Book fairs
5. Announcements and postcards
6. Web sites and links
7. Book reviews in newspapers and magazines
8. Book donation to a local school or public library, with writeup in local paper
9. Parent- and child-oriented talk radio and television shows
10. Relatives, friends, neighbors, acquaintances, strangers

11. Article about the book for newspapers and magazines
12. References in textbooks for teaching reading
13. Excerpts in children's magazines and other media
14. Spin-offs (e.g., puppet show, t-shirts, stickers)
15. Sequels

As this list shows, children's authors can choose from a wide range of publicity possibilities, some of which have been little written about. If you are interested in this article for *The Writer,* I'll gladly send it.

Sincerely,
Noelle Sterne, Ph.D.

Query to *BriarPatch*, a Canadian magazine, submitted by e-mail

Jacquie McTaggart
(address, e-mail, URL)

On opening day of the 1999 school year, the Jefferson Leadership Academies in Long Beach, CA became the first public middle school in the country to offer separate classes for boys and girls. Today 442 public schools across the United States offer some same-gender classrooms, and dozens more are in the planning stage. Do single-sex classes increase the achievement of both genders, or are they just another "innovative" flash in the pan?

As a forty-two year classroom teacher and frequent featured speaker at International Reading Association conferences, I often write articles pertaining to kids - how they learn and how society can better help them achieve their maximum potential. The piece I am pitching, "Single Gender Classrooms: Fad or Future?" will examine the pros and cons of single-sex classes, beginning with some basic, but often misunderstood facts about the different learning styles of girls and boys.

I will interview Liz Crowley, principal of the Walter Cunningham School of Excellence in Waterloo, IA, and Beth Bruno, principal at Paine Intermediate in Trussville, AL for this article. Both schools began offering a few single-gender classes in 2006, and both have added more the past two years - due to popular demand. A possible sidebar could include a list of resources for further study: Books, Web sites, and articles. I estimate 2000-2500 words for this piece. I think it would be a good fit in your September/October issue.

Focal Points:
History and statistics
Pros and cons
Quotes from some (student, teacher, parent, principal) who have "been there, done that"

My stance: Practice will continue to gain in popularity because it is meeting a need

My writing has been published in *Parenting*, *Pediatrics for Parents*, *American Educator*, *Reading Today*, *Teacher*, *The Catholic Teacher*, *Writer's Digest*, *The Iowan*, and countless regional parenting publications. I am happy to mail writing clips upon request, or send them electronically as attachments. You can also visit my Web site at *www.theteachersdesk.com* to see samples of my writing—and experience my sense of humor.

Thank you for your time and consideration.

Jacquie McTaggart

(Note that this query has no "to" address block or salutation—something I would strongly recommend including!)

Query to UK's *Home and Family* magazine, submitted by e-mail

Dear (Editor's Name Removed)

Our daughter Eleanor was a much longed for baby. For years we'd been told we'd be very lucky to have children, but then miraculously she came along. She was an angel baby and at eight months old she was happily eating whatever food we gave her. Then one day we gave her an egg sandwich and her airway started to close.

"Egg—the Unusual Suspect" is a 1400-word parenting/health article, based on my real-life story of how we discovered that our daughter has an egg allergy. Egg is the most common cause of food allergy amongst toddlers and babies and can be just as life threatening as peanut allergy, yet until my daughter was diagnosed with it, I'd never heard of it, and I bet none of your readers have either.

This article is aimed at both parents and helpers at mother and toddler groups and contains information they need to know including: the causes of egg allergy; how to test for egg allergy; hidden sources of egg such as face paints and cappuccinos, and guidance on cooking without eggs, including a recipe for an egg-free birthday cake.

The article includes two information sidebars; one on the typical symptoms of an allergic reaction and the other detailing all the names for egg used by the food and pharmaceutical labeling industry.

I am qualified to write this article from a mum's perspective as I have been living with egg allergy for the past two years and I have meticulously researched every aspect of egg allergy in order to make my life, and the lives of those who care for my daughter, including the helpers at our church mother and toddler group, easier. It is this information I want to share with your readers.

If you like the idea, I can have the article with you, complete with photographs if required, within seven days of your go ahead.

Thank you for taking the time to read this query.

Yours truly,

Dawn Copeman
Freelance Writer

Query to Writing-World.com, submitted by e-mail

Dear Ms. Allen,

Are you looking for a tasty take on success with selling books at a booth for Writing World? Having sold books at dozens of events over the past five years, I've put together a "recipe" for connecting with readers and making sales. Since so many authors try to market their books this way, I thought it would be a good fit for your site, which is so clearly focused on working writers. And working a booth is work!

This how-to article covers ten ingredients for successful events: making that first connection, standing up to convey energy, offering prospects the book, resisting the urge to loom, giving away a sample or take away to non-buyers, steering prospects to other authors, making friends with fellow vendors, eating out of sight and being ready to be "onstage," taking notes about book buyers, and enjoying oneself.

Under my pseudonym, I've sold over 30 short stories to various anthologies since 2004, and Lethe Press published Rough Cut, my short story collection last year. I've sold books at library events, book festivals, Pride events, and other venues, and honed my skills on making those one-on-one connections with readers and book buyers. Currently, I freelance edit for Torquere Press, Samhain Publishing, and Publication Services, and my recent story sales include Lycanthrope: The Beast Within from Graveside Tales and Gay City Health, Volume Two.

Thank you for your time; I look forward to hearing from you about the article.

Sincerely,

B. T. Writer
(author's name withheld by request)

Query to UK's *Heritage Magazine* (published in the US as *Realm*), submitted by e-mail

Dear Penelope Rance,

A COUNTRY HOUSE AT SEA

Would you be interested in an illustrated feature about the Royal Yacht Britannia?

The 30th June 2007 marks the tenth anniversary of Britannia's final official duty, at the handover of Hong Kong to China. From here, she sailed back to Britain and was decommissioned. She now resides at Ocean Terminal, near Edinburgh, and is a great tourist attraction. Open all year, it is the only place where visitors can see a private bedroom of the current reigning Monarch.

Britannia is not palatial and ostentatious, but warm, cosy, friendly and welcoming. Kings and Queens of Britain have built castles, and country estates, except Queen Elizabeth II, who helped design the interior of Britannia. She wanted it to feel like a country house at sea.

"A Country House At Sea" will provide a guided tour around this warm and homely yacht, focusing on the rooms that visitors can see such as the Royal Private Quarters, as well as the Officer's Quarters and relaxation areas. Many of the facts and stories illustrate how the Royal family cherished their times onboard. It was the only time when they could truly relax.

Walk around and the 1950's décor seems very out of place, until you learn that items were only replaced when they couldn't be repaired or refurbished. Step into the engine room and admire the highly polished pipes and boilers, but don't make the mistake that General Schwarzkopf did when he asked to see the real boiler room not the museum piece. So high were the standards on Britannia, the mat outside the door to the boiler room was for people to wipe their feet on BEFORE entering.

I can provide several high quality large 300dpi digital images for illustration purposes to compliment this article, and would be happy to supply everything on spec for your final consideration if you think the idea is of interest.

I envisage such an article would be between 1200 to 1500 words in length, but would be happy to meet whatever your requirements would be.

Thank you for your time. I look forward to hearing from you, and enclose a stamped addressed envelope for your reply.

Yours sincerely
Simon Whaley

Query to *British Heritage*, submitted by e-mail

Subject: Photo Feature Proposal: Chichester Flower Festival

From: (e-mail)
Date: Mon, July 13, 2009
To: (British Heritage)

Dear Editor,

When we saw the notice for the forthcoming Chichester Cathedral flower festival in 2008, we thought: Flowers, how nice. We'll be there.

When we stepped inside this 900-year-old cathedral, we realized that "nice" didn't begin to cover it. Adjectives like "awesome, stunning, and mindblowing" were more appropriate. Every niche, every tomb, every chapel in this magnificent cathedral was filled with bouquets, scenes, and arrangements on a wide range of themes, from spiritual to international. Giant bouquets of lilies hung between the chandeliers, like living stained glass; columns were wreathed with garlands. While some displays relied upon the basic bouquet, others sculpted flowers into wedding cakes, tea parties, and Christmas treats. Perhaps most amazing of all was the constant juxtaposition of living, fleeting blossoms against stones that had stood for nearly 1000 years—and might stand for another thousand.

Chichester will be celebrating its 8th biennial flower festival in May 2010—and I believe a photo feature on this spectacular event would be ideal for *British Heritage.* I have attached a selection of sample photos; more can be viewed at *www.timetravel-britain.com/gallery/chichester.shtml* High-resolution versions of these and additional photos are available.

My husband and I spent 15 months in England from 2007-2008, and became adept at photographing inside dimly lit cathedrals and similar buildings. I have been a freelance writer for more than thirty years, and am the host/editor of the popular writing site Writing-World.com (which attracts over one million visitors per year) and the British travel site TimeTravel-Britain. com. I am the author of *Starting Your Career as a Freelance Writer* and *The Writer's Guide to Queries, Pitches, and Proposals* (both from Allworth Press).

I hope you will consider this feature, as it is sure to entice visitors to this wonderful event. I have contacts within the festival who will provide additional information should the article be assigned.

Sincerely,
Moira Allen

Query to Writing-World.com, submitted by e-mail

Hi Dawn and Moira,

I have used, or presently use, Facebook, MySpace, LinkedIn, Twitter, BlogSpot, and my own Web site Wordpress blogs. That said, I'm sure there are many people with more experience out there. I'm not a person who lives with these 24x7. There would never be any time to write, which is the biggest challenge for writers who are a one-person business. The question is, is it worthwhile? Yes. Can it take over and get out of hand? Yes.

My social media connections resulted in solid online references that potential customers can see and contact, as well as many new connections. In addition, I connected with two potential jobs within the first week on Twitter. One is sending me a contract, and the other is still pending. In this market, that's worthwhile. A list of articles I could write for you in this area is below.

Social Media, Blessing or Curse?—This article would deal with the time factors and which social media are worth an investment of the writer's time.

Do you tweet, or is that twitter?—This article would cover the basics of this specific social media, including basic tips and hints, along with cautions.

Facebook, MySpace, or LinkedIn?—This article would talk about the differences in the sites and the reasons for using them, or not.

Is a blog still worthwhile?—This article would talk about the advantages and disadvantages of separate blog Web sites vs. a blog on the writer's Web site.

I'd enjoy doing any of the above articles for you. If you are looking for additional basic "how to" primers of instructions to get started for any of the sites I listed, I can do that too. In Twitter, I'm relatively new, and I haven't used all of the management tools that are available. If you need a very advanced Twitter user for an article at the expert level, I know one I can recommend. I send out tweets and use Tweetdeck, which is free. This seems to be all I need for now.

The blog article is a current topic I've been investigating. After checking into the search engine and SEO thinking now, I just moved mine to my Web sites for the benefits. Now, the challenge is to get the content built up again. Why not just more previous content to it? I'll be happy to explain in the article. <grin>

Please let me know which subjects you'd like to have me write, and I'll get started. I've written for Moira before, but it's been a long time.

Have a write-perfect day!
Penny

Moira Allen

address • city/state/zip
phone • fax
e-mail

(Date)

Marcia Preston, Editor
Byline
(address)
(city/state/zip)

Dear Ms. Preston:

The pet magazine market is an ideal place for newer writers to "break in." However, it is constantly flooded with inappropriate submissions. To break in, one must understand what these magazines want, and what they won't accept. I'd like to offer you an 1800-word article on how to write for the pet markets, covering the following topics:

- The types of articles pet markets are hungry for (e.g., care, training, health, breed), and how to write them even if you're not an "expert."
- How to win assignments from the major pet magazines (and even how to be considered for a column).
- The types of articles pet magazines don't want to see, and why ("my first puppy," "the day my cat died," talking pets, etc.).
- How to turn a personal experience article into a marketable service piece.
- Understanding the different markets (including why all dog magazines are not the same), what they expect, what they pay, and what you can expect from them.

I'm the ideal person to write this article, as I was the editor of *Dog Fancy* for two years, and am thoroughly familiar with all the major pet publications. I have been writing for the pet markets for more than ten years, and am a member of the Dog Writers' Association of America. I am the author of the award-winning *Coping with Sorrow on the Loss of Your Pet* (Alpine, 1996). I also teach professional and creative writing at two local colleges, including a class on this topic.

If you'd like to see the article, I can have it in your hands within 30 days of your go-ahead. Thanks for your time and attention; I look forward to hearing from you.

Sincerely,
Moira Allen

Moira Allen

address • city/state/zip
phone • fax

(Date)

(Editor's name)
Entrepreneur Magazine

Dear Ms. (Editor):

Thanks to a translation glitch, Microsoft was forced to pull its entire Chinese edition of Windows 95 from the marketplace. Microsoft recovered—but that's the sort of mistake few small businesses can afford! Yet thanks to the Internet, international markets are suddenly only a few keystrokes away. Just about any home office entrepreneur with a computer and a modem can create a Web page that may be accessed around the world. If those keystrokes are wrong, however, that same page can drive international business away.

I'd like to offer you a 1500-word article titled "Internationalizing Your Online Market." The article would discuss how small businesses can take advantage of "localizing" or "internationalizing" agents to tailor both their products and their marketing strategies to the international marketplace. Localizing includes not only translation assistance, but advice on "cultural correctness" in both one's product and marketing approach. For example:

- When is a mailbox not a mailbox? "Standard" computer icons often reflect images that are incomprehensible or offensive to other cultures—including images of American-style mailboxes that may have no counterpart in the market you're trying to reach.
- When are pictures of babies offensive? In Moslem countries, the display of bare body parts (even diaper-clad babies) is unacceptable, even when considered modest by Western standards.
- Is it really black and white? In the West, black is the color of funerals and white is the color of weddings. But in Asia, white symbolizes mourning and death, while red symbolizes marriage.
- Does anybody know what time it is? Depending on your market, it could be 3:30 PM, 1530, 15h.30, 15.30, or 15:30. Times, dates and currency expressions vary widely throughout the world!

My article would describe the types of services available from a localizer, the costs involved, and how to find such services. It will highlight "inter-nationalizing" a Web page to make it more effective, "culturally correct," and user-friendly in the international market. The article will include an interview with Sol Squires, president of Twin Dragons, who will share some of the blunders that can be avoided with localization help.

When even the smallest of businesses are capable of offering products and services via computer to the international marketplace, business owners need to know how to avoid the pitfalls of this type of marketing. I believe this article would be timely and useful to your audience; if you agree, I can provide the piece within 30 days of your go-ahead. Thanks for your time; I look forward to hearing from you.

Sincerely,

Moira Allen

Moira Allen

address • city/state/zip
phone • fax
e-mail

(Date)

Annette Bailey, Editor
Cats Magazine
(address)
(city/state/zip)

Dear Ms. Bailey:

Last summer, our beloved 15-year-old cat succumbed to cancer. Along the way, we learned a lot about this disease and how it affects cats.

Cancer is not an immediate death-sentence for a cat; some forms of cancer can be managed medically to prolong a cat's life with little or no discomfort. However, it is vital to recognize the presence of cancer early, and discuss options and treatments with a veterinarian as soon as possible. To help your readers do just that, I propose a 2,500-word article on "Cancer in Cats." The article would cover:

- The types of cancers most common in cats (including mammary tumors and cancers of the mouth, lips and gums—some of which are preventable!).
- How to recognize the signs of cancer early (what is that lump?).
- The symptoms and progression of various types of cancer (weight loss, diminished appetite, coughing, and wheezing can all be signs of cancer).
- The types of treatments available, pros and cons of different treatments, how treatments can affect a cat's life expectancy and quality of life, and how to find treatment (not every city has an animal cancer clinic).

The article would include information on cancer treatment from Dr. Alice Villalobos, head of the Animal Cancer Center in Hermosa Beach, CA, and from the local veterinarian who assisted me during my own cat's illness.

You are already familiar with my qualifications as a pet writer from our previous correspondence (former editor of *Dog Fancy* and associate editor of *Cat Fancy*, author of *Coping with Sorrow on the Loss of Your Pet*, etc.) If you are interested in the piece, let me know and I will be able to provide it within 30 days of your response. Thanks for your time and consideration; I look forward to hearing from you.

Sincerely,
Moira Allen

Mary Rose

(address
(city/state/zip)
(phone)

——————————, Editor
Fine Gardening
(address)
(city/state/zip)

Dear Ms. ———:

Forget-me-nots. I love their wistful name. I love their tiny blue flowers. And yes, I love that growing them is as simple as pie. Beneath rose shoots shriveling from blight, my forget-me-nots cheerfully ignore fungi brought on by yet another wet Washington spring. But in spite of their simple nature, forget-me-nots have shown up in some pretty sophisticated places: Monet grew them at Giverny, Jefferson planted flocks of them at Monticello, and Lady Chatterly's gardener found an unusual spot to strew some.

Forget-me-nots: Simply Unforgettable Spring Flowers is an exuberant thousand-word profile detailing:

- Historical background
- Varieties and colors
- Usefulness in formal, cottage, and native gardens
- Growing requirements
- Cautionary measures

Your encouraging response to a query of mine prompted me to share my love of forget-me-nots with you. I look forward to your reply.

Sincerely,
Mary Rose

[This is a good example of follow-up! Mary had submitted a previous query that was rejected, but with an encouraging personal note; she followed up immediately with this query, which was accepted. Her bullet list mirrors the publication's guidelines.]

SECTION 2
Columns & Syndication

7

Selling a Column

Your mother thinks you're the next Erma Bombeck. Your friends embrace your advice with the same awe they'd accord Ann Landers. You can't count the number of times you've been told, "You should write a column."

And perhaps you should! Columns offer many benefits. A column announces to the world that a publication regards your work highly enough to make you a "regular" rather than an occasional contributor. Columnists are generally regarded as "experts," which can help you in your quest for other assignments. Columns also provide a steady income: You know that you'll be receiving a regular check, for a regular amount.

Getting a column assignment, however, is not easy. Most publications have limited space for columns, and the competition for that space can be fierce. Because columns build reader loyalty, editors generally prefer to hold onto existing columns as long as possible, which means that opportunities for new columns are rare. To win one of those spaces, it's vital to do your homework so that you can prepare a truly dynamic proposal package.

Choosing a Market

The first question you should ask yourself is "where do I want to publish my column?" You may already have an answer—you'd like your column to appear in a favorite magazine, your local paper, or a noteworthy Web site. If you don't, take a moment to consider some of your options.

NEWSPAPERS
Newspapers represent by far the largest market for columns. Even the smallest regional papers generally run a few columns, often by local authors. Larger papers run a mixture of local and national (syndicated) columns. While weekly papers feature weekly (and sometimes monthly) columns, daily papers usually offer a mix of weekly and daily columns. Weekend editions often feature columns that don't appear during the week, including

review and "local event" sections. Some newspapers also feature rotating monthly columns, with a different author featured each week.

Newspapers also offer the widest variety of content for a single publication. Regular sections may include health, cooking, lifestyle, women's issues, religion, books, movies, local events, travel, and more—and each of those sections may have several column opportunities. (For example, a weekly cooking section might include a column on healthy recipes, another on regional specialties, another on diet and weight loss, another on baking, another on vegetarian cooking, etc.) Since newspapers are based on regional readership, they seek material that will appeal to a broad cross-section of the public, which improves your chances of breaking in.

The downside of newspapers is that many offer very low pay for columns. Even today, smaller newspapers may pay as little as $15 to $25 per column. While larger papers pay more, you still won't get rich writing for a single newspaper. However, as newspaper readership is regionally based, you can often sell the same column to more than one (non-competing) paper. (See chapter 7 for tips on how to self-syndicate your column.)

MAGAZINES

While most magazines run a selection of columns, this market can be much more difficult to penetrate. Of all publications, magazines are the most limited in the amount of space they can offer columnists. When a column slot does come up, magazine editors generally turn first to their stable of regular contributors to look for a new columnist. The best way to get a shot at a magazine column, therefore, is to become a regular contributor, thereby establishing yourself as a reliable writer who can be counted on to produce quality material on deadline and with a minimum of fuss. Once you have contributed several pieces to the magazine, you may wish to pitch a column idea to your editor; even if the idea isn't accepted, you'll have planted the idea that you are interested in writing a column when an opportunity becomes available.

Magazine columns generally offer better pay than newspaper columns, though that pay is usually monthly rather than weekly. The downside of working for magazines is the possibility of "editorial interference"—while some editors let columnists write about whatever they wish (within the constraints of the column topic), I've also worked with editors who attempt to micromanage a column by dictating topics, style, and even what they want you to say about specific topics. Be sure, therefore, that you can work comfortably with a particular editor before you offer to do so on a monthly basis.

ELECTRONIC PUBLICATIONS

A number of electronic publications are available to writers, including e-zines, newsletters, "content" Web sites, and more. Such markets often defy conventional description. Your first thought might be to look for e-zines or e-mail newsletters that cover your interest area, but that's just the tip of the electronic iceberg. Many commercial sites (such as online pet-supply stores) offer "content" sections to attract visitors, and feature a number of regular columns. Other sites focus on pure content, and offer thousands of articles and columns.

Finding these sites can be a challenge, but breaking in is often relatively simple. Online, space is far less limited than in print, so electronic publications can often afford to run more columns. Columns are usually archived, so readers can locate not only your current offering but everything you've written to date.

Payment for online columns varies widely—anywhere from $15 or $20, to $300 or more. E-mail newsletters generally offer the lowest rates (and seek columns under 1000 words). E-zines tend to fall within the mid-range, while commercial and "content" sites generally pay higher rates. There are no "rules," however; judge every site on its own merits.

Most electronic publications ask only for electronic rights to your column (though there are exceptions), which leaves you free to market the same column elsewhere in print.

Columns and Credentials

What kind of column do you want to write? While the potential for topics is virtually infinite, most columns fall within one of five basic categories: How-to/informational, advice, op-ed, review, and humor. Each requires a certain set of credentials.

HOW-TO/INFORMATIONAL COLUMNS

Look in any publication, and you're likely to find one or more columns that teach you how to do something. In your local newspaper, you'll find gardening columns, cooking columns, health columns, parenting columns, and a host of others. Larger papers often feature columns on managing finances, buying and selling real estate, improving/maintaining/decorating your home, caring for your pet, and even more esoteric subjects. Travel columns tell you where to go, what to see, how to get there, and how to save money. Self-help columns tell you how to improve your personal life and relationships.

Magazines offer a similar array, tailored to the subject matter of the publication. A health magazine might offer columns on fitness, diet, or alternative health care. A pet magazine may offer tips on training, medical care, and behavior. A more general women's magazine may host columns on fashion, beauty, household hints, health, and a dozen other topics.

To break into the "how-to" column field, you need to know how to do something and how to do it well. Unlike a freelance article (for which you can interview experts), a column generally relies on *your* expertise, *your* credentials. Don't try to write a gardening column if you've never picked up a rake! However, if your keyboard is covered with muddy fingerprints from your last potting escapade, a gardening column might be perfect for you—especially if you have the ability to explain complicated techniques and concepts in simple, easy-to-follow terms.

ADVICE COLUMNS

Advice columns often overlap with "how-to" columns in that they, too, offer instruction. Advice columns are based on reader questions, "Dear Abby" and "Ann Landers" being perhaps the best-known examples. Though such columns are popular, most publications offer only a few advice columns (compared to the number of "how-to" columns), making this a more difficult field to break into. It's especially difficult to penetrate the "personal self-help" advice column market, as a handful of well-known columnists are syndicated to even the smallest newspapers, rarely leaving room for an additional columnist.

To pitch an advice column, you need to be able to demonstrate two things: Your credentials for giving the advice, and your personal appeal as a columnist. Readers who might consider asking your advice need to know why you're qualified to answer their questions, and your answers need to be sufficiently interesting to those readers who *don't* write in, but simply read your column for information or entertainment, to build a following. A good approach to such a column would be to choose a specific aspect of life—e.g., dating, the office, parenting, etc.—that has a broad appeal yet isn't being covered by a syndicated columnist.

Often, specific credentials will be required for an advice column. An editor seeking a parenting columnist, for example, is likely to require someone with a degree in psychology. A medical advice columnist will usually be expected to have a medical degree. Similarly, a pet-health column will typically be written by a veterinarian. Before you attempt to pitch an advice column, therefore, be sure you have the necessary credentials to answer that first question: "What qualifies you to give this advice?"

OP-ED COLUMNS

Everyone has an opinion, and op-ed (opinion/editorial) columns have been long been a staple of newspapers and general-interest magazines. Op-ed columns can cover just about any topic: Politics, world events, social issues, special interests, even personal topics. Newspapers and general-interest magazines are more likely to seek op-ed pieces on issues of interest to the largest possible audience (such as politics, current events, and general social issues). Smaller publications, such as local and regional newspapers, may feature op-ed columns that relate directly to local events (or local perspectives on larger issues). Special-interest publications feature op-ed pieces that relate to those interests. Finally, many publications offer opportunities for op-eds on purely personal matters.

To sell an op-ed column, you generally need more than an interesting opinion. You also need to give the reader (and an editor) a reason why *your* opinion should be heard. Sometimes this is a matter of credentials or experience: If you have twenty years' experience in international affairs, your opinion on world events might be a hot commodity. Sometimes it is a matter of demographics: Do you speak for a particular "group" that seeks a voice? Sometimes it's as simple as being "local" and being able to offer an opinion that is representative of your community (or, conversely, challenging to your community). The primary question an editor may ask of a would-be op-ed columnist is "what segment of my readers will want to hear what you want to say?" To pitch an op-ed column, you may need to explain not only what you are speaking about, but whom you are speaking *for.*

REVIEW COLUMNS

Just as nearly every publication has some form of how-to column, nearly every publication also offers some type of review column. Subjects most commonly reviewed include:

- Books, movies, and music
- Arts, events, and (live) entertainment
- Products (including computer products and games)
- Restaurants (and other "on the town" locations)
- Travel destinations and accommodations

Some publications offer reviews in only one or two of these areas; others offer review columns for all of them and more. Keep in mind that these subjects can also be applied topically. For example, a pet magazine is likely to feature reviews of products and books relating to pets. A travel magazine may feature reviews of destinations, accommodations, restaurants, books on travel, and even, perhaps, helpful electronic gizmos for the traveler. A computer publication is likely to seek reviews of new software, hardware, games, and possibly books. A local newspaper is likely to seek reviews of local attractions (such as restaurants), movies, books (including books by local authors), and anything else that will appeal to the audience of that area. Online publications also offer review columns, while a handful of sites consist of nothing *but* reviews. The larger and more general the focus of a publication, the broader its range of review columns (and the greater the possibility that you may be able to break in with a column that covers something not currently reviewed by that publication).

The good news is that this type of column often requires no special credentials. Review columns blur the line between information and entertainment; while their stated purpose is to inform readers about the quality of a product or event, many such columns are popular simply because of their style. Consequently, for most consumer publications, all that is required is an ability to discuss a book, product, or event intelligently and interestingly.

The bad news is that because no special credentials are required, this is often the first place that would-be columnists look for work. Review columns offer an extra appeal: the fun, even the glamour, of being able to do things you would do anyway (read books, watch movies, eat out) and then get paid to write about them. To earn a space, you'll have to ensure that your column rises above the competition.

Finally, don't imagine that review columns are a ticket to free movies, free dinners, free travel, or free books. Most such products are sent directly to publications, not to reviewers—so you have to obtain a column slot before a publication will pass those products on to you.

HUMOR COLUMNS

Humor columns are among the hardest to launch, for several reasons. First, humor columns generally fall into the category of "entertainment," and most publications devote only a limited amount of space to pure entertainment rather than information. Second, what is funny to one person (or writer) often isn't funny to another. It's tough to tickle an editor's funny bone, and even tougher to build a reader following. Third, the market is already saturated; if your local paper already carries Dave Barry, it's not likely to want or need a second humor column. The fact that most of us know the major humor columnists by name is an indication of how few such columns exist (or become successful). That doesn't mean you shouldn't try; it simply means that you should not expect humor to offer you an easy entry into the world of columns.

OTHER COLUMNS

The categories listed above are certainly not the only possible types of columns; they are simply the most common. Other types of columns do exist.

One such column is the "slice of life"—personal glimpses into your own world, your life, your thoughts and feelings. These, however, are tough to sell: you have to find a way to convince the editor, and reader, that your life is not only worth writing about but worth reading about. (Your opinions, on the other hand, might fit into the "op-ed" category.)

Another tough-sell is a purely "informational" column (as opposed to a how-to column)—e.g., a column that offers facts or trivia that may be interesting, but that don't have any direct application to people's daily lives. While certain special-interest publications may offer purely factual columns, these are hard to find in more general-interest markets. If you want to write this type of column, see if you can present it in a "how-to" format—e.g., if you're writing about azaleas, remember that most people aren't that interested in the history or botanical details of the flower, but would be more likely to want to know how and when to plant them and what varieties to choose for the garden.

The Basic Column Proposal

No matter where you hope to sell your column, your basic proposal should include the following elements:

- A query
- Three to six sample columns
- Clips of other (relevant) published work
- Supporting material (optional)

THE QUERY

A query for a column is very similar to that for an article. However, instead of proposing a single piece, you are proposing an ongoing series, so the goal of your query should be to present a rationale for why the target publication would want to cover your subject on a regular basis.

Instead of going into detail about any single column, therefore, your query should present an overview of the nature and purpose of the entire column. Describe the subject, and explain why this subject is of sufficient importance (or interest) to merit ongoing coverage.

The Hook

The goal of your hook is to establish not only that you have a worthwhile subject to cover, but a subject that is too large to be handled in a single article. Your hook should also offer convincing evidence that a large number of the publication's readers would be interested in this subject on an ongoing basis.

Any of the types of hooks listed in chapter 2 can serve this purpose. Suppose, for example, that you are proposing a column on natural health alternatives to a general-interest women's publication. Any of the following hooks might pique an editor's interest:

- **Problem/Solution:** Many women today are becoming increasingly frustrated with the limitations of "traditional medicine." Often, traditional techniques—or harried HMO doctors with not enough time—just don't seem to answer women's questions or meet their needs. More and more women are seeking alternatives—and seeking accurate, helpful information to guide them toward those alternatives.

- **Informative**: Natural remedies have become big business. No longer confined to strip-mall "health stores," they now line the pharmacy shelves of every supermarket. Now, more than ever, women are in need of accurate, reliable information on the products competing for their health dollars—and on how to safely incorporate natural health care into their lives.

- **Question:** Are you bewildered by the array of natural products on your local supermarket shelves? Do you wonder whether these products are safe, whether they can actually meet their claims, or how to choose between them? If so, you're not alone; thousands of women face the same decisions every day.

- **Personal Experience/Anecdote:** When I had my first baby, I wasn't prepared for the violent reaction I would have to XXX drug. Yet it was all my doctors could offer. The next time, I vowed to be prepared; I studied alternatives, and found natural solutions that eased my pain without ruining my health. Since then, I've talked to many women who wished they had the same options...

- **Attention-grabber:** Nature can be the death of you—even when it's attractively bottled in a supposedly "safe" product on your supermarket shelf. While natural remedies offer a host of helpful alternatives to traditional healthcare, it's vital to know what you're doing—what's in that bottle, how much you can safely take, whether it actually works, and how it might react with other natural products.

The Pitch

Your hook should lead directly into your pitch—and your pitch should clearly describe the type of column you are proposing. Be sure to include a catchy but descriptive column title in your pitch: A good title helps "fix" your idea in an editor's mind.

Your pitch should include two additional pieces of information: The length of the column and its frequency. If you're pitching to a monthly magazine, the frequency is predefined; however, if you're pitching to a newspaper or online publication, you should state how often you would like your column to appear. If possible, include the section of the publication in which your column would fit—for example, the "Tuesday Health Section" of your local paper.

A good pitch to follow the hooks above might read:

> I'd like to offer you a [monthly, weekly] column covering the many facets of natural health care. Titled "Your Guide to Natural Health," this column would fit well within your "To Your Health" section. It would run between 750 and 1000 words, and cover such topics as:

The Body

The body of a column query should list a selection of topics that would be covered in your column. A bullet-point list often works well for this:

My column would cover such topics as:

- Traditional home remedies: Which ones work, and why.
- How to read and understand the labels of "natural" products.
- Why "natural" doesn't necessarily mean "safe" and how to use such products safely.
- Understanding the health claims of natural products: What they're based on, whether they're true.
- Product interactions: Knowing which natural products can be taken together and which can be harmful.
- Teas, tisanes, and distillations: How to best prepare a natural remedy.
- Natural remedies for pregnancy and childbirth problems.
- (etc.)

Be sure to provide enough information on each point to ensure that the editor can clearly determine what the column will be about.

The Credentials

As I mentioned above, columns are generally based on the writer's personal credentials. You're much more likely to sell a column based on your own skills, education, expertise, or experience than on interviews with other experts. Columnists dispense wisdom, counsel, and advice; therefore, readers expect them to be "experts" in their own right. Since an inaccurate column can damage the credibility of the entire publication, editors will want to be sure you have the credentials to qualify you for the job.

The Close

The final paragraph of your query should offer a potential start-date for your column. If appropriate, it may be the place to specify your terms: the rights you are offering, and in some cases, the fee you expect. In most cases, however, you'll leave these matters to be negotiated after the editor approves the column idea.

SAMPLE COLUMNS

Unlike an article proposal, a column proposal only begins with the query letter. The heart of your proposal will be the columns themselves—the proof that you can deliver what your proposal promises.

Most editors expect to receive at least three, and sometimes six, sample columns with a proposal. Needless to say, these should be your best work; this is your first and only chance to demonstrate both the value of your information and the quality of your writing style.

Format your columns as you would an article submission, with each column beginning on a separate page. If your column is likely to require fact-checking (or if the publication routinely fact-checks columns and articles), provide a list of references with each column. (One way to do this is to provide footnotes throughout the column. These are strictly for editorial use, and will be removed when the column is actually printed.) Add a brief "about the author" bio to the end of your columns.

Don't use the same topics for your sample columns that you've listed in your query. Your query should present a list of topics that goes beyond your samples, to demonstrate that you have plenty of material for an ongoing column.

CLIPS

Good clips are often essential to make the sale. While your column may demonstrate that you can write well, your clips demonstrate that you write well enough to have been accepted and published, preferably by reputable publications. Be sure to select clips that relate in some way to your column. If you don't have clips that relate directly to the subject matter, use clips that relate to the general type of column you're proposing—for instance, if you're offering a how-to column, send along clips of other how-to articles that you've written, even if they aren't on the same subject.

Your clips needn't necessarily be from consumer publications, or even material for which you were paid. If you are basing your column on professional or educational credentials, and have contributed to professional journals or in-house publications at your place of employment, these may be sufficient to help establish your expertise and demonstrate that you have written about your subject before.

A published book makes an excellent clip. Being able to state that you are the author of a book on your column subject is one of the best ways to establish your expertise and authority. If you can, send the publisher a copy of the book itself. Otherwise, send a photocopy of the cover and one or two chapters, and copies of any especially favorable reviews (particularly reviews that have appeared in reputable publications).

SUPPORTING MATERIAL

In addition to your query and sample columns, you may wish to provide some supporting material to back up your credentials. Such optional material might include:

- A publications list (highlighting publications relevant to the column).
- An expanded author bio.
- A photo. (You will often need a photo to run with the column, but many writers prefer to send in such a photo only after the column has been accepted.)

THE SUBMISSION PACKAGE

Unlike article queries, column proposals should generally be submitted by surface mail, for two reasons. First, you are submitting a large package, which would create a very long e-mail message—something an editor might be unwilling to read online, and equally unwilling to print out. Second, column proposals do not lend themselves to a quick response, which eliminates the primary value of submitting by e-mail. Submitting a package by surface mail enables an editor to review your submission thoroughly, and perhaps pass it around to others before making a decision.

Submit your column package in a professional manner. Use a 9 x 12 mailing envelope so that your materials will arrive flat and unrumpled, and include a SASE for the editor's response. (A letter-size SASE should be sufficient; just indicate that you don't need to have the materials returned.) Be aware that it may take longer to make a decision on a column proposal than it would on a regular article query; wait at least six weeks before following up.

The exception, of course, is when submitting to electronic publications. When submitting to an online market, you should send your proposal by e-mail unless the market's guidelines indicate otherwise. Unless the market indicates a willingness to accept attachments (most don't), include everything in the body of a single e-mail. Make sure that you have saved your material as a text-only file, and checked for any odd characters that can result from "smart quotes" and other special formatting. (See chapter 3 for a list of tips to observe when formatting an e-mail query.) Often, you can avoid submitting actual clips and simply refer the editor to a Web site that offers some of your previously published (and preferably relevant) material.

The final stage of the process involves "negotiation." Once an editor decides to accept your column, you'll need to negotiate an acceptable contract and rate of payment. What constitutes "acceptable" in either category can vary widely from writer to writer and publication to publication. Keep one thing in mind: If you have any thoughts of moving on to syndication, you'll need to retain the rights that enable you to do so. But that's another chapter!

8

Self-Syndicating Your Column

Once you've been writing a column for a few months, you may want to consider the next step: Marketing that column to more than one publication. This is particularly appropriate for newspaper columns, as newspaper readership is generally based on region rather than interest, and thus rarely overlaps. You can often sell the same column to newspapers in different states, or even papers in different counties or cities within the same state, as long as you are certain that there is likely to be little reader overlap.

Many writers dream of national syndication, but this is considerably harder to achieve, at least in the beginning. (See the next chapter for more information.) It's usually easiest to start by marketing your column to an ever-expanding list of newspapers until you've built enough of a following to justify a larger distribution. In short, you'll want to begin by syndicating *yourself.*

"Self-syndication" simply means offering a column on a nonexclusive basis to several different publications that are not in direct competition with one another. The best place to start is with local and regional newspapers. Because the distribution of such newspapers is generally limited to a specific town, city, county, or region, such a paper will not be concerned with the fact that your column also appears in the next county or even the next city. (See chapter 5 for Amy Chavez's explanation of the "100-mile rule": Don't submit the same material to two newspapers within a 100-mile radius of one another.)

Choose a Topic

The previous chapter discussed several types of columns. If your goal is to self-syndicate, you'll want to choose a subject that crosses regional boundaries or that can be sold to a variety of publications within a certain geographical area.

Some topics, such as health tips or parenting, are universal (or at least tend to work well within the bounds of your own country; other countries may have different health systems or different ideas about parenting). Other topics, however, tend to be more localized. If you're writing a gardening column, for example, you'll need to tailor it to the region you're familiar with, addressing the issues of climate, soil conditions, plant types, etc., that apply to that region. It would be difficult to sell a column on Northwest gardening tips to a newspaper in Arizona. The subject of your column, therefore, will often be the first consideration in determining where to market it.

The farther afield you choose to market your column, the less "commonplace" it should be. While you may be the only person writing about parenting for your home-town paper, thousands of other writers are covering this topic for other publications throughout the country. To break into a wider market, therefore, you'll need to develop a column that contributes something unique within the field—something that will enable it to compete with other columns that address similar topics.

The same applies to "review" columns. Reviews of books, movies, and music may cross regional boundaries (if you can create a compelling reason for an editor to buy *your* reviews rather than those of a local or nationally known reviewer). Reviews of restaurants and events, however, tend to be much more localized (though you might be able to pitch such a column to a travel page as a "destination" piece).

In short, don't waste too much time trying to export a column that has only a limited local value. Focus, instead, on ways that you can give your column a broader appeal—or, consider launching an entirely new column that you can market to multiple publications from the start.

Select Your Markets

You might be amazed to discover how many local newspapers exist in your state or region. You can locate such newspapers through any of the dozens of electronic "newsstands" on the Web. You can get even more detailed information about many papers through the *The Gale Directory of Publications and Broadcast Media*, which can be found in the reference section of your local library. While researching newspapers online is easier, Gale has the advantage of providing important information about circulation, frequency, and editorial staff. If you have decided, for example, that you only want to target newspapers that are distributed daily and have a circulation of over 20,000, you may wish to turn to Gale.

Amy Chavez notes another resource in chapter 5 of the annual *Editor & Publisher International Year Book*. Available in most libraries, the *Year Book* "lists addresses and editors of U.S. and Canadian daily newspapers, as well as alternative newspapers and specialty newspapers covering topics such as parenting, seniors, ethnic groups and real estate. *The E&P Year Book* also gives you valuable information on how often the newspaper is published (daily, weekly, bimonthly), its circulation figures, whether the paper has a Sunday magazine, and a list of the paper's weekly sections and special editions."

Pre-screening newspapers by content and circulation is a wise precaution. You don't want to waste time or money submitting columns to weekly "Pennysavers," or papers that are clearly too small to have any budget for freelance (or at least nonlocal) submissions. In addition, if a city or region is served by more than one newspaper, you won't want to submit to both simultaneously.

Some regions are served both by local papers and a larger state or big-city paper. Since you don't want your column to appear in both (or more accurately, your editors won't appreciate it if your column appears in both), you'll need to decide which to target first. This may not be as easy a decision as it sounds. While a big-city paper may pay more (and will reach a larger audience), it is also likely to demand more rights (or even all rights), and is also more likely to want to post your material on its Web site, which can limit your ability to distribute that column elsewhere. Smaller papers, though offering lower pay, may be less demanding of rights and less likely to archive your work on its Web site.

Define Your Terms

Your basic syndication submission package should include a simple description of the terms you are offering, including:

- Column length (usually 750 to 1,000 words is best)
- Column frequency (daily, weekly, biweekly, monthly)
- Rights offered

Rights are a key issue in self-syndicating a column. Indeed, you should start thinking about "rights" long before you consider self-syndication; you should think about this issue when you sell your very first column to your very first paper.

Markets of all types are placing increasing demands on writers for their rights. More and more publications (including small-town newspapers) want writers to sign over all rights to their columns, or even produce them as "work for hire" (which means that the newspaper owns the copyright to the material from the beginning). You may find that publications that pay as little as $10 to $50 per column still expect you to fork over all rights to that piece.

If you have any intention of selling your work elsewhere, you must ensure that you retain the right to do so. Typically, you will want to offer a newspaper "one-time nonexclusive rights" to your column, perhaps with the guarantee that the column will not appear in a competing publication. An alternative is to offer "exclusive regional rights," and define "region" as narrowly as possible. The region should be limited to the area of the newspaper's general readership; if the paper is read only in Yakima, Washington, for example, don't let your contract restrict you from selling the same column to another paper in Seattle or Tacoma.

In some cases, a newspaper will want "first" rights. This may work if your first column sale is to your local paper; it gives you the ability to resell that column a week later to all your other markets. Since only one publication can ever be "first," however, think carefully before granting this option.

Don't be tempted to accept more money for "all rights." The goal of self-syndication is not to earn a huge amount from any single publication, but to gain the widest possible distribution for your piece. Payment for columns is always fairly limited; you're not likely to get an offer above $500 from even the largest paper. If you can sell the same piece to twenty newspapers that offer $50 apiece, you've already doubled that figure—and quite possibly doubled your readership as well. (If you have hopes of moving on to national syndication, readership figures will be vital to your success. It is better to be read not just by a large number of people, but by a large number of people distributed across a wide range of markets.)

Also, make sure that the paper using your column does not automatically offer its columns for distribution to other newspapers. A columnist recently brought this issue to my attention: She had been providing a column to a local paper at no charge, and discovered that the parent group owning the paper had been making the column freely available throughout the country, without her knowledge or permission (and certainly without a contract specifying that the company had the right to do this). However, ultimately this worked to her best interest, as she was able to demonstrate that her column had wide appeal and had already been "picked up" by more than twenty-five papers when she made the jump to self-syndication.

Finally, you'll want to determine a minimum rate you're willing to accept. Some small newspapers still offer as little as $10 per column, but that amount can add up quickly if you can sell your column to several papers. Debbie Farmer, who syndicated her column "Family Daze," sets her fee by a standard formula: 50¢ per 1,000 subscribers.

Prepare Your Package

Self-syndication has one downside: expense. Many newspapers still prefer to receive column proposals by surface mail than by e-mail. This means that to pitch your idea to a wide range of markets, you'll have to invest in postage, printing, and envelopes.

Your submission package will be much the same as that described in the previous chapter, including:

- A cover letter describing your proposed column (be sure to list the terms you are offering)
- Three to six sample columns
- Clips
- Supporting materials, if desired
- A SASE, or
- A self-addressed, stamped postcard that provides "check boxes" for an editor's response

Many editors prefer a postcard to a SASE, as it enables them to quickly check off the appropriate response, rather than having to prepare a formal letter of acceptance or rejection. Your postcard might read something like this:

Date: _____

Dear (Your Name):

Thank you for submitting your proposal for a column titled "Natural Health Tips for Seniors."

_____ We would like to use this column on a weekly basis. We will pay you a fee of $ _____ for one-time, nonexclusive rights (per your guarantee that the column will not appear in a directly competing publication).

_____ We regret that we cannot use your column.

(Signed) _____

Editor's Name: _____

If you plan to submit your column to a large number of newspapers, you'll probably want to have all your materials printed in bulk. Have your cover letter printed on a high-quality paper stock; your clips and column samples can be printed on plain bond paper. Most print shops will also be able to print your return postcard. To save costs (and weight), print clips double-sided.

Follow Up and Move On

If you don't hear anything from your top prospects within a month of your mailing, don't hesitate to follow up. Often, material gets lost on a busy editor's desk, and a polite phone call may be all you need to close a sale. (In this case, a letter or card also stands a high risk of being lost in a shuffle of papers, so a phone call is actually a better follow-up mechanism.)

Don't be surprised if an editor wants to modify the terms of your agreement. Some may wish to suggest a lower price, or a different word count. It's up to you to decide whether to accept such modifications. If you will be distributing your column to a large number of publications, attempting to tailor the material to each one individually may not be worth the effort. On the other hand, if you've received little response to your mailing, this can be a good way to build a solid relationship with one or two newspapers, which can lead to better rates and additional assignments later.

If you still don't hear anything after following up on your initial mailing, don't be surprised. Many newspaper editors simply do not respond to material they don't plan to accept, so you may never receive any word from many of your markets. Don't be insulted; simply move on to the next prospect.

Self-syndication is a wonderful way to build your portfolio. Be sure to ask for copies of the issues in which your column appears, or at least for a tearsheet of your column. Once you have a regular column with a local paper (even if it's not local to *you*), you can list yourself as a "contributor" or "stringer" to that publication. This may be just the stepping-stone you need to propel your column into the big leagues—such as national syndication.

How I Became a Syndicated Columnist
by Debbie Farmer

About two years ago I decided I didn't have enough excitement, frustration, and uncertainty in my life, so I decided to become a syndicated family humor columnist.

I starting writing monthly family humor articles for the local Mother's Club newsletter while my children were napping. About six months later, I brought column samples to the editor of a tiny, independent newspaper and it began running my column every two weeks.

I stayed with that paper long enough to generate several months'-worth of clips and some fan mail, then approached the features editor of the larger daily newspaper. Now I was competing with established syndicates who had professional columnists, but I offered the editor something she couldn't get elsewhere—a local family humor columnist.

The bigger daily gave my column a catchy name ("Family Daze") and started publishing it weekly. I finally began to take my writing more seriously. I figured out that the only chance I had of earning pay that reflected the hard work I put into each column was for it to be picked up by a major syndicate that could market it to hundreds, perhaps thousands, of papers. This became my goal—right along with every other freelance newspaper columnist in the world. But since ignorance can be bliss to a budding columnist, I was naïve enough to think that I could beat the odds.

I quickly learned, however, that I had a better chance of breaking into a major syndicate if I self-syndicated my column into as many papers as I could manage. I sent out packets to editors that contained a cover letter, publishing history, six column samples or clips, and a price/distribution sheet. I put everything into a folder with a clear cover with my cartoon logo on the first page showing through.

Kathleen Purcell, who self-syndicated her column "The Corner Booth" to dozens of newspapers, suggests using a bright blue cardboard folder with a business-card die-cut centered about 1/3 of the way down the front cover. She says, "I selected six of my favorite columns, dropped my photo (digitally) onto the upper left quadrant (just like it would appear in a real column), and ran them off on my printer. Those I put in the right pocket of the folder. In the left pocket I put my bio, list of papers where my column was running, cover letter and three business cards (one for the editor, one for the secretary, and one to pass out to other editors at conferences). The cover letter explained how I billed, how much I charged (50¢ per thousand circulation, according to the newspaper's circulation figures published in *The Gale Directory of Publications and Broadcast Media*), when they could expect to receive columns, and how to contact me if they had a problem."

I also use a standard pricing formula of 50¢ per 1,000 circulation. This means that I receive amounts between $50 per column (from my local paper) to $1.50 per column (from my smallest independent paper). The average price range is generally $10–$15 per column. Of course you have to find the marketing system that works best for you, your schedule, and budget.

Since everyone's pitching style will be different, do what's comfortable for you. I tried to keep my pitch short and sweet—preferably with no begging. OK, just a little begging. I highlighted my publishing history, reader appeal, and professional awards.

Kathleen Purcell's "pitch" takes specifics of the publication into consideration. She says, "For small, community papers I said my column built reader loyalty, would *not* offend advertisers, supported community values, and appealed particularly to women with children (easily the bulk of their readership.) For larger papers I said my column was unique, timely, built readership, and provoked discussion."

After two years, my persistence finally paid off. Well, almost. "Family Daze" is now published weekly in over two-dozen newspapers, I've sold articles to national parenting magazines, and I have a trial offer pending with a national syndicate. It just goes to show that with a little bit of moxie, persistence, determination, and luck, you can successfully syndicate your newspaper column. Just don't quit your day job—yet.

A Successful Proposal
by Diana Lynn Tibert

Canadian author Diana Lynn Tibert offers another example of a successful column proposal. This simple pitch demonstrates several key elements that can help make a sale. She notes, for example, that while this column is relatively new, she has written another column for six years—demonstrating that she has staying power, meets deadlines, and as she notes, "the well of ideas never runs dry." Her credentials indicate that she has more to offer than just writing skills; she has expertise in the proposed subject area.

Diana writes that at the time of submitting this query, "my column was only three months old and published in only four newspapers. This query sold my column to *The Kings County Record*. With little tweaks here and there, I reused the query and sold my column to several other publications. My column is now four years old and appears in ten newspapers.

"This query was sent through e-mail, but I don't slack on format. I create the e-mail as if I were mailing a letter: date at the top, name and address of the person I'm sending it to, salutation, proper paragraphs, my signature, and contact information. Below the query, under a short dotted line, I include samples of my writing. In this case, I sent the column that introduces me and the column."

(Date)

[Interim Editor]
Publication Name: Kings County Record
Mailing Address
Phone Number

Dear Mr. _____,

The holidays are over, the lights are extinguished and winter has set in. What is there to do? It's time to pull out the binders and scribbled notes and start working on the family tree again.

This time of year, many individuals pass the long days researching their family trees. On the Internet, in the archives and newspapers, they continue the search to knock down brick walls and extend the branches to find new family members.

What better time to pick up the local newspaper to find information on how to help them with their search?

"Roots to the Past," a genealogy column just months old, will fill the need of the many individuals who are just starting to search their family tree and for the researcher who has been growing their tree for years.

My "Roots to the Past" column has been welcomed by the many readers of the *Halifax Daily News, The Western Star, The Journal-Pioneer,* and *The Citizen.* One column was so popular that the Cumberland County Genealogical Society requested permission for it to be reprinted in their newsletter, *Cumberland Roots.*

Since beginning the column in November, I have had several requests from New Brunswick residents regarding queries and where they can read the column. However, at the moment, my column is not published in the province.

My professional writing career is more than six years old. In that time, several hundred articles have been published in newspapers, magazines and e-zines. Dozens of photographs have been published alongside these articles. My credits include *Canadian Gardening, Plant and Garden Magazine, Saltscapes Magazine, Guysborough Journal,* and several others.

My experience with columns is extensive. My "Garden Tales" column, which currently appears in four Nova Scotia newspapers (*Weekly Press, Dartmouth Laker, Bedford Magazine,* and The Southender), will celebrate its sixth anniversary this March. Not only are all deadlines met, but the well of ideas has never gone dry.

My passion for writing and photography is matched only by my passion for genealogy. I have been researching my family tree for more than fifteen years. My family tree grows in Nova Scotia, but it also has roots in Newfoundland, Prince Edward Island, New Brunswick, and in the western provinces and the United States. I am English, German, Scottish, Mi'kmaq—in other words, Canadian.

I would like to offer "Roots to the Past" to the *Kings County Record.* Below is the introductory column for you to read.

Thank you for your time. I look forward to hearing from you.

Sincerely,

Diana Lynn Tibert
www.thefamilyattic.info/Tibert.html

9

How to Become a Syndicated Columnist

by Amy Chavez

Most column writers dream of becoming syndicated. Syndicates distribute your articles to newspapers and magazines, with the profits split between you and the syndicate. Representation by a major syndicate guarantees a wide readership for your work.

Getting syndicated is tough, though, especially via the print medium these days, since so many newspapers are dying out. With fewer print channels for syndicates to sell to, you may be better off considering a column for an online audience. For your column to get syndicated in print, it really has to stand out.

It must also be appropriate. Many submissions received by syndicates are more suited to magazines (which don't work on an immediate, time-sensitive basis) rather than newspapers. Op-ed pieces, review columns, and commentary, for example, must be relevant to what is happening right now—not what happened three months ago. Magazines also target niche audiences, whereas newspapers—and newspaper columns—must appeal to a more general audience.

Ideas that are appropriate for syndication are those that lend themselves to weekly, twice-weekly, or even daily news or updates, such as a column about technology or stocks. Columns that provide a voice for a certain population of people are popular: For example, Ted Rall (Universal Press) represents the voice of Generation X, while Leonard Pitts (Tribune Media Services) speaks for African Americans. Such opinion columns draw from the news, a never-ending resource for material. Advice columns on subjects such as personal finance, parenting, and relationships are also appropriate, while horoscopes and crossword puzzles are staples in syndication.

Unfortunately, all these topics have been taken. What you'll need to do is uncover a new idea that doesn't compete with anything already out there, yet isn't too narrow in scope. For example, a column on healthy, timesaving recipes for working mothers might be appropriate, whereas a column on cookbook reviews would be too narrow for syndication.

Since syndication slots are limited, competition for them is stiff. To replace an existing columnist, or fill the shoes of a columnist who is retiring, your column has to be dramatically better than anything else coming across a syndicate's desk. That means your idea has to be fresh and new, offering something the syndicate doesn't already have.

This is not as easy as it sounds. "Although syndicates say they want new ideas in theory, some of them don't seem to want to sign them in reality," noted David Astor, a former senior editor of *Editor & Publisher Magazine*. For the print media, an appropriate idea is one that is new but not too risky. Riskier ideas are better suited for online media.

Show the Need for Your Column

If your material has already been published elsewhere, you've proven that there is a need for your material. Thus, self-syndicating your column (as described in the preceding chapter) is an excellent place to start. Once you've gotten your column into several publications (preferably in different regions, to demonstrate that it is not simply of local interest), you can put together a package of sample columns to show to a syndicate. The more papers you can sign up on your own, the better your chances are of convincing a syndicate there is a need for your column.

In order to know what syndicates are looking for, keep up with the trends. Some syndicates offer "syndication packages," whole broadsheets containing several articles that newspapers can simply add as a section to their paper. Syndication packages can cover topics such as food, health, technology, parenting, and dozens of other areas. Some packages cover a variety of topics; others focus on specific subject areas. For example, when car racing increased in popularity, syndicates began to offer weekly packages of NASCAR information. Another company offers sudoku syndication packages to college and university newspapers.

When newspapers buy a package, they pay a set price for the entire section. This is good for columnists because syndicates have to sign on more writers to fill the sections. The pay, however, can be less than a standard 50/50 split. Syndication packages tend to pay one set price for your article, no matter how many packages are sold.

How to Approach a Syndicate

Before you send out your submission, do your homework. Doing so will save you time and prevent you from making costly mistakes that will only further delay your pursuit of syndication.

Get a copy of the *Editor & Publisher Syndicate Directory*, updated annually and available from the E&P Web site, which lists all the syndicates in the United States as well as all the names of syndicated columns and columnists (including those self-syndicated). Contact names and addresses are listed for all syndicates, as well as their Web sites. By visiting syndicate Web sites, you can quickly find out what kind of columns they already carry. Since many columnists are self-syndicating their columns these days, knowing who these people are, what kind of columns they write, and where their columns appear will help you decide if your column idea should be pursued or not.

Read the latest news about syndicates and syndicated columnists at *Editor and Publisher Online* for industry gossip, current acquisitions, and editorial changes. This is also a great place to spot trends and opportunities. (At the E&P Web site, click "Departments," then "Syndicates.")

Once you decide which syndicate to approach, be sure to read the submission guidelines (usually posted on their Web site). Most syndicates want to see about six sample columns. If your work has already been published in other places and you have received feedback from readers, include some copies of their letters in your package. Even negative letters are useful; the fact that you are able to stir people's emotions and create controversy can be an excellent selling point. Also, make sure that you obtain letters of recommendation from editors who are running your column. Other things to include in your package are articles about you or your work that have appeared in publications, your publishing history and a bio.

It takes time and effort to put together an attractive package to send to a syndicate. But remember, the most important part of your package is your column idea. It needs to be more than good; it needs to be phenomenal!

SECTION 3
Selling A Nonfiction Book

10

Preparing a Nonfiction Book Proposal

Take a look around any bookstore, and you'll quickly realize that the vast majority of books offered for sale are nonfiction. Nonfiction titles cross the spectrum of ideas and experience. Some appeal to a small, focused niche of readers; others have an audience of thousands.

The good news is that the nonfiction book market is fairly open to new writers, provided that you have a marketable idea and the skill to present it in a readable (and hopefully interesting) form. The even better news is that you can often sell your nonfiction book *before* you write it, by presenting a convincing proposal to the right publisher. This means you won't have to start writing without a commitment from a publisher (and quite possibly an advance). It also means that you can get feedback from the publisher before you start, so that your book is tailored specifically to that publisher's needs.

Finding the Right Publisher

The first step in selling a nonfiction book is to find the right publisher to sell it to. Locating an appropriate publisher means more than grabbing a directory of markets and looking in the topic index. Just because a publisher offers books on "dogs," for example, doesn't mean that it's the right publisher for your dog book. You can waste a lot of time sending out proposals to inappropriate publishers—or save a lot of time by targeting the right publisher on your very first try.

Here are some steps you can take to find that publisher:

1. **Check your bookshelf.** Take a look at the references you use in the subject area you're writing about. Do certain imprints stand out? If so, these may represent publishers who produce the kinds of books *you* use for research—which means that your own book might fit well into their line-up. Make a note of any imprint that appears more than once on your bookshelf.

2. **Check a bookstore.** Browse through the shelves as if you were looking for titles you might want to buy in the relevant topic area. Again, do certain imprints stand out? Do you find that you pick up books by a specific publisher more often than any other? If so, this is another indication that the publisher matches your interest area—and that you might match the publisher's interests as well. While you're browsing, ask yourself these questions:

- **Do you like the look and feel of the publisher's products?** Is the paper of high quality? Is the cover attractive? Does it make you want to pick up the book and browse? Is the type easily read? Would you want your book to be presented in a similar fashion?

- **Does the book "look" like the book you're planning?** One thing to consider, for example, is illustrations: If the publisher likes to use lots of color photos, can you supply them? Conversely, if your book requires artwork and you see no illustrations in the books you're reviewing, will you be able to convince that publisher of the need for art?

- **Does the style and presentation match your own?** Pay attention to the "language" of the books you've selected. Do they match your style and tone? If you write in a conversational style, don't try to pitch to a publisher whose books are all written in a highly technical or academic style.

- **Do your credentials match those of the publisher's current authors?** Take a look at the authors' bylines. Would yours be comparable? Or does this publisher require academic degrees or professional experience that you lack?

- **What is the price range of the publisher's books?** Does it match the "buying range" of your target audience? You may like the idea of presenting your work in glossy coffee-table format, but will your audience be willing to shell out $30 or more to buy it? Or would you be better off with a publisher who offers more reasonably priced editions?

3. **Check the Web.** Once you've located two or three publishers who seem to be likely candidates, look for their Web pages. On the publisher's Web site, you should be able to review the publisher's current catalog and submission guidelines. Take a look at that catalog: It will tell you not only what authors the publisher features, but also whether it has produced (or will shortly be producing) any titles similar to yours. If the publisher has recently offered a book much like the one you're about to propose, it isn't likely to want another (especially as the two books would be in competition with one another).

4. **Review the submission guidelines.** Make sure your proposal matches the publisher's requirements. Are you offering the right kind of information and supporting materials? Is your book the right length? (If it isn't, can you cut it back, or expand it, as needed?) Does your book fit into the range of desired topics? Make sure you know exactly what the publisher wants you to submit, and submit precisely those materials.

5. **Review the publisher's terms.** Most print publishers don't post copies of their standard contracts online (though many electronic publishers do); however, they will usually provide an overview of the basic terms they impose on authors. Make sure you aren't submitting your book to a work-for-hire publisher, or you'll lose the copyright. Make sure you understand what royalties are offered, on what basis (e.g., retail price vs. net profits), and when they will be paid. Knowing these things in advance will prevent you from making the mistake of accepting a bad offer, just because you feel that any offer is better than none.

Essentials of a Proposal

Once you've found an appropriate publisher, your proposal must answer three basic questions: "What is this book about?," "What is the market for this book/idea?," and "Why are you the right person to write it?" To answer those questions, you'll need to prepare a package that consists of the following elements:

- **Overview**. This section is usually divided into several subsections, including:
  - ◆ Content (a general summary of what the book is about)
  - ◆ Rationale (a discussion of the potential market for the book, as well as why it should be published "now")
  - ◆ Competition (a review of other books on similar topics)
  - ◆ Format (the length and presentation of the proposed book)
- **Chapter-by-Chapter Outline**. This section provides a list of chapter titles, and usually a brief (one-paragraph) description of each chapter.
- **Author Credentials**. This is where you'll answer the all-important question, "Why are you the person to write this book?" Your bio should be at least half a page to a page in length.

The Overview

TITLE

While your title may be the last thing you decide upon, it will be the first thing a potential editor sees when reviewing your proposal. Author Amy Shojai (whose successful proposal appears at the end of this section) points out that a title "must not only describe the book and/or concept, but be that elusive thing that editors/agents describe as 'sexy.' In other words, the title must strike an instant chord of recognition with the editor. One of my favorites, still, is my book, Competability: Building a Peaceable Kingdom Between Cats and Dogs." At the same time, she notes, "don't get too attached to titles, either. Editors change them all the time, often for something that's boring (after all the trouble you went to in finding a killer name!)."

CONTENT

What is your book about? Presenting a coherent, well-defined answer to this question is crucial to selling your idea. Your topic must be both broad enough to justify a book-length manuscript and specific enough to focus on a definable market niche.

For example, if you're a pet writer, you wouldn't want to pitch a book about "dogs." That's far too broad a topic (as evidenced by the hundreds of "dog books" already on the shelves). Instead, focus on a more specific topic that you're qualified to write about, such as medical care of dogs, traveling with dogs, hiking with dogs, breeding dogs, training dogs, etc. Even then, you may need to narrow the field. Amy Shojai's proposal for *New Choices in Natural Healing for Dogs & Cats: Over 1,000 At-Home Remedies for Your Pet's Problems* (published by Rodale Press), for example, doesn't attempt to cover every aspect of "medical care" for pets, but focuses on "natural health care."

The first part of your overview should offer a general summary of the content of your book. Don't go into excessive detail; instead, try to convey the general focus and purpose of your book, including the benefits it will offer to readers. (The concept of "benefits" is key: Your overview should clearly indicate what readers have to gain from your book.)

Amy Shojai explains that her book "examines the world of nontraditional medicine for dogs and cats, and offers real-world applications to the many health conditions that affect our pets." Note, again, that this is a very general overview of the subject matter. At the end of her proposal, however, she includes a "therapy thesaurus" that lists "(about) 100 common dog and cat illnesses/conditions." That list is enough to give the publisher a clear idea of the topics to be covered (from acne to wool-sucking), without cluttering the overview itself with excess detail.

RATIONALE

Besides explaining what your book is about, your overview should also provide an idea of the audience for that book. "Back up the need for the book with stats," says Shojai. "Editors want numbers; don't just say 'everybody who loves pets will buy my book.' Tell them how many owners there are who have dogs who chew used bubblegum and would benefit from your book, 12 Steps to De-Gumming Da Dog."

Shojai's approach is to offer broad statistics that define the potential of the market: "66.2 million cats and 58 million dogs are kept by Americans."

She then narrows that market to the "most likely" readership: Those who "welcome pets into their hearts and homes as full members of the family. This pet-generation is eager to provide quality care for their furry families…" She further defines the market by noting that the "national obsession with health and fitness" also applies to pets—and that a large number of pet owners are also interested in alternative health care options.

By highlighting a growing trend (the interest in alternative health care), Shojai also indicates why her book is *timely*. Her proposal conveys the impression that the time to target this market is *now*, while the trend is growing—but before the market is saturated with books on the topic. Be sure that your proposal answers the vital question: Why publish this book *now*?

Though I've listed "Content" and "Rationale" separately, these should not necessarily be separate components of your overview. In most cases (as the sample proposals in this section illustrate), they will be tightly interwoven. As you discuss content, you should also present your rationale for why this particular content will be important to your target audience at this particular time.

COMPETITION

Your overview should also discuss the competition that currently exists for your book. If you perceive little competition for your book (few books on the market on the same or similar topics), you may decide to cover this topic in your discussion of "content" and "rationale." If, however, your book faces steep competition (i.e., many books have already been published on similar topics), you may wish to break this out into a separate section, so that you can address the competition in detail.

Before you can discuss the competition, however, you must first research it. Hopefully, you've already done this before you started working on your book: It's vital to know what has already been written, so that you don't end up reinventing the wheel. Your publisher will also want to know that you've reviewed the competition, and that you can offer something new and different.

Amy Shojai sums up the need to study the competition in a nutshell: "The competition section is vital; it's probably the most important part of any proposal. [It's a] balancing act here, though—I try to *never* slam the competition, but just to put my proposal in a favorable light compared to whatever might be out there. In this case, I felt that some of the competition was quite good—just way, way out of date, which meant my proposal was timely. Of course, I added lots of new elements the competition doesn't have, too."

Your discussion of the competition should list specific titles (including author, publisher, and publication date). It should then explain how your book differs from those titles: how it improves, differs from, or goes beyond what has been written before. For example, Shojai lists several representative titles in her proposal, then notes that while most of her competitors focus on single therapies, her book will present a range of approaches. She sums up her description of the competition by stating that, "No book to date offers the comprehensive balance, positive approach and step-by-step advice of *Healing at Home Naturally*."

Several years ago, when I proposed a book to Allworth Press, one significant competitor was one of Allworth's own titles. To demonstrate that my book filled a niche not addressed by that title, I prepared a chapter-by-chapter comparison of the two books, noting points that would be covered in my book that were not covered in the existing title, as well as points addressed in the other book that would not be covered in mine, to demonstrate that I was avoiding overlap. My goal was not to suggest that my book was "better" than the existing book (not always a good thing to try to tell a publisher!), but rather, that it would meet a different need in the market.

What if you can't identify any competition for your book? This is not necessarily a good thing! Shojai notes, "If there is no competition, find some. Put something in, even if it's a stretch, because if nobody has done the topic before, the publisher/editor will figure there's a reason—probably because it's not a saleable idea. You *want* books on your topic to be out there and successful; that means you have a ready-made market. Then it's a matter of making your book different enough, bringing something new to the table, to make the idea viable." Chapter 11 looks at ways to research your competition via Amazon.com.

FORMAT

Even if your book is not yet written, your publisher will want an idea of its anticipated format. This section may be as short as a paragraph; it should list the book's title and subtitle, the number of words you anticipate, and any other information that will be relevant to the actual production of the book.

For example, Shojai's proposal notes that her book will be organized in two sections, the second of which will be in the form of a "thesaurus." She also mentions the use of sidebars, and an appendix that will include a glossary, directory, and resources.

A proposal for a medical history textbook by Dr. Robin Anderson is even more specific about format, offering the outline of a typical chapter:

- Introduction—general overview of chapter and chapter themes
- Body
  - Text with large margins
  - Subheads to break chapter into components
  - 10-12 illustrations, sidebars, or vignettes
  - Use of bold face to accent key terms unfamiliar to reader
- Conclusion

Be sure to mention any illustrations or other artwork that will accompany the book—e.g., charts, diagrams, figures, tables, line drawings, photographs, etc. If you plan to use color illustrations, make sure that the need for such illustrations is clear, as these will involve extra production costs.

MARKET

While you presented a rationale for the type of audience your book is likely to attract earlier in your proposal, you may also wish to add some specifics about how to reach that audience. Shojai, for example, lists a variety of pet and health magazines that target the same market as her book and cites circulation figures for each. She also provides a list of organizations that might be interested in her book (and, possibly, in promoting it).

This information isn't absolutely necessary at this point. However, keep it in mind—because you'll be asked to provide it if and when your proposal is accepted. By presenting it in your proposal, you'll have demonstrated, again, that you have done your homework, and can offer the publisher not only a high-quality book, but also valuable support in selling that book.

Chapter-by-Chapter Summary

While this may be the largest part of your proposal, in terms of pages and word count, it is the most easily explained. Simply provide a list of planned chapters, and a brief (one- to two-paragraph) overview of the contents of each.

Of course, this may be more easily said than done. If you haven't actually begun to write the book, you may not have any idea how many chapters it will contain, or what will go in each. If you don't, guess. Your publisher will expect this information in your proposal—but will also understand that it isn't written in stone.

One way to develop such a summary is to work from your existing outline. If you haven't developed an outline yet, this exercise will accomplish two tasks in one. Dividing your planned content into chapters is a good way to determine the logical organization for that content—and also a good way to discover whether you have too much information in one area and not enough in another.

There are no "rules" about how many chapters a book can or should contain. However, if you're familiar with other titles in your subject area, you'll probably have a good idea of how many chapters those titles contain, on average. "Ten" is always a nice, round number. Five chapters or fewer may make your book seem too short, even if each chapter is packed with information; more than twenty chapters may make the book seem too long or unwieldy. (Remember, you can always adjust the number of chapters later in the writing process.) There are no "rules" for chapter titles, either. Some writers, like Shojai, let chapter titles speak for themselves. Others write expansive descriptions of each chapter.

Author Bio

No matter how convincing an outline you put together, publishers will still have one "make-or-break" question: What are your qualifications for writing this book? How can you prove that you know what you are talking about?

Your bio should answer this question in the space of (about) a single page. It should be written in narrative format, and in third person—e.g., "John

Smith is an award-winning decoy carver who has practiced—and taught—the craft for more than twenty years..."

Before you attempt to put together an author bio, be sure you know what credentials are *expected* of you by the publisher you're approaching and by the market you are attempting to target. For example, if you're writing a scholarly treatise, you'll want to seek an academic publisher, and you'll be expected to have the right academic credentials. If, however, you're writing a book for a more general audience, you will want to find a publisher who can reach that audience—and who may be more interested in your writing ability than in academic degrees. In other words, research the market first!

A publisher is likely to expect credentials in one or more of the following categories:

- Educational background
- Professional background/expertise
- Personal experience/expertise
- Previous writing credits

If your book focuses on "scholarly" information, chances are good that you'll be expected to have academic credentials. For example, a book on military history or recent archaeological discoveries is more likely to sell if it is written by a "qualified" military historian or archaeologist. There are exceptions, but you're going to have to present a very convincing argument for your proposal if you don't have a publisher's "first choice" of credentials.

If your book focuses on business or technical information, you may be expected to provide relevant professional experience. For example, if you're writing a book on corporate management, you'll have a much better chance of selling it if you are a CEO, or at least an experienced manager. If you can combine that expertise with a degree in business management, so much the better—but the practical experience will, in this case, generally outweigh the academic credentials.

If your book addresses more popular "how-to" or "self-help" topics, you may be able to market your proposal on the basis of professional *or* personal expertise. For example, if you're writing about dog training, the fact that you've been a professional trainer for years would carry more weight than a degree in veterinary medicine. If you're writing a book on how to build your own sailboat, the fact that you've built three such boats in your garage (and, perhaps, sailed them around the world without sinking) will be more significant than a degree in engineering.

Personal *experience* can be a tricky credential. It is, of course, essential for a book that is, itself, an *account* of your personal experiences (e.g., a memoir or account of a specific life event). It is usually less helpful, however, in marketing how-to or self-help titles. A good guideline to consider is, the more impact your book might have on a reader's well-being, the more credentials you will be expected to have. While you might sell a book on fly-fishing on the basis of a weekend hobby, you may have trouble selling a book on child-care if your only "credential" is having been a parent.[1]

Previous writing credits can be useful *if* they are relevant to the book you are proposing. Shojai, for example, cited the fact that she had already written ten nonfiction pet books and more than 250 articles on pet care. This might have been sufficient to sell her proposal, even without her professional credentials (veterinary technician, spokesperson for Purina brand pet foods).

If, however, your writing credentials don't relate to your proposed topic, they will carry very little weight. Rodale Press would probably not have been impressed if, for example, Shojai had written ten books on gardening. Writing experience is generally the last credential publishers look for; while such experience does indicate that you can write (and even that you can write a successful book), it doesn't necessarily indicate that you are qualified to write *this* book.

Supporting Materials

Your basic proposal package—overview, chapter-by-chapter summary, and bio—should provide all the information that an editor (or agent) would need to make a decision. In some cases, however, you may wish to include certain supporting materials, such as:

- **Resume or curriculum vitae.** Include this if it supports the credentials described in your bio. If it doesn't, omit it.
- **Publications list.** Again, if this supports your bio, include it. Or, include an edited list that focuses on those publications that *do* support your proposal, leaving out those that are irrelevant. (You can title this "Selected Publications List.")
- **Writing samples.** Some authors (and publishers) discourage the inclusion of samples of previously published work. Include them only if they are relevant to your proposal—and include no more than three samples.
- **Business card.** It's always a good idea to include a professional-looking business card (or two) with your proposal, so that an editor or agent can easily contact you.
- **A SASE.** Need it be said? Yes, you should include a SASE with your proposal! If your entire proposal weighs less than one pound and you would like it to be returned, then include a manila envelope with enough postage for its return. More typically, however, you should simply include a stamped, self-addressed #10 envelope for the editor's or agent's response.

---

[1] Before someone writes to tell me that they know someone who sold a book on just that type of topic with no more credentials than I've mentioned, let me hasten to say that there are exceptions to every rule, and many books *have* been sold with virtually no author credentials. If you *don't* have the credentials, however, you will have to work that much harder to make the rest of your proposal convincing.

- **A "reply" postcard.** If you would like to know when your proposal was received, you can include a self-addressed postcard that the recipient can toss in the mail. Just put the name of the publishing house or agent on the reverse; the postmark itself will give you a date for delivery confirmation.
- **A product sample.** In very, *very* rare cases, it might be appropriate to include a "sample" of whatever it is you are writing about. For example, if you're writing a book on "how to create your own personalized greeting cards," it might be appropriate to include a sample card in your proposal package. I've heard of authors sending a batch of cookies along with a cookbook—but I'm not sure I'd recommend it!

Don't Send:

- **Your photo.** A prospective publisher or agent doesn't need to know what you look like, your age, your race, or any other information that would be conveyed by a photo. Save the publicity shots until after your book has been accepted.
- **Testimonials or reviews.** If other folks have said nice things about your work, that's great—but don't share them with your editor or agent. Let your work stand on its own.
- **Irrelevant writing samples.** If a sample doesn't support the subject matter of your proposal in some way, don't send it—even if it's the only writing sample you have.
- **Anything unprofessional.** It's probably best that you don't include greeting cards, personalized bookmarks, business pens, or other "gifts" with your proposal. Don't try to rationalize that such objects will help "get an editor's attention." They may—but they won't improve your chances of selling your book.

One other item that you may not be expected to submit is "sample chapters." In this, nonfiction proposals differ dramatically from fiction proposals. When submitting a fiction proposal, you will generally be expected to have completed the book—and thus you can be expected to have the first three chapters available to send with your proposal. A nonfiction proposal, however, may be submitted before you've written the first word of the book itself, and thus sample chapters are often not necessary. (Always check the publisher's or agent's guidelines to be sure!)

Even if you *have* written the entire book, however, a proposal is usually a far better way to market that book than sending out the entire manuscript. Don't expect your manuscript to speak for itself, no matter how good it may be. Instead, use your proposal as an opportunity to speak *for* your manuscript: to convince an editor that there is a market for your book, and that it can "beat" the competition.

When to "Pitch" Instead of "Propose"

A good book proposal can sometimes lead to an assignment that you don't expect. If all the elements of your proposal demonstrate to a publisher that you would be a good author to add to their "stable," but they can't use the book itself, you may be asked to present an alternate idea.

In this case, you'll often be asked to "pitch" rather than "propose." Most likely, the publisher will ask you to suggest two or three book topics, with a brief description of each. That description should cover content and rationale, but you won't need to go into details about the competition or attempt to develop an outline. You also won't need to provide the same level of detail about your own credentials, as you've already established those in your original proposal. (You may, however, need to provide a few lines to indicate why you would like to write, or are specifically qualified to write, the book you're now "pitching.")

A pitch can take the form of a simple letter (formatted like a basic query). Often, the publisher may wish to receive this via e-mail, which is a good idea, as you want to get your pitch in as quickly as possible.

Following is a portion of the "pitch" letter I submitted to Allworth Press, after my initial book proposal to that publisher was rejected:

> Dear Mr. Crawford,
>
> Thank you for your kind words about my proposal, "How to Launch Your Writing Career." Yours is probably the most encouraging rejection letter I've ever received!
>
> Thank you also for the invitation to suggest some additional book concepts for possible consideration. Following are three topics that I believe might be of interest to Allworth Press:[2]
>
> ## 1. Writing in Cyberspace: How to Build Your Writing Business Online
>
> Thus far, most Internet books for writers (including Arco's recent *Writer's Guide to Internet Resources*) have been much the same. They discuss the basics ("This is a URL") and provide an overview of Internet resources of interest to writers.
>
> I'd like to go beyond that, and develop a book that focuses on "applications": specific ways in which writers can

---

[2] Only the pitch for *Writing.com* is included here! Ironically, Allworth later revisited my original proposal for "How to Launch Your Writing Career," which became *Starting Your Career as a Freelance Writer*, published in 2003 (with an updated version scheduled for 2011).

expand their business and sales, and enhance their writing skills. Some recent topics I've explored include:

- How to research and market to international publications
- How to promote a book on-line
- How to get the most out of an on-line critique group
- How to protect one's electronic rights

Other topics that might be appropriate for this type of book include:

- How e-mail etiquette applies to electronic queries and submissions
- How to research a market on-line
- How to locate contacts and conduct e-mail interviews
- How to promote one's work through a Web site
- Participating in (or offering) on-line writing workshops and classes
- Pros and cons of writing for electronic markets (such as e-zines)
- Alternate markets (e.g., becoming a "guide" for a Web site such as Miningco)

Resources are important and should be included, but I would prefer to see such references grouped together in sidebars or at the end of a chapter. (It can be frustrating to try to relocate a URL that is buried in a paragraph of text.) Ideally, I'd like to compile an updateable CD-ROM of writing-related links to accompany the text.

This could be the book that picks up where [Allworth's] Tim Maloy's *The Internet Research Guide* leaves off!

Thank you for the opportunity to pitch these ideas to you. I hope that at least one of them excites your interest. Please feel free to contact me by e-mail; I look forward to discussing these or other topics with you further. Thank you again for your interest in my work.

The request for a "pitch" can take you by surprise. You may not be prepared to suggest a topic other than the book you've already planned. But if a publisher makes such an offer, it's wise to do your best to come up with something, even if you feel you're really "reaching" for ideas. You never know when a "quick pitch" is going to result in a long-term relationship.

11

Researching the Competition
on Amazon.com

In the previous chapter, I mentioned the importance of reviewing the competition for your book in a book proposal. A potential publisher will want to know what other books are available on your topic and what makes your book different from, or better than, those books.

But what if there are a great many books on your topic? How can you possibly review them all, even if you could afford to buy them? This was a question I faced when crafting a proposal for a new edition of my book, *Coping with Sorrow on the Loss of Your Pet*. A check of a major pet loss Web site revealed no fewer than 82 books on pet loss!

Fortunately, my search led me to another Internet resource that enabled me to review this competition and discuss it intelligently in my proposal, without buying a single book. That resource was Amazon.com.

Amazon.com is a great place to begin your research into the competition. Try searching on keywords related to your topic; chances are such a search will produce a list of titles. Be sure to check the "Listmania" column on the right side of the page; this is where readers compile their lists of "recommended" books on the topic, which can help refine your search.

Once you've developed a list of books on your general topic area, you can then use a variety of Amazon.com features to determine just how those books compare to your own. These features can help you answer just about any question a publisher might ask about the "competition" for your book.

How Is Your Book *Different* From the Competition?

While many books may be written on a subject, you'll quickly find that they aren't all the same. Some will be written from a different perspective, or about a different aspect of the subject. Some may be more general than the book you want to write; others may be more specific.

One of the first questions to ask is whether a book targets the same audience as yours. Of the 82 books on pet loss, I found that more than one third were aimed at children, which ruled them out as "competition." Several others were technical books written for professionals (psychologists and therapists). This also reduced my list to a more manageable size.

Once you've eliminated books that are targeting a different audience, it's time to look more closely at those that remain. Your question now is "what makes this book different from mine?" Start by checking the title and subtitle of each book. I quickly discovered, just from reviewing titles, that a significant percentage of the available books on pet loss were autobiographical—the author's personal account of the loss of a beloved pet. Since my book is a "how-to" book, it was easy to explain how it differed from books in the "personal experience" category.

I was also able to determine that many books on the list focused on a single aspect of pet loss (e.g., whether pets have an afterlife). Since my book was designed to cover "all" aspects of pet loss, again, this made it easy to define another subcategory of "different" books—in this case, books that were more narrowly focused than mine. Conversely, if you're writing a narrowly focused book, explain how your book offers more "in-depth" information than books that offer more general "overviews" of the topic.

Once you've exhausted the information that can be gleaned from titles, it's time to check for an official summary. In many cases, the publisher or author will provide a capsule description of the book, which may be all you need to determine how the book differs from your own. If a summary is not available, check the reader reviews; readers often summarize the books that they review. If that doesn't help, see if the book includes a "Search Inside" option. If it does, you should be able to review the table of contents, the index, and even a sample chapter.

How Is Your Book *Better* Than the Competition?

Once you've eliminated those books that offer substantially different information from your own, you may find that there are still a number of books that, unfortunately, look a great deal like the one you're proposing. If someone else has already covered the same topic, how can you prove that there's a need for your book? The answer is to show that your book is somehow better than the others—without actually trashing the competition!

One of the easiest ways to build such an argument is to find out what people are saying about the competition. The most obvious way to do this is to check those reader reviews again.

Before you do, keep in mind that actual "ratings" are meaningless. A book that has only one review can have a five-star rating, while another book that has garnered dozens of rave reviews can have a lower rating simply because it also has one or two negative reviews. A more important measure of a book's popularity is the actual number of reviews. If a book has been in print for five years and has only one or two reader comments, chances are that it hasn't been very popular.

Next, focus on what the reviews actually say. Are they positive, negative, or somewhere in between? Do certain criticisms come up again and again? Look for comments that apply not only to individual books, but also to entire categories of books within the competition.

For example, I found that the books that seemed most directly competitive with my own were those written by therapists and psychologists—people with credentials that I lack. However, I found a consistent theme in the reader comments on these books: Readers complained that they were often too cold, too clinical, too psychological. Many complained that such books spent more time explaining the psychological basis of grief, but not enough on discussing actual coping strategies. This gave me the perfect opportunity to explain that my book was "better" because it was written in a warm, compassionate, and accessible tone.

Another item to check is the length of the book, by checking the page count in the book description. Is your book considerably longer (and therefore, presumably, more comprehensive) than the competition? I was surprised to discover that many of my competitors' books were only 50 to 80 pages long.

You can also check the book description to determine *when* your competitors' books were published. If most of your competition is five to ten years old, you can easily make the argument that your book will be more current than most of the existing books on the market.

A final item to review is the pricing of the competition, particularly if you have an idea of the price range in which your book is likely to fall. If, for example, you expect your book to cost around $16.95, and you find competing books selling for $25 to $50, you can argue that readers will be more likely to buy your book simply because it is less expensive!

Pulling It Together

Your publisher does not expect a capsule description or review of every single title on the competition list. Instead, divide the competition into subcategories that you can discuss as a group. Provide four or five representative titles for each subcategory. For example, I devoted one paragraph to a discussion of how my book differed from "personal experience" pet loss books, and another on how it differed from "books written by psychologists."

Don't hesitate to use the information you've found online to support your arguments. Consider quoting selections from reader reviews of the competition—particularly those that highlight the need for the book you want to write. Keep in mind that even a positive review of a competitor's book can support your case. For example, if a reviewer notes, "the one problem with this book was that it seemed far too short," use that comment to demonstrate the need for a longer, more comprehensive book on the subject.

If you wish to provide a more detailed comparison of titles, create a list or table as an appendix to your proposal. List the competition by title and author and include any other information you consider relevant, such as publication date, publisher, or page count. Add a brief, one-sentence explanation of how the book is different from, or inferior to, your proposed title. Such a table provides evidence that you've researched the competition, without overwhelming the main proposal.

And only you need to know that you did that research in a single day, without spending a penny!

12

Pitching to International Book Publishers

by Huw Francis

You have a great idea for a nonfiction book. You're also an international writer—or, you believe that your book would have international appeal. Globalization trends have made readers around the world more open to reading about international subjects. How can you turn this to your advantage and make your book stand out from the thousands of ideas editors and publishers see every year?

As the world becomes increasingly global, it is now practical and common for raw material to come from one country, be processed in a second, and be sold in a third. In the publishing world the infrastructure exists to allow text to be moved quickly around the world to print books close to their distribution market—or somewhere with low overhead. My first book was written in Turkey, required the input of people worldwide, was published in the UK, and was distributed on four continents.

Where in the World Should You Look for a Publisher?

Whatever your nationality and no matter where you live, you should look for the most suitable publisher in the world for your book, not just the best one in your home country or country of residence. Finding the perfect match between publisher and proposal is more important than proximity, and working with the best publisher for your book benefits both of you. The publisher has a product that enhances its catalogue and suits its existing target market, and you will see bigger returns through higher sales.

TARGET MARKETS

Publishers concentrate on specific markets. Even global publishing houses have imprints and subsidiaries that specialize in individual markets and/ or countries not targeted by other imprints within the same company.

Consequently, it is important to identify the target market (both demographically and geographically) for your book before you start approaching publishers. By doing this you can target your submissions to publishers who already produce books for that market.

The determining factor is not simply the type of book you want to write. A more important question is, "where will people buy that book?" Most of the likely readers of a book on adopting a Chinese baby will be outside of China. A book on adopting a baby in the United Kingdom, however, will be of most interest to UK residents. The first step toward deciding whether to target an international publisher, therefore, is to determine where your target market lives.

This selection of publishers is important because you not only have to demonstrate that there is a market for the book, but also that the target market is accessible to that particular publisher. For example, while there might be large market for an English-language book on day trips from Paris, not all American publishers are going to be able to reach it. A French publisher, or a U.S. or European publisher with a French office, would probably be a better choice because many tourists will buy the book once in Paris. A French-based publisher of English-language books is also likely to have a distribution agreement with companies in the United States and United Kingdom, so your book can still be bought by people before they travel.

It is essential to research the distribution network of a publisher you are considering. Distribution networks vary enormously, from local to international, and cannot be determined just by looking at the country in which the publisher is headquartered. In addition, once you find a publisher with, say, a French office, you must then determine whether that office or another international office actually makes acquisitions. Some regional offices operate purely for distribution, while others operate as local imprints.

Marketing

When you are marketing a book to a publisher in a country where you do not live, or are not a national, you will face some special obstacles that most local writers have no concept of. Finding a way past these obstacles can also help you develop your book to enhance its international appeal and make a publisher more likely to accept your proposal.

In general, the publishing industry has standard formats and procedures that are designed with domestic submissions in mind, and which all authors are expected to follow even if they are submitting from abroad. As an international writer, you need to follow this process as closely as you can. However, you will need to adapt and bend the rules to suit your unusual circumstances.

For instance, you must show publishers why *you* should write the book, rather than someone local. This means that you not only have to show that you can do it as well as a local, but that you are better placed to do so. The credentials you offer to make this point should be reflected in the content of your book (or proposal). For example, if you are pitching a book on the premise that you are an American living in Paris and writing a guidebook for U.S. and UK tourists, your book should include destinations and restaurants that American tourists will want to see, not destinations that would appeal to Japanese tourists.

Being in a different country or of a different nationality complicates the task of demonstrating your credibility to a publisher. From the start, publishers are likely to be concerned that you may be remote, difficult to contact and communicate with, and also more expensive to deal with (telephone calls, faxes, mail, etc.). They may also (unfairly) associate all the worst stereotypes of your country of residence or nationality with you.

Establishing your credibility is a multi-leveled task and involves the following.

YOUR IMAGE

First impressions count for a lot in publishing. No matter where you live, you wish to project a professional image. Other chapters in this book explain what publishers expect to see in terms of professional style and presentation.

WRITING ABILITY

When trying to sell a book proposal internationally, it is important to show not only that you can write well, but also that you can write for the target audience of your book. If you have not written and published articles or other books on the subject or for the target audience, then the best way to prove your ability is to write two or three chapters of your book and include them when you approach the publisher. At least one of these chapters needs to be a completed product, not an early draft. The other chapters, even if not finished, will support the primary chapter and demonstrate your dedication to the task of completing the book. This will help improve your image as well as demonstrate your writing ability.

When writing the sample chapters, it is important to make sure your grammar, spelling and word usage are those in use in the country of the publisher. U.S. English should not be used in a submission to a British publisher (unless your book is aimed at Americans living in, or visiting, the United Kingdom), and British English should not be used for an American publisher.

Word usage can be very important, and getting it wrong can mean not getting a contract. Some perfectly acceptable U.S. words are rude in the United Kingdom (fanny definitely does not mean backside in the United Kingdom) and some words have different meanings ("quite good" means very good in the United States, but if someone in the United Kingdom said your book was "quite good," they are actually saying that it was nothing special).

SUBJECT QUALIFICATION

Why should a reader believe what you write? Would you buy a travel guidebook written by someone who had never been to the country? The publisher needs to be convinced that you are qualified to write on the subject.

If you already know your subject well, all you have to do is state, in some detail, how you obtained your knowledge. For a book on adopting a child from China, you might be able to say, "Over the last three years my partner and I have been through the complicated and drawn-out process of adopting a child from a Chinese orphanage, and we now have a wonderful Chinese daughter."

If you have no experience or knowledge on the subject you want to write about, state how you will gain it. For a book on buying property in Belize, you could say, "I have been planning to buy property in Belize for some time and in a few months I will be moving to Belize with the sole purpose of doing so." You should also outline why you believe it is possible to buy property in Belize and how you plan to do so.

THE MARKETABILITY OF YOUR BOOK

Who is going to buy the book, where will they buy the book, and why? Though the publisher will take responsibility for selling the book, you need to prove that there are enough people who are sufficiently interested in the subject to spend up to $15 on a book about it.

Publishers want to see more than a bald statement of, "I know there are lots of tourists and many expatriates in France who would love this book." Facts and figures are essential. How many expatriates live in France? How many of them speak English as a first language? How many speak English as a second language? How many U.S. tourists go to Paris every year? How many tourists are returnees? Where do expatriates in France buy their books? Where do U.S. tourists buy their guidebooks (U.S. bookshops, airports, or French bookshops)? How many books does each expatriate and tourist buy per year or trip? In what other countries is there a market where subsidiary rights can be sold?

Proposing a marketing plan using online forums, Web sites, and trade publications you already interact with and that reach an international target audience is also beneficial, as it will widen the potential market for the publisher.

Submitting Your Proposal

Identifying suitable publishers takes time and effort. *The Writers Market* can give you information on North American publishers, while *The Writers Handbook* and *The Writers Market UK and Ireland* offer information for UK, European, and British Commonwealth countries. *The Writers Handbook* also includes comments from writers who have worked with specific publishers.

Such reference directories should only be the start of your research, however. Most publishers, even smaller ones, have Web sites that include their catalogue, philosophy, details of their target market, and submission guidelines.

Despite the common perception that there are standard ways of writing to all U.S. publishers and standard ways of writing to all UK publishers, every publishing house is made up of different people with different ideas. The best way to determine the style your cover letter should take is to thoroughly review the publisher's Web site. This will give you a good understanding of house style and allow you to incorporate buzzwords and key phrases into your cover letter and proposal. If the Web site is written in a pedantic and technical style, follow that. If it is written in an easygoing style, relax your own style, but still maintain a professional and serious tone; flippancy is unlikely to endear you to publishers, even if they do publish joke books.

An increasing number of publishers are including online submission forms on their Web sites or accept e-mailed submissions. These can be particularly useful for international writers, as they speed up submission times, improve communications, and demonstrate to the publisher that you are technically capable of supplying the text of your book electronically.

Your research will also give you an idea of whether you need to send your proposal directly to an editor or to a centralized submissions office. If in doubt, call the editorial assistant of the editor of a book similar to yours and ask how to proceed.

SURFACE MAIL SUBMISSION

When you send a surface mail submission, always send a SASE. Be sure that it either has the correct return postage in the stamps of the country *of the publisher* (not your own country's postage), or that you include an appropriate number of International Reply Coupons (IRCs) for a response. Two IRCs are usually enough to send a regular letter from one country or another; more will be needed if you actually want your proposal or manuscript returned. However, IRCs are not popular with publishers (they require a trip to the post office to redeem them), so stamps are much preferred. Check with the Web site of the target country's post office to see if you can order stamps online—or ask a contact in that country to mail you stamps.

Make sure that you include your full name and contact details. When submitting a book proposal internationally, an e-mail address is also very important. Most of the publishers who expressed interest in my own proposal and asked for further information did so via e-mail. Those that are not interested will also often let you know by e-mail, when they would not bother to send a letter.

E-MAIL SUBMISSIONS

E-mail submissions allow you to avoid the vagaries of the international mail system and deliver your proposal quickly. Because of the rise in e-mail viruses, it is a good idea to send the text of your proposal in the body of the e-mail, just after your cover letter. However, the drawbacks of e-mail submission are that the layout and format of your proposal may be altered or lost and you may not be able to send artwork and sample articles. If you have a personal Web site with samples of your published work, some publishers are happy to refer to it, so be sure to mention it.

If you feel that you really need to send your proposal as an attachment, check with the publisher first to ensure your formats are acceptable and they are willing to risk opening your file on their computer. The Adobe Acrobat .pdf format is most readily accepted and can be easily created using the OpenOffice software package.

ONLINE SUBMISSIONS

Online submission usually entails filling out a form designed by the publisher, which means that you *won't* be able to submit your carefully crafted proposal. To avoid spelling errors and to make sure that all the important information in your proposal is included, print off the forms to use as a guide. Then, type your responses in your word-processing program, proof them, polish them—and then cut-and-paste them back into the online forms.

Electronic submission works! That's how I sold my proposal.

As an international writer, don't downplay your international status; play it up. Highlight the positive aspects of why a non-national or non-resident should be writing this particular book. Actively raise the publisher's interest by demonstrating why you should be writing the book from your perspective and location. Expressing confidence in your abilities and knowledge, without boasting, is the best way to make a publisher believe in you.

(Huw Francis's successful proposal for his most recent book, *Live and Work in Turkey*, is included in the samples at the end of this section.)

13

Electronic and "Do-It-Yourself" Publishing: Viable Alternatives?

Trying to sell book—whether nonfiction as discussed in this section, or fiction as discussed in the next—can be a confusing and frustrating task. While some authors are successful with their very first submission, others send off proposals to publisher after publisher, and wait months after each submission only to receive another disappointment.

What should you do if the procedures outlined in this book don't "work"? Should you try something different? Many writers are convinced they can do better with a "do-it-yourself" approach to publishing, such as electronic publishing, print subsidy publishing, self-publishing (print or electronic), or print-on-demand (POD) publishing. Are these, indeed, viable alternatives to "traditional" or "commercial" publishing?

The answer depends in part on what you hope to achieve with the publication of your book. Do you want an advance of several thousand dollars? Do you want your book to reach thousands, or even hundreds of thousands, of readers? Do you want your book to be available throughout the country in brick-and-mortar bookstores? Do you want it to be available through libraries? Do you want it to be reviewed in major book review venues—or, for that matter, in your local paper?

If the answer to most, or all, of these questions is "yes," then going the "DIY" route is probably not for you. Self-publishing, subsidy publishing, and electronic publishing rarely achieve these goals. Let's take a quick look at the downsides of these options first:

- While a handful of electronic publishers may offer a small advance, you will receive no advance at all from self- or subsidy-publishing, including POD.
- In most cases, readership of electronic and subsidy-published books remains in the hundreds, not the thousands. For most

POD titles, a sell-through of 500 copies is considered very good. Skillful self-publishers are often able to push those numbers into the low thousands—but it's very difficult to achieve the same readership as a commercially published book.

- Very few "brick and mortar" bookstores carry electronic or DIY books, with the occasional exception of self-published books by local authors. It's very, very rare for a DIY book to achieve national bookstore distribution.

- Libraries rarely carry e-books, and though they *will* buy self-published and even the occasional subsidy/POD title, it's almost impossible to get such books into the main library distribution chains—so you're often stuck trying to market to one library at a time.

- Major book review venues (such as *Kirkus, Editor & Publisher, Library Times, New York Times*, etc.) won't touch DIY books. The situation here has actually worsened; it was once not quite so difficult to get a self-published book reviewed, but now that the market has been flooded with subsidy/POD titles, many reviewers have simply ceased accepting any type of DIY book. While you may be able to get coverage locally, it's just about impossible to achieve national coverage for e-books or DIY books.

- Many industry organizations, such as the Romance Writers of America, won't recognize DIY books as "published" in terms of an author's publication credits or consider them for awards. The RWA does recognize certain e-publishers as having sufficient distribution to be considered "commercial," but not all organizations do.

Does that mean these options are useless? Not at all. Many writers *have* made the DIY approach work for them. However, a successful DIY publisher is one who understands that the key to this approach truly is *doing it yourself*. It means going far beyond being just a writer, and taking on the tasks that would normally be handled by your publisher. At the very least, these will include marketing and promotion—and depending on how much you want to spend, it can also mean doing your own copy-editing, proofreading, interior design, book production, cover design, and more. If you become a self-publisher, you'll need to take on the roles of accountant, warehouse, and shipper as well. Of course, you can hire help at every step along the way, but every element that you choose to pay for eats into your book profits.

Now let's look at each option in more detail.

Electronic Publishing

Ten years ago, electronic publishers were cropping up across the Web like mushrooms after rain. The rush toward e-publishing was fueled by a variety of assumptions, including the notion that there were thousands of "great books" out there that were being ignored by "traditional publishers" whose cared only about the almighty dollar and not a whit about literature. Many would-be publishers also assumed that e-publishing would be a great way to make a profit, as it involved little up-front cost (and, unless one chose to publish on disk, virtually no "production" costs). A third assumption was that today's Web-savvy readers would be delighted to access books online, particularly if e-books could be offered at lower prices than print books.

Unfortunately, many e-publishers soon discovered that there were, in fact, thousands of books out there that were being ignored by "traditional" publishers for very good reasons: They were awful. They also discovered that many readers weren't, in fact, that anxious to read books online (or to pay for e-readers). The market for e-books was not the vast, untapped source of wealth many expected it to be (including many mainstream publishers and big-name authors).

Today, only a handful of those e-publishing pioneers have survived, and they survived by doing exactly what any other successful publisher would do: They selected only the best material they could find. That means e-publishing is no longer a venue where "just anyone" can break in: One's chances of being accepted by a high-quality e-publisher (such as Booklocker, which specializes in nonfiction books, and Ellora's Cave, which specializes in romance—particularly erotic romance) are not much better than the chances of being accepted by a print publisher. However, it also means that the successful e-publishers have managed to build a significant following, so if you are accepted, your chances of getting a decent readership are much higher than they were a decade ago. More authors have also been able to make the transition from e-publishing to print publishing, precisely because they *can* demonstrate that they have a large following.

With e-publishing, the author usually has more control over the publishing process (and publishers are less likely to ask for changes and revisions). Contracts are generally less restrictive than print contracts (e-publishers rarely try to lock in any rights *other* than electronic publishing rights) and can usually be terminated by either party after a specified period of time (as the issue of a book going "out of print" in e-publishing is irrelevant). Publication usually occurs more quickly, though some e-publishers report that it may take six months or more to bring out a new title.

E-publishing can be a viable option for either fiction or nonfiction titles. In the area of fiction, it can be a good option for books that are too short to be considered a commercial "novel" (bestselling author Diana Gabaldon e-published a novella for precisely this reason several years ago; it has now been anthologized in print!). It's also a good option for subgenres that don't currently have a large print audience, such as paranormal romance. In the area of nonfiction, it's a good way to target a niche audience that is willing to obtain information electronically. So e-publishing has definitely become a respected option—but that doesn't mean it's an "easy" way to publication, or that it's necessarily your best choice.

Self-Publishing

Many writers are confused about the distinction between "self-publishing" and "subsidy publishing," partly because subsidy publishers today try to use the term "self-publishing" to describe their business model.

There is a difference, however. If you take your book to another publisher—whether it's an e-publisher, a subsidy print publisher, or a POD publisher that organization is officially the "publisher" of your book. You may have to assign some of the rights to your book to the publisher (though most POD publishers do not require any transfer of rights). The publisher will control the production of your book and pay you a royalty on every sale after they deduct their costs and profit.

When you self-publish, *you* are the publisher. You own your book outright; you don't sign away any rights to anyone else. You arrange for the production of the book, as well as its promotion and distribution—and whatever you earn over the cost of producing that book is yours to keep. You can set your own price, offer quantity discounts, and print as many copies as you like. Since you'll usually be dealing with a book *printer*, the per-unit cost involved in self-publishing is usually much lower than that of POD publishing, which enables you to offer bookstore and distributor discounts, and also reduces the cost of sending books out to reviewers.

It also means that you have all the *responsibilities* associated with being a publisher—including accounting, taxes, sales tax, and possibly the need for a local business license. You may find that your garage becomes a book warehouse and your kitchen table a mailing counter. And above all else, it's entirely up to you to find a *market* for your book, reach that market with your sales message, and then get the books to the customer.

Self-publishing garners marginally more respect in the book industry than subsidy publishing—but it has never gained a *lot* of respect. Unless you plan to really dedicate yourself to the business of *publishing*, it's very difficult to get your book into bookstores and libraries, have it picked up by major distributors, or gain national reviews. Typically, you'll find yourself marketing directly to the customer, one book at a time. Nevertheless, many self-publishers (myself included) have managed to sell thousands of books this way, so it's not an option to dismiss lightly.

However, if your goal is to be a writer rather than a publisher, it's an option to consider with great care. Becoming a self-publisher can mean spending far more of your time publishing than writing. If you're not interested in starting and running a business, and giving it the time and energy required to make it a success, this may not be the option for you.

Print Subsidy Publishing

Originally, the only form of "subsidy" publishing available was traditional print subsidy publishing, in which books were printed in just the same way as by a commercial publisher, only at the author's cost. An author who chooses traditional print subsidy publishing can expect to pay thousands of dollars to have a few thousand copies of a book produced—copies that may never leave the publisher's warehouse. Unlike self-publishing, you don't *own* those books once they're printed; they're still the property of the publisher. You'll receive royalty payments if and when the publisher sells the book (which puts you, once again, in the role of marketer and promoter). But if you wanted to actually own those books, you'd have to pay for them—again!

Worse, you may find yourself stuck with a contract that is every bit as restrictive as that of a commercial publisher—and one that can be hard to get out of if a commercial publisher actually decides to accept your book. Not surprisingly, this is considered one of the least beneficial options for an author who is considering the DIY approach.

Print-on-Demand Publishing

The last decade has seen a huge increase in the number of books being published via print-on-demand (POD). A large percentage of these are "personal" books—i.e., they aren't intended for a mass audience, but just for the individual, family, or friends. But authors who are frustrated with the process of trying to reach a commercial publisher are also turning to POD in droves. Some are happy with the results; a great many are not.

There are a number of well-known POD publishers in the marketplace, offering a wide range of services at a wide range of prices. Publishers like Xlibris and iUniverse charge various fees up front—Xlibris fees currently start at $400 for their most basic package, and go as high as $14,000 for the "Platinum" package, while iUniverse fees start at $600 and go up to $4200. At the other end of the scale, Lulu.com charges no up-front fee to get started; you pay only for the books you order, for only the cost of production. For books sold to customers, you'll receive a royalty that is based on the difference between the production cost (and the publisher's markup) and the retail price you set on the book. (Not all POD publishers allow you to set your own retail price.)

The advantage of POD publishing is that the publisher generally does most of the work—which means you can get a good-looking book produced for a fraction of what a print subsidy publisher would charge. And, of course, if you can do the work yourself—particularly if you can design your own interior and create (or arrange for the creation of) your own cover— you'll save even more by going with a publisher like Lulu.com, Blurb.com, or Amazon.com's CreateSpace program (which gives you an ISBN and gets you onto Amazon at no charge). You also don't have to pay for a large print run of books up front, as you do with self-publishing. Books are printed when ordered by the customer, which means you aren't storing boxes in your garage or shipping them from your kitchen. You also don't have to go through the hassles of setting yourself up as a publishing company, getting a business license, collecting sales tax, and all that.

One significant downside of POD publishing, however, is that the per-unit cost of a book tends to be very high. On Lulu.com, for example, it currently costs $5.01 to create an 84-page black-and-white book; a 200-page book costs $7.10. (By comparison, a print run of 500 copies of a 200-page book at Morris Publishing via a traditional sheet-fed press gives you a per-book cost of $2.88.) This means a significantly lower profit for you (especially once the publisher has added their own markup to the production cost)—and it means that POD books must often be priced higher than comparable commercially produced books. For example, if you have to price your paperback mystery novel at $14 just to make a couple of dollars in profit per book, it is no longer competitive with other mysteries that are typically priced at $8, which tends to discourage would-be buyers. Higher POD prices also mean that it's virtually impossible to offer significant quantity discounts to booksellers, distributors, or other bulk buyers. (Bookstores also refuse to stock POD books because they are not returnable.)

As with any other form of DIY publishing, POD publishing means that you must handle all the marketing and promotion for your book. If, however, you've targeted a niche market and know how to reach it, POD can be much easier than self-publishing. Once your book is in the POD system, all you have to do is drum up sales and point your customers toward the book's sale page. If you don't want to have to actually start a self-publishing business, this can be an excellent option. It's rarely successful for fiction, but *has* worked well for many nonfiction books.

Why Not Self-Publish First, Then Seek a Publisher?

Many writers wonder whether it might not be best to self-publish or POD-publish a book first, then submit the "published" book to commercial publishers. This notion stems from the mistaken impression that something that "looks" like a book will carry more weight than a mere manuscript. Perhaps it is because, as authors, we yearn for the sight of our own work in "book" format—and we imagine that editors and publishers will be similarly impressed.

Unfortunately, nothing could be farther from the truth. Rightly or wrongly, this form of publication smacks of desperation. The message it sends to a publisher is not, "Wow, look, a real book!" but rather, "This person couldn't get published any other way." In other words, it makes a *negative* impression, not a positive one.

Commercial publishers generally do not view a self-published or subsidy-published book as "published" in any sense that counts. The only way that you would be able to impress a publisher with such a book is by actually demonstrating a track record of *sales.* If you can prove, for example, that your self-published novel has already sold 10,000 copies just through your marketing efforts alone, a publisher might be tempted to consider it (though many won't just on general principles).

Though commercial publishers won't regard your book as "published" in a positive sense, they may regard it as "published" in a negative sense—i.e., they may treat it as a "previously published" work, even if you haven't sold a single copy. Since most publishers purchase only original manuscripts, the very act of self- or subsidy-publishing your book could automatically disqualify you from achieving commercial publication. In short, this option not only won't help you find a traditional print publisher, it may actually decrease your chances of ever doing so.

The bottom line is that while there *are* alternatives to the standard submission route, and many authors *have* used those alternatives successfully, you must know what you are doing if you decide to try the DIY route. Otherwise, you may find yourself even more disappointed by the alternative than by your original course—and, possibly, out a considerable amount of money (and perhaps a share of rights) as well.

14

Sample Nonfiction Book Proposals

Following are three samples of successful book proposals: Amy Shojai's "Healing at Home *Naturally*: Alternative Pet Care that Works!" (published by Rodale Press as *New Choices in Natural Healing for Dogs & Cats: Over 1,000 At-Home Remedies for Your Pet's Problems*); Simon Whaley's *Best Walks in the Welsh Borders* (published by Frances Lincoln, U.K.); and Huw Francis's *Live and Work in Turkey* (published by How To Books, U.K.).

While each proposal incorporates the various elements described in the previous chapters, each author handles these elements in his or her own, unique way—demonstrating that your voice as an author is as much a part of creating a successful proposal as following a formula!

Healing at Home *Naturally* Alternative Pet Therapies that Work!

by

Amy D. Shojai
A Book Proposal[1]

Meredith Bernstein Literary Agency
2112 Broadway, Suite 503A
New York, NY 10023

[1] Proposed by Amy Shojai; published by Rodale Press as *New Choices in Natural Healing for Dogs & Cats: Over 1,000 At-Home Remedies for Your Pet's Problems.*

Healing at Home *Naturally*:
Alternative Pet Therapies that Work!

Overview

More Americans than ever before share their lives with pets. Consequently, the national obsession with health and fitness has spilled into the pet arena. Owners seek the best possible care for their four-legged friends, yet many of the pet-generation have lost faith in traditional medicine. They yearn for a simpler, more natural method of promoting good health for themselves—and for their pets. HEALING AT HOME *NATURALLY* examines the world of non-traditional medicine for dogs and cats, and offers real-world applications to the many health conditions affecting our pets.

There is a wall dividing conventional from alternative medicine, when in fact pets—and people—benefit most from complementary therapies of both. HEALING AT HOME *NATURALLY* will open a window in that wall to find common ground between the two, debunk the myths, and explore the possibilities.

There are a wide variety of alternative therapies available to pet owners; however, many remain investigational at this time and some may seek only to profit from the "natural revolution" rather than promote the health of the pet. The therapies covered in HEALING AT HOME *NATURALLY*: Alternative Pet Therapies that Work! have been carefully chosen for their track record and proven benefits. My book is a no-nonsense look at which alternative therapies really work, and how to use them safely and effectively at home. Not only cure, but prevention will be addressed. Information will be supported by direct quotes from expert veterinarians and others in the field. Readers can follow the advice set forth with confidence, knowing that years of study and practical experience—and the positive response of pets—supports the text. Further, the text offers concrete advice on when and where to seek qualified veterinary care—both alternative and traditional—when an expert's help may be required.

66.2 million cats and 58 million dogs are kept by Americans, and most welcome pets into their hearts and homes as full members of the family. This pet-generation is eager to provide quality care for their furry families, but the appropriate tools are needed to make informed decisions. HEALING AT HOME *NATURALLY*: Alternative Pet Therapies that Work! is the first book to offer how-to advice on applying alternative cures to specific health conditions. My book empowers owners to make the best alternative choices for their cherished pets.

Competition

HEALING AT HOME *NATURALLY*: Alternative Pet Therapies that Work! could not be more timely. More than 40 percent of United States households keep dogs, 38 percent keep cats, and all are seeking answers to pet health questions that conventional therapy seems unable to answer.

Several books address the pet owners' growing interest in alternative therapies. Most, like *THE NEW NATURAL CAT* by Anitra Frazier and Norma Eckroate (Nal–Dutton, 1990) and *THE NATURAL DOG* by Mary L. Brennan and Norma Eckroate (Nal–Dutton, 1994) deal with behavior problems, nutrition and specific nursing care using a holistic approach. Other books, like *THE HEALING TOUCH: The Proven Massage Program for Cats and Dogs* by Michael W. Fox (Newmarket, 1991) and *COMPLETE HERBAL HANDBOOK FOR THE DOG AND CAT* by Juliette D. Levy (Faber & Faber 1991) provide in-depth coverage of a single alternative therapy.

Nearly all "natural" pet titles address dogs and cats in separate texts, and promote a single alternative approach to good health. My book stands out as featuring only the best, scientifically proven, safe and drug-free healing methods available for both dogs and cats. No book to date offers the comprehensive balance, positive approach and step-by-step advice of HEALING AT HOME *NATURALLY*: Alternative Pet Therapies that Work!.

Book Format

HEALING AT HOME *NATURALLY*: Alternative Pet Therapies that Work! will be a 125,000 word (about 500 page) book. The proposed work examines the best alternative health care protocols as they relate to pets, and suggests how best to benefit from these non-traditional therapies.

The book is organized in two parts. The first half explores the world of alternative medicine, describing the meaning of the term "natural" and touching on the difference between safe and effective protocols compared to investigational "trendy" modalities.

Following this overview, the specific protocols advocated by the book are addressed. The traditions and principles behind each alternative treatment are explored in individual chapters. A poignant example of a pet helped by a given therapy introduces each of these chapters to illustrate how the protocol works, and the potential benefits.

The second half of the book is the "THERAPY THESAURUS" section, similar in format to the highly successful *THE DOCTOR'S BOOK OF HOME REMEDIES FOR DOGS AND CATS* (Rodale, 1996). A comprehensive A to Z listing of (about) 100 of the most common dog and cat illnesses and conditions is presented, followed by the alternative therapies which may be best applied to each to effect a cure. Where appropriate, sections as they apply to dogs or cats—"For Dogs Only" or "For Cats Only"—will be included.

The author incorporates the expertise of recognized alternative and conventional pet health care professionals gleaned from personal correspondence, interviews, and other technical sources. Each illness, condition, or symptom is first described, followed by easily digested tips and advice presented in direct quotes from these experts describing home-care application for cures. Each entry will be summed up in a "Prevention" section.

Sidebars offer more detailed information where appropriate. Boxes of information, such as "The Homeopathic Medicine Chest" and "Medicating Your Pet" offer succinct information necessary for applying the book's recommendations. A "When To See The Expert" box offers advice when an illness or condition requires attention beyond the scope of home care. In these instances, readers will be advised to seek the help of their alternative and/or traditional veterinary specialist as needed.

The text is written in an engaging, entertaining style that educates and informs without resorting to dry jargon. Check lists, charts and/or tables, along with striking line drawings are included to clarify or illustrate information and demonstrate treatments.

An Appendix offers: 1) "GLOSSARY," a list of alternative medicine terms and their meanings; 2) "DIRECTORY," with contact information for alternative pet care resources; and 3) "RESOURCES," a further reading list on the subject of alternative health care. Finally, a detailed index will be included to more easily access information.

Target Audience

<u>HEALING AT HOME *NATURALLY*</u>: Alternative Pet Therapies that <u>Work!</u> will appeal to those members of the pet-generation who yearn for a simpler, more natural method of promoting good health for themselves—and for their cats and dogs.

Suggested Marketing

- Direct mail
- Print advertisements placed in pet and health magazines:
  - "natural" publications, i.e., *Natural Health, Natural Pet, Natural Remedies*, and *The Natural Way*
  - *Animals (MSPCA)*, circ. 100,000
  - *Cat Fancy*, circ. 303,000
  - *CATS*, circ. 127,000
  - *Dog Fancy*, circ. 276,000
  - *I Love Cats*, circ. 200,000
  - *Parade*, circ. 37,000,000
  - *USA Weekend*, circ. 17,500,000
- Submit the book for review
- Place in both book stores and pet "super stores" like Petco, and "natural" product stores
- Press releases, including to cat and dog organizations, i.e.:
  - Cat Writers' Association & Dog Writer's Association (writers, editors, publishers, broadcasters, etc)
  - Cat Fancier's Association, American Kennel Club and others (umbrella organizations for cat & dog clubs)
  - ASPCA, and other animal welfare organizations
  - American Holistic Veterinary Medical Association
  - International Veterinary Acupuncture Society
  - National Center for Homeopathy
- Subsidiary rights potential:
  - selected chapters excerpted in magazines or through newspaper syndicates
  - library sales/book club deals

To coincide with the book's publication, book signings should be scheduled at book stores, cat and dog shows, and animal welfare and natural health organization meetings and events. The subject matter lends itself well to the popular issues of many television and radio talk shows, such as the *Today Show* and others. The author frequently appears on television and radio in connection with her writing, and is willing to vigorously promote the book in these venues and in person.

Author Biography

Amy D. Shojai is a nationally known authority on pet care and behavior who began her career as a veterinary technician. She is the author of ten nonfiction pet books and more than 250 published articles and columns, and is the spokesperson for Purina brand pet foods (an Author's Resume is attached).

Most recently, she contributed 16 chapters to the Rodale Press book *The Doctor's Book of Home Remedies for Dogs and Cats*, which is approaching 500 thousand copies sold. She has three forthcoming pet books; *The Purina Encyclopedia of Cat Care* and *The Purina Encyclopedia of Dog Care* will be published by Ballantine, and *Competability: Building a Peaceable Kingdom with Cats and Dogs* by Crown. Her work also appears online with the Time Warner "PetPath" and with Purina's "Tidy Cat" Web site.

Ms. Shojai has written widely in the pet field on training, behavior, health care, and the health benefits of keeping cats and dogs. She is the founder and president of the international Cat Writers' Association, is a member of the Dog Writer's Association, and has won numerous awards for her books and articles.

Ms. Shojai frequently speaks to groups on a variety of pet-related issues, and has often been interviewed on radio and television in connection with her pet writing. Most recently, she represented the "cat side" and won a nationally televised tongue-in-cheek debate (NBC Today Show, Fox, CNN and others) arguing whether cats or dogs are the more appropriate White House pets.

PROPOSED OUTLINE

HEALING AT HOME *NATURALLY*:
ALTERNATIVE PET THERAPIES THAT WORK!

INTRODUCTION:
Conventional versus Alternative, and What's "Natural"

PART I: OVERVIEW—PRINCIPLES THAT WORK & WHY

Chapter 1	Acupuncture and Acupressure: Getting the "point"
Chapter 2	Chiropractic: Major and minor adjustments
Chapter 3	Holistic Therapy: The mind/body connection
Chapter 4	Homeopathy: When less is more
Chapter 5	Massage therapy: Need to be kneaded
Chapter 6	Nutrition: Eating the cure
	(Includes "cancer" diets, vitamin/mineral supplements, fasting)
Chapter 7	Water Therapy: It's all wet—and works!

PART II: THERAPY THESAURUS
A to Z directory of (about) 100 common dog and cat illnesses/conditions with recommended alternative care; brief one to five paragraph introductions followed by succinct tips on home treatment/care from the experts; topics including but not limited to: [the A-Z topical directory has been omitted.]

APPENDIX A

"GLOSSARY," alternative medicine terms and definitions

APPENDIX B

"DIRECTORY," contact information of alternative pet care resources, i.e., veterinary holistic practitioners, acupuncturist, chiropractors, etc.

APPENDIX C

"RESOURCES," further reading list

INDEX

Best Walks In The Welsh Borders

A book proposal

by

Simon Whaley[2]

[2] Proposed by Simon Whaley; published by Frances Lincoln (U.K.)

About the Book

Best Walks in the Welsh Borders will provide a variety of walks through the English/Welsh borders for families or dedicated walkers. Although the area is often referred to as the Welsh Marches, I believe that many people do not understand this designation, and therefore using the phrase "Welsh Borders" in the title helps readers immediately identify the location. Walks will be graded as "Easy," "Moderate," or "Strenuous" depending on the terrain and their length, which will vary from between three and nine miles.

The Welsh Borders provide a diverse range of walking opportunities, including the Clwydian Hills in the north, the Shropshire Plain, the South Shropshire Hills, the mid-Wales hills, the meandering Wye Valley through Herefordshire, and the Black Mountains in the south.

The beauty of the Welsh borders is that they are relatively quiet, with many people heading towards the popular Brecon Beacons and Snowdonia mountains, yet ironically the area is easily accessible. Sections of the area are within a 90-minute drive from the huge conurbations of Cardiff and South Wales, Cheltenham and Gloucester, Birmingham, Wolverhampton, Stafford, Stoke on Trent, and Chester. Telford, Shrewsbury, and Hereford are even closer. To give an example, one of the proposed routes would include **Carding Mill Valley** in the Long Mynd, in Church Stretton, Shropshire. Here, the National Trust caters for **250,000 visitors** in the Valley each year.

Each route description will take the following format:

- Basic Facts of the Route (Map to use, distance, where to park (or use public transport), whether there are ant public toilets)
- Introduction to the walk, detailing the waterfall(s) encountered, what else may be seen on route and who this is suitable for,
- A route description of about 1,000 words,
- A map, highlighting the route,
- Tourist Information—contact telephone numbers,
- Interesting facts. Two or three small paragraphs detailing interesting facts of items of interest along the route.
- Suggestions for other areas to walk in the immediate area.

I have included the first section of the book, which includes an Introduction, and basic information concerning public transport, maps and safety, as well as a breakdown of the contents page.

Illustrations

I also envisage including illustrations for each walk, hopefully of each waterfall, and other viewpoints along the way. I have a Canon EOS 300D, capable of providing 300dpi images of larger than A4 in size, which is more than adequate for this size of book. If preferred, I also have a Nikon SLR camera, and would be able to supply images in 35mm color transparency format as an alternative.

Book Length & Delivery

Based on the number of walks and the information to be supplied, I envisage that **Best Walks in the Welsh Borders** will be approximately 40,000 –45,000 words in length. In light of the number of walks needed to be undertaken, and the traveling involved, delivery of a complete manuscript would be approximately 12 months after receiving a favorable decision from yourselves.

Competing Books & Frances Lincoln Best Walks Series

Having carried out research in my local bookstores, in libraries, and on the Internet, I have located two books that cover areas of this borderland. *Family Walks in South Shropshire and the Welsh Borders* was published in 1990, and *Walks in the Central Welsh Marches* was published in 1985. Both of these are rather old and difficult to obtain now. Jarrold's Short Walk Series have a book which covers the Heart of England (Shropshire, Herefordshire, and Worcestershire and Birmingham) but it doesn't cover the Welsh side of the border. They have another book in their Pathfinder series entitled *Mid Wales and the Marches*, but this doesn't cover the northern and southern areas that my proposed book would.

I feel that **Best Walks in the Welsh Borders** would fit neatly alongside your Best Walks in North Wales, (and still provide an opportunity for Best Walks in South Wales in the future?) whilst also complementing your Poucher Guides and new *Freedom To Roam Walker's Guides*.

About Simon Whaley

I am 34 years old and a full-time writer. I have written numerous articles for a variety of national magazines including *The Lady, In Britain, Heritage, Dogs Monthly, Water Gardener, Self Build and Design, Cumbria and the Lake District Magazine*, and *Hotel*. I am also the best-selling author of *100 Ways For A Dog To Train Its Human* and *100 Muddy Paws For Thought* both of which are published by Hodder & Stoughton. This year will see Hodder Children's Division publish *Puppytalk—50 Ways To Make Friends With Your Puppy* and Ignotus Press publish *Running A Writers' Circle*.

However, I believe that I am the best person to write this book because I already have a track record in producing walking routes. I am regular contributor of walking routes for *Country Walking* magazine, covering South Wales and the Welsh Marches. Living in Church Stretton, Shropshire, means that I'm only one hour away from the extremities of the Welsh borders. I am also the provider of the monthly route description for *Country & Border Life* magazine, a county magazine that covers the northern section of the Welsh Marches (from Llanidloes in the south to Denbigh in the north). I am also an occasional contributor to *Walking Wales* magazine, a small A5-sized quarterly magazine.

In 2004 I was commission by the Welsh Tourist Board to provide ten pages of information for their *2005 Walking Wales* tourism brochure.

From a marketing point of view, I hope that *Country Walking, Country and Border Life,* and *Walking Wales* would be willing to publicize the book if provided with review copies. I'm sure the Welsh Tourist Information Centres would also be good outlets for the book as well as bookshops in Chester, Shrewsbury, Hereford, Worcester, Gloucester, Abergavenny, Newtown, Birmingham, and Welshpool. The National Trust has a strong presence in the area and would also provide excellent opportunities for further sales, particularly as a few of my proposed walks provide opportunities to explore some of their properties.

Appendices

To follow is a selection of further information that I feel is relevant to this proposal. I have included:

- A list of the routes in the Welsh Borders appearing in this book.
- A map, pinpointing the routes, to give an indication of the geographical spread across the Welsh borders.
- A copy of my writing curriculum vitae.
- A selection of routes published in *Country Walking* magazine.
- A selection of routes published in *Country & Border Life* magazine.
- A selection of routes published in *Walking Wales* magazine.

Please note that I always provide the images to accompany the route descriptions, and further examples of my photography can be seen on the Web site of the Photographic Agency, Alamy. Typing my name into the search box will provide thumbnail images.

BEST WALKS IN THE WELSH BORDERS

1. **Moel Famau** – A climb up to the folly at the summit (the Jubilee Tower), with excellent views across to Snowdonia, the Cheshire Plain, and the Dee Estuary.
2. **Llangollen** – Climb up to Castel Dinas with great views of the Dee Valley, and an opportunity to explore Llangollen.
3. **Bangor-is-y-coed** – A gentle walk along the banks of the River Dee through the fertile fields.
4. **Ceiriog Forest** – Forest walks through this remote landscape.
5. **Ellesmere** – A gentle walk around Shropshire's Lake District
6. **Pistyll Rhaeadr** – A route to a waterfall with a drop higher than that of Niagara Falls.
7. **Grinshall** – A route around a surprising sandstone hill, in the Shropshire Plain and through the historic village of Clive.
8. **Lake Vyrnwy** – A glorious route in the hills by this picturesque reservoir and RSPB centre.
9. **Breidden Hills** – Rodney's Monument at the top has glorious views over Shropshire and Welshpool.
10. **The Wrekin** – A walk for all the family with good views from this isolated hill, west of Telford, overlooking the Ironbridge Gorge.
11. **Welshpool** – A wander around this picturesque border town with an opportunity to visit Powis Castle.
12. **Stiperstones** – With enigmatic names like the "Devil's Chair," these rocky outcrops near the border provide a dramatic backdrop for an outstandingly rural walk.

13. **Montgomery** – Perched on a cliff, the castle here had dramatic views across this area. The walk joins these remains with the earthworks of an earlier castle.

14. **Long Mynd** – Perfect for a family day out, this route uses one of the quieter valleys to reach the summit before returning into the popular Carding Mill Valley with its National Trust Tea Shop.

15. **Wenlock Edge** – A 17-mile-long escarpment give great views over Shropshire to the Long Mynd and the Welsh Hills.

16. **Brown Clee Hill** – The highest point in Shropshire gives good views towards the Birmingham conurbation as well as the Malvern Hills.

17. **Bishops Castle** – Hilly enough to feel rural, yet it's also a fertile farming area, Bishops Castle is perfect for those after walk drinks. It has its own brewery!

18. **Kerry Ridgeway** – Follow in the footsteps of the ancient drovers who took their livestock along this ridge to market.

19. **Clun** – The Clun valley inspired AE Houseman – this walk demonstrates why.

20. **Craven Arms** – Home to the Secret Hills Discovery Centre, it's the ideal base to explore the local hills as well as the nearby fortified Manor House, with idyllic Elizabethan Gatehouse.

21. **Knucklas** – Right on the English/Welsh border, Knucklas has an impressive viaduct which carries the Heart of Wales railway line across the valley – one of the most scenic railway lines in Britain.

22. **Mortimer Forest** – A good climb from the medieval market town of Ludlow is High Vinnals, the highest point of the Forest and a good spot to see Deer.

23. **Elan Valley** – Perfect for seeing Red Kites and other Birds of Prey, Elan Valley's reservoirs provides drinking water for Birmingham.

24. **Llandrindod Wells** – A Victorian border market town on the Heart of Wales railway line, this route visits a nearby isolated church.

25. **New Radnor** – Forest walks amongst the highest hills to see the Water-Break-Its-Neck waterfall.

26. **Croft Castle** – A quiet walk through the fishponds valley up to Croft Ambrey hill fort.

27. **Hergest Ridge** – From Kington, Offa's Dyke climbs up onto Hergest Ridge with wide sweeping views across Wales and Herefordshire.

28. **Aberedw** – Above the fast flowing waters of the River Wye, Aberedw has the perfect craggy outcrop as a viewing platform.

29. **Dinmore Hill** – Half way between Leominster and Hereford lies Dinmore Hill. The road goes over, the railway goes under, and this route goes round.

30. **Dorstone** – In the Golden Valley, popular with the author C.S. Lewis, lies Dorstone, with its castle and a steep climb up to Arthur's Stone.

31. **Hay Bluff** – With incredible views over the Wye valley, it's just a stone's throw from the book town at Hay on Wye.

32. **Abbey Dore** – An idyllic walk in the Golden Valley and along the banks of the River Dore.

33. **Mordiford** – Elgar enjoyed fishing here where the Rivers Lugg and Wye meet.

34. **Sugar Loaf** – An iconic hill seen from miles around, retrace Rudolph Hess's footsteps to its summit, from the delightful town of Abergavenny.

35. **Symonds Yat** – Perched high above the River Wye, this route takes in the meanders of this route as it near the sea.

(Huw Francis contact info)[3]

Acquisitions Editor
How To Books Ltd
Spring Hill House
Spring Hill Road
Begbroke
Oxford OX5 1RX

(Date)

Dear [Editor],

Please find attached the proposal for Living and Working in Turkey.

I believe there is a need for such a book for the following reasons:

- 34,000 Britons and approximately 20,000 U.S. citizens already live in Turkey and rapid economic growth, fueling increased trade with Europe and the USA, will lead to continued expansion in these numbers.
- The Turkish government has recently stated that they wish to become the 'next Spain' and build 1 million properties for sale to international buyers. 100,000 foreign nationals currently own property in the country and recent changes in property ownership rules and the introduction of mortgages in Turkey will stimulate demand for holiday and retirement homes in line with the government's plans.
- There are currently only three books on the market offering advice on moving to and living in Turkey and these are very limited in scope.

Having lived in Turkey for five years and since worked with a number of companies to assist them do business in the country and move key personnel to Istanbul and Izmir, I am well placed to write the book.

I will be able to deliver the completed manuscript within nine months of contract signing. If you have any further questions please do not hesitate to ask.

Yours sincerely,
Huw Francis

---

[3] Proposed by Huw Francis; published by How To Books (U.K.) in 2009 as *Live and Work in Turkey*.

Living and Working in Turkey
by
Huw Francis

Living and Working in Turkey

By Huw Francis, B.Eng. P.G.Dip., MIEx

Table of Contents

Introduction

An Overview

Turkey has long been a popular destination for northern Europeans and in 2005 over 21 million visitors spent $18 billion in the country.

Like in Spain, many tourists have dreamed of returning to live and work in the country and so far 100,000 foreign nationals have bought property in Turkey. Britons are a sizeable number of the foreign residents and 34,000 live there permanently with an additional 4,000 living there part time. Most of these British residents are of working age with only approximately 1000 of them being retirees.

Though Turkey's progress to joining the EU as a full member is likely to be slow, and is by no means assured, there is an existing customs union and Turkey enjoys preferential trading links with the EU as an associate member of the community.

The Turkish government has also declared its intention to build and sell 1 million homes to foreigners in the next ten years and become the "new Spain" and the "country of choice for people looking to buy a home on the Mediterranean."

As the trading links grow some high profile British companies have set up operations in the country, among them HSBC and Tesco. There is also an active Turco–British Chamber of Commerce and a number of U.K. regions have associate organisations representing them in the country.

With a strong state education system and growing international trade links, English is widely taught in schools and private tuition companies, this has also lead to ongoing demand for English speaking teachers and lecturers at private schools, international schools, English medium universities, and EFL companies.

These strong trading, educational, and tourism links and Turkey's increasing European focus will see a growing number of expatriates and retirees moving to the country.

Having lived in Turkey for five years, Huw Francis will be able to provide a strong sense of what it is like to live in the country and guide both new arrivals and those who know the country, as they decide where they want to live and then settle in after arrival. This is especially important in Turkey as, despite its closeness to Europe, it is markedly different in terms of culture, religion, and social attitudes.

Living and Working in Turkey will be between approximately 80,000 words in length and Huw Francis can deliver the manuscript within nine months of contract signing.

Target Market

Living and Working in Turkey will be of interest to working expatriates, those considering buying a holiday home, and retirees as it will give a sense of what it is like to live in Turkey, as opposed to being a tourist. Whether the reader is older or younger, a corporate executive, an accompanying spouse, an academic, a student, or a retiree, the content of *Living and Working in Turkey* will be pertinent to their needs.

Whilst aimed primarily at British readers it will also provide information for Canadian, American, and other English-speaking readers who are also resident in significant numbers.

Competitive Books

- *Culture Shock! Turkey* (*Graphic Arts Books, January 2007*). Primarily concentrating on the social and etiquette aspects of being in Turkey and giving few details on the practicalities of living, working, and buying property in the country.
- *Buying in Turkey: A Complete Property Buyer's Guide 2006/07* (Apogee Publishing; June 2006). A booklet aimed purely at people looking to buy property on the southern coast of the country.
- *Buying a Property: Turkey* (Cadogan Guides, December 2004). A more detailed book, but also aimed at people looking to buy property for their retirement. Now significantly out of date due to recent changes in the property and financial rules governing purchase of property by foreigners.
- *Living and Working in Turkey* by Huw Francis will be different as it will be the only book to cover all aspects of living and working in the country for individuals, families, and retirees.

About the Author – Huw Francis

Huw Francis is well placed to write *Living and Working in Turkey* as he spent five years living and working there with his family.

Huw Francis grew up in Wales then attended Cranfield University in England, where he graduated in Engineering. He subsequently worked as an engineer for four years before moving to Hong Kong and changing career to work as a communications and marketing consultant with companies such as Camus, Goldman Sachs, Hughes Electronics, and Morgan Stanley.

After four years in Hong Kong he moved to Turkey for five years and then France, working as an independent business consultant and freelance writer. Along the way he married a Scot in Hong Kong and had two children, one in Hong Kong and one in Turkey. He also gained a post-graduate Diploma in International Business from Central Connecticut State University.

Huw Francis has written *Live and Work Abroad: A Guide for Modern Nomads* (Vacation Work Publications, 2001) and updated *Live and Work in Italy* (Vacation Work Publications, 2002) to make it more useful to American readers. Articles by Huw Francis have been published, in English as well as French, Spanish, and Korean translation, in the magazines, newspapers, and Web sites of sixteen countries. He has also contributed chapters to

The Writer's Guide To Queries, Pitches & Proposals, by Moira Allen (Allworth Press, U.S., 2001) and *A Career In Your Suitcase 2*, by Jo Parfitt (Summertime Publishing, U.K., 2003). Most recently Huw Francis wrote a full-length feature article on Turkey for *Morning Calm*, the in-flight magazine of Korean Airways.

As an independent consultant, Huw Francis has worked with international organisations on corporate relocation policy and practice, business development, and marketing strategy. His clients have included The British Council Education Counselling Service, Tesco PLC, and Compass Ltd.

Promotion Proposal

In Turkey there are a number of expatriate organisations and Web sites that provide information for people moving to the country and they can be approached to review the book and the author could write articles for their publications.

UKTI produces a magazine on international trade opportunities for British businesses and prints articles on different countries and working abroad and may be interested in profiling Turkey and highlighting the book as an essential resource.

Many Turkish schools, universities, and higher education institutes attract staff from overseas and *Living and Working in Turkey* will be an excellent resource for their staff and reduce the need for expensive welcome packs to be produced. Details of the institutions can be provided by the author.

There are also publications covering international relocation, study abroad, and retirement that often look for articles and books to review and can offer great opportunities to reach an audience already looking to move, but not sure where to go or how to do it.

Numerous international HR and expatriate relocation conferences take place around the world and Huw Francis has previously spoken at such events and can do so in the future. These events always provide opportunities for speakers to sell their books, or the event bookstall will stock and promote them.

Reviews of *Live and Work Abroad: A Guide for Modern Nomads*, by Huw Francis

University of Edinburgh Careers Service, Phoenix Magazine.

"A most comprehensive guide to living and working abroad."

*Peter Van Buren, Traveling Internationally with Your Kids –
www.travelwithyourkids.com.*

"Much of this book is stuff I wish I would have known 15 years ago when I started my own life as a nomad. This book is of use to everyone just starting out, with enough good content that even expats higher up the learning curve will find much of value."

Carrie Shearer, International HR Consultant.

"... this book, aptly listed as a guide for modern nomads, is a must-read for anyone going on or living through an expatriate assignment. During my years in International Human Resources I think I read every book written about the expat experience, looking for the one that I could recommend to our staff. I'm pleased to say that this book satisfies my craving and, after twenty-five years, I can stop my quest."

Diane MacPherson, Mobility Services International, Newsbreak.

"New guide for 'modern nomads' puts a more positive spin on the expat experience. 'Much of the published literature aimed at people living overseas seems to assume that many expatriates do not really want to be living abroad, and that their main aim is to reach the end of their difficult posting and return to normality,' say Huw Francis and Michelyne Callan, co-authors of the just-released *Live and Work Abroad - A Guide for Modern Nomads*. While Francis and Callan acknowledge that there certainly are expats who view their life this way, it's a foreign concept to them. Instead, they have put together a resource designed to help expats make the most of their overseas experience. The end result is terrific. *Live and Work Abroad* is a comprehensive resource that takes a decidedly positive, yet realistic look at the many challenges present in the expat experience and provides practical, real-life advice for getting through them and on to good things this experience brings."

The Outline

Living and Working in Turkey

Chapter List and Outline

Chapter 1
Introducing Turkey – History, Religion, People, Politics, Government, Economy, Geography, and Regions.

This chapter will provide a compact, but comprehensive, overview of the country, its disparate regions, and various ethnic groups.

Chapter 2
Getting there – Flying, Overland, and Ferries/Sailing.

As a large country, with seven countries having land borders with it as well as an extensive coastline, there are numerous ways to enter and leave the country, which provides plenty of choices for residents and tourists alike. This chapter will highlight the various options available and their restrictions where appropriate.

Chapter 3
Bureaucracy – Visas and work permits, importing personal belongings, vehicles, and pets.

Covering the important aspects of the paperwork necessary to live and/or work in Turkey.

Chapter 4
Accommodation – Renting, buying, and utilities/services.

This chapter will looking at the process of renting accommodation and setting up electricity, gas, telephone, and other services. The process of buying property will also be covered in this chapter.

Chapter 5
Daily Living - Language, public holidays, education, public services, pets, police & crime, social life, churches, bereavement, and media.

Covering the social and practical sides of living in Turkey, this chapter will provide information on a wide variety of issues that are important in helping people enjoy living in a foreign country.

Chapter 6
Working in Turkey – Opportunities for expatriates doing business in Turkey.

Sources of jobs and employers in Turkey will be discussed as well as some of the cultural issues of working and doing business in the country.

Chapter 7
Setting up in business – Business types, proscribed occupations, business support organisations, investment regulations, repatriation of profits.

This chapter will provide information for people looking to set up their own business in Turkey and cover the various options available as well as the investment climate.

Chapter 8
Retiring to Turkey – Regulations, prime locations, pensions.

Specifically written for people considering or planning on retiring to Turkey and addressing the additional and/or separate issues important to them.

Chapter 9
Finances – Banking, taxes, mortgages, and insurance.

An overview of the banking and other financial services on offer in Turkey as well as the tax system and reciprocal arrangements with other countries.

Chapter 10
Travelling and Leisure – Travel and leisure options in Turkey.

Looking at the options for travel within Turkey and sports and leisure activities available around the country.

Chapter 11
Health services and social security.

An overview of the state and private healthcare systems and social security arrangements for non-Turkish residents.

Appendix A
Embassies, consulates, tourist information services, relocation services, universities, international/private schools, private healthcare providers, banks, job listings newspapers, ISPs, satellite/cable operators, travel/transportation providers, etc.

Appendix B
Books on Turkey and by Turkish authors. Turkish films.

Appendix C
Further reading and resources.

SECTION 4
The Fiction Proposal

15

A Novel Proposal

It's not hard to find ghastly statistics about the number of novels that are rejected by "New York Publishers." Vanity/subsidy presses (both print and electronic) trumpet the fact that thousands, if not hundreds of thousands, of first-time novels are passed over by the commercial press every year. But why?

One very simple reason so many novels "fail" is that the vast majority of first-time novelists are unfamiliar with the submission process. Most new novelists simply wrap up their book and mail it off—only to have it languish for months, unread, in a stack of similarly ill-prepared manuscripts. Worse, many publishers (particularly the larger mainstream publishers) refuse to even consider unsolicited manuscripts, which means that such submissions will either be returned unread or, if the writer has failed to include proper postage, be consigned to the dumpster.

Given the volume of submissions generated by hopeful writers every year, editors and agents simply have no time (or patience) to deal with those who don't follow standard submission procedures. While a good proposal is no substitute for a good novel, it *can* make the difference between having your novel reviewed by an editor—and having it become landfill.

Submitting Your Novel: A Step-by-Step Guide

So what, exactly, is "standard procedure"? Fortunately, it is virtually the same whether you are submitting your novel to a print publisher, an electronic publisher, or an agent. Here are the basic steps you'll need to take:

1. **Finish your novel.** This is the most important step in the process. Gone are the days when an editor or agent might accept an author's work-in-progress, based on an outline and a few sample chapters. In today's publishing market, if you haven't finished your book, no editor or agent will be willing to work with you.

All too often, new writers never make it to the finish line—so no matter what your "potential" may be, you must first prove that you can deliver the goods.

2. **Search for potential publishers.** Who might be an appropriate publisher for your novel? What publishers might make good second and third choices? Don't try to answer these questions by reaching for *The Writer's Market* and looking up every publisher who produces books in your genre. For this kind of market research, you need to go to the market itself.

    • **Check your bookshelves.** Presumably, you own a number of books in the same genre in which you're writing. If you write romance, you should be reading romance; if you write mysteries, you should be reading mysteries. Chances are, you've also saved your favorites—books that you'd be willing to read again. Who publishes those books? Scan your shelves to see what imprints appear most frequently: These are the publishers who produce the types of books you like to read. Would your book fit among their titles?

    • **Check your local bookstore.** Browse the sections where your book would be most likely to appear. Again, what imprints do you see? Take a look at the actual books produced by different publishers. Do you like the quality of the production? Are the covers attractive, or do they look cheap? Do you recognize any of the authors? Do the cover blurbs appeal to you and entice you to read further? Jot down the names of publishers that produce the types of books you might be willing to buy.

3. **Look for publishers' guidelines.** *The Writer's Market* and other market guides can help you here, but don't stop at their listings. Go online, and locate the Web sites for the publishers you've chosen. Search the site for "author guidelines" (which may also be labeled "submission guidelines" or "for authors"). Also, check the publisher's online catalog. Do you see a mix of known authors and newcomers? If a publisher offers only "big names," you may have difficulty breaking in; if, however, a publisher features only unknowns, you may not be able to expect much in the way of an advance or promotion.

    Pay careful attention to the "wants" specified in the publisher's guidelines. Make sure your novel fits within those guidelines. For example, does a publisher purchase horror novels "but no vampire stories," which yours just happens to be? Does your novel fit within the specified word limits? There's no point in submitting a 200,000-word novel to a publisher that won't accept manuscripts of more than 100,000 words. Never assume that you can be "the exception"; submitting a novel that falls outside a publisher's guidelines simply sends the message that you haven't done your homework.

Finally, determine exactly what procedure must be followed to submit to that publisher. Most publishers fit into one of the following three categories:

- **Accepts unsolicited manuscripts.** This means that you don't need an agent to approach the publisher and you don't need an "invitation" (usually based on a query). It does not necessarily mean that you can submit a complete manuscript; the publisher may prefer to start with a synopsis and sample chapters.

- **Does not accept unsolicited submissions.** This does not mean that you need an agent; however, it does mean that you must query the publisher before submitting even a synopsis and sample chapters. If the guidelines don't make clear exactly what you can and cannot send, contact the publisher to find out, because if you send the wrong materials, they will be returned unread.

- **Accepts only agented submissions.** In this case, your only hope of selling to this publisher is through an agent. Don't even bother with a query, as it won't be considered. This publisher will only accept material that has been "pre-screened" by a reputable agent.

4. **Prepare your package.** While some publishers do accept entire manuscripts, most prefer a "proposal" package that usually includes a cover or query letter, an outline or "synopsis" of your novel, and three sample chapters (the first three chapters of your book). Agents generally require the same materials; in fact, the procedure for approaching an agent is almost identical to that for approaching a publisher. Be sure you know exactly what the publisher (or agent) expects, including any limitations on page count, word count, etc. The rest of this section will discuss the specifics of preparing that all-important package.

The Query

There is no specific "formula" for a winning novel query. Some writers like to start off with a dramatic hook: "What if a nuclear explosion leveled New York, and you were one of a handful of survivors?" Others prefer a more straightforward approach: "I am seeking representation for my 75,000-word mystery novel, *Death Dines Out...*"

As author Lynn Flewelling notes, "The query letter is an elegantly concise piece of promotional writing. You have exactly one page to introduce yourself and your novel—just four or five clean, tight paragraphs, each with its own specific purpose. That doesn't sound so hard. We are writers, after all, right? But the devil is in the details, especially for a newcomer with no track record or flashy credentials." Typically, a novel query addresses many of the same questions as a periodical query, including:

1. **Your reason for choosing this agent or publisher.** Make sure the recipient of your proposal knows that you selected them with care. If you chose a publisher based on certain book titles, or an agent based on authors that agent already represents, say so. This will demonstrate that you've done some market research—which is the mark of a professional. But don't "suck up" by telling a publisher how much you love their books, or that you've named your first-born child after the lead character in their most popular series.

2. **The basics about your book.** Make sure your query specifies the type of book you've written (e.g., its genre), its length (word count), and a working title. If you're writing in a genre that has several subcategories ("cozy" mystery, "paranormal" romance), be sure to specific the appropriate category. Be sure that your book actually fits the publisher's guidelines: If the publisher only handles hard-boiled detective novels, don't bother submitting a "cozy" mystery. If your book defies categorization, do your best to categorize it anyway: Being able to "place" a book within a particular genre is a key selling point. You may wish to describe your book as "a cozy mystery with romantic elements," but don't try to pitch "a genre-busting blend of mystery, romance, time travel, and technothriller." If an agent can't determine how to best market the book you've written, he or she will be much less interested in reviewing it.

   As mentioned above, your book should be complete—and you should indicate this in your query. But what if your book is part of a series? There's no hard-and-fast rule about this one; some editors and agents like the idea that you have more than one book to offer (presuming they like the first one), while others prefer to take a "wait and see" approach before offering to handle more than one book.

3. **A brief synopsis.** Your query letter should include a short overview of the book's plot and major themes. Don't attempt to summarize your entire novel in two paragraphs; this is a "pitch," not an outline. Consider approaching this section as if you were writing the copy for the back cover of your published book: What elements would be most likely to attract a reader's attention? These might include:

   • **The primary characters.** In your query letter, you'll only have space to introduce two, or at most three, major players in your novel—usually the key protagonists and, possibly, the antagonist.

- **The basic plot.** Most stories answer a "what if" question: "What if an exiled Russian countess falls in love with a rugged American frontiersman?" "What if a nuclear blast destroys New York in 2050, leaving only a handful of survivors?" "What if a local busybody is murdered, and the prime suspect is the detective's own father?" Identify the basic "what if" question that drives your plot. (Remember that "plot" isn't just the sequence of events that occurs in your novel; it's the *reason* for those events.)

- **The setting.** Where and when does your story occur? How important is that setting to the story? If your setting is essential to the plot—e.g., your protagonists are exploring a strange planet that confronts them with a series of perils and obstacles—say so. If, however, your setting is merely "background," don't spend too much space describing it. Remember, too, that many settings can be conveyed in a few words: If your story takes place in a medieval fantasy universe, you won't have to explain that this world includes castles and serfs and bad plumbing.

- **The primary source of conflict.** What are the key obstacles your characters face? Where does the conflict come from? With whom (or with what) do your characters struggle? Is the conflict primarily internal or external? Is it with another character, with society, or with the forces of nature? Focus on the conflict that is central to the plot as a whole—e.g., your aristocratic heroine's struggle to escape the duties of her position so that she can be with the man she loves—rather than specific details, such as the arguments she has with her family and friends.

- **The theme.** Does your story have an underlying message? What is it "about," beyond the actual plot? What issues does it explore or reveal? What questions does it raise? Don't confuse "theme" with preachiness; your novel doesn't have to be a sermon to raise intriguing questions or ideas in the mind of the reader.

4. **The market (readership) for your book.** Who would be most likely to buy your novel? Try to define a specific audience. No novel will appeal to "everyone," and the writer who thinks otherwise will only appear naïve.

   A good way to describe the potential market for your book is to mention comparable titles or authors. You might suggest, for example, that your book is likely to appeal to "fans of mystery writers such as P.D. James or Patricia Cornwall." Never suggest, however, that your book is just like that of another author, or is "just as good as" some other popular title. You don't want to give the impression that you're trying to imitate, or compete with, what's already on the market. Your book should stand on its own merits.

Should you link your book to a trend? Only if it is an enduring trend with a long-standing, established audience. For example, there may never be a shortage of fantasy novels about dragons, but the interest in fantasy novels about vampires tends to wax and wane. Be especially cautious about linking your book to hot new trends; publishers were flooded with Harry Potter knockoffs. Remember that your book isn't likely to appear on the market for at least two years after acceptance, by which time today's hot trends may be yesterday's cold news.

5. **Your credentials.** If you have relevant credentials, list them. If, for example, you have sold several short stories to reputable markets within your genre, list those credits. Don't, however, list "sales" to low-paying or nonpaying markets, Internet sites where you can post your own work, or self-published/vanity published novels (unless they have a spectacular sales record). Mention any experience or expertise you have that relates to your novel—for example, mention your degree in history if your novel has a historical element. If your novel is set in Greece and you spent three years in that country, say so.

Nonfiction writing credentials rarely carry much weight in the fiction community. They are worth a mention because they demonstrate that you can write professionally and have been able to sell your work (especially if you've managed to sell a nonfiction book or two). However, by themselves, they won't sell your story. Even if you've been writing nonfiction for years, your novel will still be treated as the work of a "new" author.

Never discuss (or apologize for) your *lack* of credentials. Never mention, for example, that this is the first thing you've ever written, or that you've never been published before, or that you have no relevant background. If these happen to be true, say nothing.

6. **What to avoid.** As with any query, there are certain things you should never include in a novel proposal, including:

- **Hype.** Never tell an editor or agent how "good" you think your book is. Don't describe it as "exciting" or "a sure-fire success." Hyping your own book is a sure sign of inexperience; editors and agents prefer to make those judgments for themselves.
- **Flattery.** Don't try to convince an editor that you've read every book the publishing house has published. The editor doesn't care what you think of other books; s/he is only interested in the quality of *your* material.
- **Negative information.** If your book has already been rejected twenty times, don't say so. It is true that many books are rejected repeatedly before becoming "overnight

bestsellers." Editors and agents, however, tend to respect the judgment of their peers, and there is no point in telling them that those peers have already passed judgment against your novel.

- **Irrelevant personal information.** Don't mention how old you are, your marital status, or how many children you have, unless this somehow relates to your novel. An editor doesn't need to know that you are a housewife who has written her first novel at the kitchen table. Don't explain *why* you wrote the book (e.g., as therapy, or because everyone told you that you ought to write down the story of your life).

- **Testimonies**. If your mother loved the book, or your spouse has been urging you to send it to a publisher for years, or your writing group thinks you're brilliant, or your writing instructor gave you an "A," that's great. Explaining any of this to a publisher or agent, however, is like scrawling "newbie!" across your manuscript in big red letters. Don't do it.

The Fiction Query Letter
by Lynn Flewelling

There I was, with a book I was burning to sell and no idea how to go about it. It quickly became clear that the most important tool I needed was a great query letter. It's a writer's introduction, our calling card and, hopefully, our foot in the door.

For us nobodies, it's basically a cold sales job; we've got one page to engage an agent or editor's interest, make him want to flip the page to scan our carefully chosen sample chapters. Write the letter like it's the one thing standing between you and success. It just might be.

Here's the query letter that sold several agents on *Luck in the Shadows* and ultimately led to a two-book contract with Bantam:

Dear (Agent/Editor's Name):

I am seeking representation for my fantasy adventure novel, *Luck In The Shadows*, complete at 170,000 words. I am enclosing a synopsis and a sample chapter. The sequel, *Stalking Darkness*, is nearing completion and another free-standing book featuring the same characters is in outline form.

I love thieves and spies—those sneaky people who live by intuition, skill, and inside knowledge. In fantasy, however, they are often portrayed as dark, ruthless characters or relegated to second string roles, a la Falstaff, as useful or amusing foils for more conventional heroic types. *Luck in the Shadows* gives the rogues center stage.

Seregil is an experienced spy for hire with a murky past and noble connections; Alec is the talented but unworldly boy he rescues and takes on as apprentice. "I admit I've cut a purse or two in my time," Seregil tells Alec soon after they meet, "and some of what I do could be called stealing, depending on who you ask. But try to imagine the challenge of overcoming incredible obstacles to accomplish a noble purpose. Think of traveling to lands where legends walk the streets in daylight and even the color of the sea is like nothing you've ever seen! I ask you again, would you be plain Alec of Kerry all your life, or would you see what lies beyond?" Alec goes, of course, and quickly plunges into danger, intrigue, and adventure as their relationship deepens into friendship. The interaction between these two forms the core of this character-driven series.

I've been writing professionally for ten years and am currently a freelance journalist. My articles appear regularly in the *Bangor Daily News, Preview! Magazine,* and *Maine In Print.* I've covered everything from software to psychics; my interview credits include Stephen King, Anne Rice, and William Kotzwinkle.

Thank you for your consideration of this proposal. I look forward to hearing from you soon.

Sincerely,
Lynn Flewelling

First things first. When approaching any market, make certain you're writing to the right person. If you're using a reference book, make sure it's the latest edition. Addressing your query to someone who left the agency three years ago shows a lack of research on your part and can prejudice some readers against you before you've even begun your pitch. The same goes for spelling their name wrong or addressing them by the wrong title or gender.

Reading the market news in trade journals can help keep you up to date on who's where. Most agents and editors say that a brief call to their office to verify the information is also acceptable.

Now, on with our dissection:

Paragraph 1: The Opening

This brief opening accomplishes a number of things. It states what you're selling, how long it is, and that it's complete. The "synopsis and sample chapter" mentioned in this paragraph are the items this particular agent's listing asked for. Giving them what they want— no more, no less—demonstrates that you've done your homework and are approaching them as a professional.

If you have other related works underway, it's a good idea to mention them here, showing that you're not a one-shot wonder. If you don't, however, don't worry about it, and don't bother mentioning other works in a genre the agent or editor does not handle.

Paragraph 2: "Why I Wrote this Book"

Those of you who are basing your science fiction epic on your Nobel prize-winning research in human genome mapping won't have much trouble with this one. For those of us "nobodies" with less stunning credentials, it can be a bit daunting. Most of the sample letters I found while researching queries were written by people who were, as stated above, basing their latest novel on their own research or some life-changing personal experience. In every case the author had an impressive publishing background of some sort, and none of them were first-timers.

I, on the other hand, had simply written a book I really liked, so I said that and let the enthusiasm carry it. Keep it simple and direct. Don't go on at length about your literary influences or what book first turned you on to the genre. Just be sincere.

Paragraph 3: Give 'Em a Glimpse of the Goods

You can't tell the whole story; that's what the outline or synopsis is for. Just give them the flavor, introduce the protagonist, and above all, demonstrate that you can write well. How you present your book here is just as important as the story itself. Make your thumbnail description concise but lively. Try to capture what or whom the book is about. In short, consider this paragraph your book's audition scene, and know that this paragraph is the one most likely get you rejected for the right reasons.

"Right reasons?" you ask.

Absolutely. Most editors and agents are book lovers just like the rest of us, with the same subjectivity of taste. If an agent doesn't like books about dragons and that's your main focus, then they aren't going to want your book and you don't want them representing it. With agents, you want an enthusiastic representative for your work.

With editors, you want someone who's excited by the prospect of polishing your manuscript into a salable book and getting it on the shelves.

A wise friend once observed that the ratio between rejections and acceptances is about 12:1. What happens generally is this: Agent One reads your carefully crafted query and thinks he's seen your idea a hundred times before; Agent Three thinks it's the freshest treatment he's seen of that idea in ages; Agent Seven just plain hates that sort of plot; Agent Eleven can't get enough of it. Simple persistence and faith are required to run this gauntlet, and rejection letters do have their uses. We'll return to this shortly.

Paragraph 4: Experience and Background

Got it? Flaunt it! Don't got it? Keep quiet.

While the freelance writing I mentioned in my query by no means guarantees that I'm a good novelist, it does suggest that I probably know how to string words together. I also tried to be creative in my spin on the subject. I've written dozens of feature articles for local papers; the ones I chose to mention in the query were selected to highlight my interest in the fantasy field, and in literature and authors in general.

If your background has no bearing on the novel in question in some readily apparent way, it's best to just leave this paragraph out, or keep it brief.

Paragraph 5: Your Standard Polite Good-Bye

Don't press for response times, hand down ultimatums ("You've got two months, then I'm sending it somewhere else"), or offer to call. The agent's or publisher's market listing should include an estimated response time. Be patient and don't expect them to meet their own deadlines to the day. However, if you don't hear back for a month after the listed time, a polite phone inquiry is usually appropriate.

The Novel Synopsis

Sooner or later, you will need to provide a synopsis of your novel to an editor or agent. In some cases, you'll be expected to send it with your initial query; in others, you'll be asked to send it only on request.

Few things terrify the first-time novelist (or even experienced novelists) so much as the demand for "the dreaded synopsis." Condensing the salient points of a 100,000-word novel into a five- to ten-page summary is no easy task. But it can be done.

The first step is to understand the purpose of the synopsis. While it is a selling *tool* for your novel, it is not a *sales pitch* (like the overview in your query letter). The primary goal of your synopsis is to demonstrate that your story is coherent, logical, well thought-out, and well organized. It should show that your characters act and interact in a realistic, consistent fashion; that the plot unfolds logically and at an appropriate pace; that plot twists don't seem contrived or coincidental; that the story will hold the reader's attention from beginning to end; and that the ending (the "resolution") is believable and satisfying.

While some publishers still ask for a chapter-by-chapter synopsis, most now prefer a "narrative" synopsis that follows the flow of the story as a whole. This format enables you to focus on the key points of the story, without having to "say something" about each individual chapter. This enables you to focus on the primary plot and major characters, without confusing the issue with subplots and secondary characters.

A synopsis should generally be formatted like a regular manuscript. Some writers double-space; some single-space. Some use a cover page that includes the book title, author's name (or pen-name), author's contact information, and the word-count of the book as a whole. Others include this information on the first page of the synopsis itself, as with an article or story.

How long should it be? If the agent or publisher doesn't give any guidelines on maximum length, a good rule is to allow one page of synopsis per 10,000 words of novel—up to a maximum of ten pages. Shorter is better; if you can say it in five pages, don't stretch it to ten.

A synopsis is written in the present tense: "Andrea returns to her home town for the holidays, to find…" Try to avoid long blocks of text; break it up into shorter paragraphs.

Put character names in CAPS or boldface the first time they appear. Try to limit the number of characters you actually name in your synopsis; too many names become confusing. (Thus, instead of saying, "Andrea shares her concerns with her best friend, Ginny," it would be better to leave the friend unnamed unless she plays a major role in the action.)

What should your synopsis cover? What should you leave out? If you ask ten different writers this question, you're likely to get ten different answers. In chapter 18, you'll find one author's analysis of the ideal novel synopsis, followed by a sample synopsis, which is then analyzed in detail in chapter 19.

The Proposal Package

Once you've written a synopsis for your novel, you've accomplished the most difficult—and most important—part of the proposal process. You may have to edit that synopsis for different publishers, but you have the basics.

The final thing that most publishers and agents will request from you is "three sample chapters." These must be *the first three chapters of your book*—not three chapters that you choose at random. Need I say, therefore, that it is in your best interest to polish those three chapters to the best of your ability? Review them. Edit them. Run them by a critique group. Ask someone to help you proofread them. Make sure that they are the best example of your work that you could possibly send. Format them according to basic manuscript format principles (double-spaced, ample margins, indented paragraphs, no extra spaces between paragraphs, numbered pages, etc.).[1]

Do not send any of the following items with your proposal:

- A personal (or publicity) photo.
- An expanded bio, resume, or curriculum vitae. (In some cases, it might be appropriate to include a list of relevant publications.)
- Samples of other published (or unpublished) writings.
- Letters of reference or recommendation.

Now it's time to assemble your package. Be sure to include a SASE. If you would like confirmation that an editor or agent received your query or proposal, include a self-addressed, stamped postcard for an immediate response. Just type a line on the back that reads something like:

Dear Author,

We have received your manuscript, "title," on

(Date): _____.

We hope to be able to respond to your manuscript by

(Date): _____.

(Signed): _____

The second line is optional, but useful if you'd like an estimate of when you can expect to hear from the editor or agent.

If you have a professional business card, add one of those as well, as it will make it easier for the recipient to keep track of your contact information.

If your total proposal is more than twenty pages, sandwich it between two 8.5 x 11 pieces of cardboard (e.g., cardboard from the back of a notepad), and secure it with a rubber band. This will prevent the pages from being damaged in shipping. Choose a sturdy envelope that will hold your proposal snugly. (Too large an envelope will allow your proposal to slide

---

[1] If you have any doubts about proper manuscript format, see my article, "A Quick Guide to Manuscript Format," at *www.writing-world.com/basics/manuscript.shtml.*

around and become battered; too small an envelope will cause it to bend and crimp the pages.) If your proposal is too large for an envelope, use a thin stationery box instead.

After you've assembled your package (but before you seal it), weigh it. If it weighs less than 13 ounces, you might wish to include a SASE of sufficient size, and with sufficient postage, to allow the return of your entire proposal. If, however, the proposal weighs more than 13 ounces, it's better to include a letter-size SASE for a response only, and allow the editor or agent to discard the proposal itself (assuming it isn't wanted!).

Now that your proposal is out the door, there is one more thing for you to do: *Wait.* Response times for publishers and agents are notoriously slow, especially if your work is unsolicited. Agents may take from two to four months to respond; publishers may take between six months and a year. (Electronic publishers tend to respond more quickly—usually within less than two months.) Check the response times listed in the publisher's (or agent's) guidelines, and assume that in many cases, these may be underestimates.

If the specified response time has elapsed and you have heard nothing, follow up with a polite letter or e-mail inquiring as to the status of your proposal. Wait two weeks, then follow up again. If you still receive no reply, you may wish to send a final letter withdrawing your proposal from consideration (it's important to do this to avoid confusion or accusations of "simultaneous submission) and send it to the next agent or editor on your list. Don't be surprised if you have to repeat this several times.

Given that it *can* take months to receive a response to a query, is it acceptable to query several agents or editors simultaneously? The answer used to be "no"—despite the fact that publishers might take as long as six months to respond to a submission. However, that seems to be changing toward a more realistic understanding of the writer's dilemma.

A.C. Crispin conducted a survey of agents and publishers on this topic, and reported the results in the *Science Fiction & Fantasy Writers of America Bulletin*. She found that the agents and editors agreed that simultaneous *queries* were acceptable. Two of the four agents queried were also willing to review partial works (e.g., synopsis and sample chapters) or even complete manuscripts submitted simultaneously to other agents; the other two would not. Similarly, two of the publishers were willing to review multiple submissions; one was not, and one accepted only agented submissions.

The bottom line, then, would seem to be this:

- It is generally considered acceptable to send simultaneous queries to multiple agents and/or editors.
- If you do send out multiple queries, inform the agents/editors that you are doing so. This is basic courtesy, and if you omit this step, you're likely to alienate an editor or agent who might otherwise have been willing to review your package.

- Though some agents and editors are willing to review simultaneously submitted packages or even complete manuscripts, this is not yet a widely accepted practice. Agents and editors are more likely to respond to your query by requesting an exclusive review of your submission package.

The key at this point is persistence. Your goal is to find an editor or agent who will believe in your book as much as you do. That person may not be the first on your list, or even the fifteenth or twentieth. But if you're willing to persevere in the belief that such an editor or agent is out there, you're a thousand times more likely to achieve publication than the writer who despairs after the first or second rejection.

16

Seeking an Agent

Many writers assume that finding an agent is a necessary first step toward getting published or that it may be impossible to get published without an agent. This is not necessarily true. One of the first steps you should take is not necessarily to *find* an agent, but to determine whether you actually *need* one.

A good way to answer this question is by reviewing the guidelines of publishers in your genre or interest area. If most of the publishers in your genre (and especially the "top" publishers) accept only agented submissions, then you would be well-advised to seek an agent before attempting to market your manuscript.

If, however, most of the publishers in your field or genre accept unagented submissions (including unsolicited submissions and submissions by invitation only—e.g., based on an initial query), then you may wish to proceed without an agent. You could, for example, hunt for an agent and a publisher simultaneously, or seek an agent *after* you've received an offer from a publisher. (At that point, it's wise to ask the publisher for a recommendation, as you may want to find an agent who can help you negotiate that particular contract.)

In making this decision, it's also important to know what an agent will do for you, and what an agent will expect from you.

What an Agent Offers a Writer

The primary function of an agent is to find a publisher for your work. Agents work almost exclusively with book-length manuscripts (fiction and nonfiction); they rarely handle short fiction or articles. There are occasional exceptions, but generally speaking, if you are trying to market short stories or articles, you should be handling this on your own.

An agent will also help you negotiate a book contract. This is a key advantage, as an agent is literally *your* representative in the industry. The agent works for *you*, and will strive to get you the best deal possible in terms of money, rights, etc.

An agent will also attempt market the subsidiary rights to your book, which can be a lucrative field that you might have great difficulty tapping on your own. An agent is the best person to sell translation rights, international rights, audio-book rights, electronic rights, movie rights, etc. Often, an author can reap an even greater income from subsidiary rights' sales than from the original book sale.

In the processing of handling these transactions, your agent will serve as an "escrow" account for your funds. Generally, your advance and royalties, and any other monies, will be sent directly to your agent, who will subtract his/her commission and pass the rest to you. (Your agent is not an accountant, however; don't expect help with writing expenses and taxes.)

It's important to realize that an agent is *not* an editor. While some agents will offer suggestions on how a book can be polished into a more marketable form, many agents will work only with books that are already market-ready. An agent will *not* line-edit your work, correct your spelling and grammar, or do any other basic editorial tasks.

In some cases, an agent will provide you with a contract that spells out what is expected on both sides. Many agents, however, do not work with contracts. Don't assume that having a contract is "good" or that not having one is "bad." What matters is being able to work well with the agent; if you can't, a contract can sometimes lock you into an unwanted long-term relationship. One thing to determine before you even enter a relationship with an agent is how to end it, if it isn't proceeding as you hoped.

What an Agent Expects of You

The first criterion an agent uses in determining whether to represent an author is the quality of that author's work. While you don't have to be published to find an agent, you do have to have publishable-quality material.

Agents also seek "career" authors, rather than one-book writers. Agents want to work with writers who will provide an ongoing source of income (which means writers who plan to produce more than one book). When seeking an agent, therefore, it's wise to present yourself as an author with long-term plans, rather than someone who simply wants to find a publisher for the "book of a lifetime."

Finally, an agent expects a fee. The standard fee at this time is 15 percent of all domestic sales made by that agent, and (in some cases) 20 percent of international sales. A few agents also charge for unusual expenses, but most do not charge for the basic expenses of copying and mailing manuscripts.

Note that this fee is assessed on *sales* of your work. Until your work is actually sold, the agent will collect no commission.

What to Watch Out For When Seeking an Agent

While there are hundreds of reputable literary agents, there are also hundreds of predatory sharks swimming in the publishing pool, hunting for inexperienced writers who are willing to do (and pay) anything to "get published."

Experienced authors warn writers to stay away from any agent who:

- **Asks for a reading fee.** If an agent charges a fee (no matter how small) to read and review your manuscript, that agent is earning his/her income from would-be writers—*not* by selling work to publishers. Charging reading fees is not illegal, but agents who do so are avoided by professionals.

- **Asks for an upfront fee (e.g., "to pay expenses") to market your work.** A reputable agent won't accept a manuscript that s/he doesn't believe can be sold—so such an agent doesn't regard the basic expenses of submitting manuscripts to be a "risk." While some agents may charge for unusual expenses, the basics of copying and mailing manuscripts are considered to be covered by an agent's commission.

- **Offers to edit your manuscript for a fee.** Again, reputable agents only accept material that is market-ready. If an agent is making money from writers by providing editorial services, that agent has little incentive to try to *market* your work.

- **Suggests that you submit your manuscript to a specific editor or book doctor for editing.** While an agent *may* recommend that you seek editing for your manuscript, be wary of any who (a) suggests that you go to a specific service, and (b) implies that he or she will "accept" your manuscript after you do so.

- **Refuses to disclose information about his or her client list or sales history**.

- **Has a large percentage of sales to smaller or less reputable publishers.** Don't waste time with an agent who is likely to submit your work to small presses, electronic publishers, or (worst of all) subsidy publishers. You don't need an agent to approach those markets; what you want is an agent who can open doors that would otherwise be closed to you.

- **Asks for a higher commission.** Don't accept any excuses. Don't let an agent convince you that because you are a new writer, or don't have a track record in the industry, or have an unusual or "difficult" book, that you should pay a higher fee. If a reputable agent thinks he or she can place your work (even if it may take some effort), that agent will charge the usual fee; otherwise, he or she will simply refuse to represent you.

- **Is not a member of the Association of Author's Representatives (AAR).** While membership is not a sure sign of a reputable agent, it does mean that the agent has agreed to a certain standard of ethics.

There is one other consideration when seeking an agent, and that is whether the agent works primarily for *authors* or for *editors*. An agent who is primarily interested in working with authors will be more likely to take your work, as written, and seek a publisher. An "editor's" agent, however, tends to seek authors who are interested in handling specific assignments from publishers. This type of agent is one whom publishers will contact if they have a specific need; the agent attempts to build a stable of authors who can be called upon for assignments. While there is nothing wrong with an "editor's" agent, particularly if you'd like to be considered for assignments, you may find that this type of agent is less interested in handling your existing work and more interested in your ability to write to someone else's requirements.

How to Locate an Agent

Knowing what to look for in an agent is one thing; knowing where to look is another. Many sources of information on agents exist, but it can be difficult to track down just the *right* agent for your work.

Ideally, you want an agent who appreciates and understands the type of material you write. If you write science fiction, you want to find an agent who regularly sells science fiction, who is familiar with all the major science fiction publishing houses, who knows what an alternate universe is, and who would never, ever accept a book by a new writer who uses terms like "warp drive" and "phaser."[1] Since science fiction comes in many flavors, you should also look for someone who appreciates the type of novel you have written.

Two general sources of agent listings include *The Literary Marketplace* and *Literary Agents of North America* (both of which can be found in most libraries' reference sections). Writer's Digest Books offers an annual *Guide to Literary Agents* (which includes lists of fee-charging agents). Several Web sites (including the AAR) post lists of agents online.

Be cautious about agent listings in writers' magazines. Reputable agents generally don't want to attract submissions from amateur and inexperienced writers, and so are less likely to place advertisements in publications that have a high percentage of such writers in their readership.

Another way to find an agent is to ask another writer. This doesn't mean, however, that you should go online, hunt down a writer's Web site, and send an e-mail out of the blue asking that writer to tell you the name of his or her agent. Most writers won't share that information unless they are familiar with you and the quality of your work.

---

[1] An experienced agent will know that (a) these terms are common to the trademarked *Star Trek* universe, and (b) only a rank amateur in the science fiction genre (and someone who has not read widely in the field or read any books about *writing* science fiction) would use such terms in a serious science fiction novel.

A good way to establish that type of relationship is to join a high-quality online discussion list or newsgroup for writers, one that includes several published authors in its membership. Contribute to discussions, and share your material in critique groups. Once you become known and respected by the other members of the group, you are more likely to be able to ask those members for information about their agents.

Approaching an Agent

Approach an agent just as you would approach a publisher, and with the same types of materials. Start, for example, by researching the agent's Web site, to determine:

- What types of material the agent handles
- Whether the agent is accepting new clients
- What type of client the agent is looking for (e.g., how much experience or publishing background a client should have)
- What clients the agent currently represents and/or what titles the agent has sold
- Exactly what the agent wants you to send (e.g., a query letter, a query and synopsis, a nonfiction proposal, a complete manuscript, etc.).

Once you have determined the answers to these questions, follow the instructions in the relevant chapter of this book to prepare the requested materials.

The good news is that agents usually respond more quickly than publishers. Many will respond to a query within three to six weeks and to a larger proposal (such as a synopsis and sample chapters) within two to three months. As always, observe an agent's posted response times before following up—and always remain courteous and professional.

What should your query include? Here's some advice from best-selling science-fiction author Tara K. Harper:

Writing the Agent Query
by Tara K. Harper

What advice would I give to others who are trying to write agent queries? My automatic response to a question about a query is to say, "Be polite!" My second response is to list the following seven points that address the basic and most common mistakes made in queries.

The general advice is, for the most part, applicable to any business correspondence. For a professional writer, good communication means understanding your audience, addressing the needs of your audience, and communicating your points effectively.

Basics of Querying an Agent

- Fit the query to the agent. If the agent says he handles horror but not science fiction, don't query him about SF.
- Make your points quickly and succinctly. Don't flog a dead horse—if you do, it will only prove you can't write well for a market (in this case, your agent).
- Restrict yourself to one page if possible; two if necessary. More than that, and you should start thinking about taking an axe to your query.
- Be professional. Make sure your writing tone is confident and informative without being arrogant or obsequious.
- Don't try to be witty unless you really are witty. There's little that's worse than a flat joke—it just demonstrates that your readers will probably be as unimpressed as this prospective agent.
- Don't try to tell the agent how much he will love your work. It's up to him to decide how he feels about what he reads.
- Proof your letter carefully! Good grammar and spelling are extremely important in this first-impression query. Remember, the agent will think that if you don't care enough about your writing to proofread your one-page query letter, your 400-page manuscript will probably be in horrible (translation: slushpile) shape.

How to Write Query Letters

Before you can write your query letter, you need to know some things about your work and yourself. First, you'll need to know how to describe your story in one or two paragraphs. You will want to be able to touch on the important points, and introduce the characters and areas without putting in too many unknown terms. You will have to give the agent reason to believe that 1) you are a good enough writer to write a saleable story, and 2) you have enough self-discipline or dedication to complete the manuscript so it can be sold in the first place.

Do all query letters follow the format recommended here? Of course not. Queries are as varied as the people who write them. But I do think good query letters answer these questions:

What Kind of Story Are You Trying to Sell?

What kind of story is it? If it's science fiction, what category is it: hard-SF? cyberpunk? SF-adventure? space-opera? military SF? There are many publishing houses that handle science fiction, but some really like hack-em-slash-em-big-booms-in-space stuff. Some houses seem to handle more space-opera, some handle SF with a more scientifically technical theme, etc. A prospective agent will immediately want to know the genre for which you've written and how your story will fit into that genre.

For example, if you have written a cyberpunk science fiction story, in the first paragraph of your letter, you could include a statement like this: "Readers who enjoy cyberpunk-suspense in a near-future setting will also enjoy this story." That statement gives a prospective agent an idea of where he can try to sell your work.

Almost all stories fit into an existing category of fiction (or nonfiction). If your story truly doesn't fit into any category, you may or may not want to address that immediately in your query. Such a story may be hard to sell, thus putting you and your agent in a difficult position. For such a novel, there will be no existing readership to address, so not only will your name and the book be new, but also an entire market must be developed.

For example, it took Jean Auel years (and something like forty-two rejections) to sell her first novel, *Clan of the Cave Bear.* Partly this was because, although the story is considered romantic, there was no prehistory-romance category already in place. No one knew how the book would fit into the market or what kind of (or how many) readers would buy it. Since then, an entire category of fiction has developed. Now, you can go to any bookstand and see titles like *Daughter of the Forest, The Animal Wife, Reindeer Moon,* and so on.

Is Your Topic Popular or Gaining Popularity in the Market?

This is more difficult. The entertainment market is notoriously fickle. What is popular this month may be disdained the next. And even if you sell a story with a popular idea, it can take two to six years to get that story on the retail shelves.

However, if today's readers love dragon stories, and you've written a dragon story, you have a better chance of selling that story than if the current market hates dragons. If refugee memoirs are "in" and look like they will be "in" for a while, your leaving-your-country manuscript may be just what an agent is looking for.

Unless the ideas in your manuscript are particularly timely or farsighted, don't talk specifically about markets and topics in your manuscript. The book description should give the agent all the information he needs to determine what kind of ideas you have.

Is Your Work Similar to the Work of any Other Published Authors?

Something that can help you attract an agent is a similarity in style to another, popular author. I'm not saying you should write like other authors—you should develop your own style. However, your style may be reminiscent of or similar to the style of another published author. Even if you write in a genre other than that of the published author, being able to make a comparison will give an agent some idea of which editors (and readers) enjoy that style of writing. For example, if you can say that readers who love Mary Higgins Clark will enjoy your work, then if the agent is interested in the market for readers of M.H. Clark, he might be interested in you too.

Similarly, if your SF/fantasy has a beauty of prose but is technically detailed, perhaps you could say: "This book combines the emotional depth of prose similar to the achievements of Orson Scott Card with the technical detail of work such as that seen from Greg Bear." If your work is military action/suspense, then you could give your agent a good idea of market placement with a statement like this: " Readers who like the realistic, gritty detail of military engagements in the style of David Poyer will also enjoy this book."

There are two things to be careful of here. The first is attaching yourself to an already saturated market. If there is no more room for books along the lines of Anne Rice's vampire work, then saying that your work is similar to that work means a quick ticket to the slush pile. (Of course, as my publisher says, there's always room for another good book.) If the market is saturated by a single author's extensive number of releases, you're going to have to come up with a very good reason why the agent should try to sell a publisher on yet another unknown who writes in the same style.

The second danger is attaching yourself to an author who writes in the same genre but whose style really isn't at all like yours, or whose style is so varied that your statement of similarity is ineffective. For example, SF/fantasy author Piers Anthony writes books that are dark (such as Chthon), but also very light, facetious stories (such as the Xanth series). To say simply that you write in the style of Piers Anthony can be misleading. Better to specify that readers who enjoy Piers Anthony's darker, more serious work will enjoy your novel, or that readers who enjoy Piers Anthony's Xanth series will enjoy your new novel.

Think of it this way: You're not trying to attach yourself to someone else's coattails. What you're trying to do is give a prospective agent an idea of the style in which you write. Mentioning a known writing style that is similar to yours can give an agent an idea of what kind of readers will like your work. That tells him whether or not he has the contacts to be able to work effectively to place your manuscript. The more specific the information you can give, the better the agent can determine whether or not he will be interested in representing you.

What Is Compelling or Interesting About This Story?

Include a synopsis of your story—why is it compelling, poignant, exciting, terrifying, whatever. Don't tell your agent that he will love the poignancy or excitement of the story. Just tell him about the story. Let him make his own judgment about your work once he sees it.

One way to write the synopsis is as though you were writing a blurb for the back cover of your book. For one thing, this helps keep the description short. For another, it concentrates the plot into a few major points. If you can't figure out how to describe your story in one or two paragraphs, you may need to take a closer look at what you're trying to say in the book.

Some people advise including a blow-by-blow plot description with your query. If you really feel you must include an outline, try it, but I think it's premature at this stage. It's an editor, not a prospective agent, who will want detailed description of your book. Remember, the agent is looking at your work for only three things:

- Is there a market for this kind of story?
- Do I know a publisher/editor who is interested in trying new authors who have written this kind of story?
- Do I think this story is written well enough to sell?

He doesn't need an outline to tell him these things. He needs a quick summary of how your work answers those questions. (Of course, he'll probably forgive you for including that four-page outline if it's really that fantastic.) Later, when he has agreed to represent you, then he will want details—and a copy of the manuscript, of course.

Do You Have Any Name Recognition?

If you have built name recognition for your novel-length fiction through the publishing of short stories, you are in good shape. It will be important for you to point out that you have a solid history of readership. For example, perhaps, in two years, you have had nine short stories published in professional magazines, and one story published in an anthology. In that case, you should include a statement like this:

> "In the past two years, I've had nine short stories published in professional magazines, such as *Asimov's* and *Omni*. In 2006, one of my stories, XXX-title, was included in the *XX Anthology* as one of the featured stories."

Such a statement tells the agent that your work was either popular enough or interesting enough to be included in top-of-the-field magazines, and that you have developed a readership. That will be useful information in getting a publisher to look at your book-length fiction.

If you are bringing name recognition from another field, you might mention that also. This is not necessarily a strong selling point, but it can help. If your name recognition is not in the genre in which you are now writing, mention it last.

What Are Your Qualifications for Writing Fiction?

Everyone has one good story in them—that's what the old adage says. But that doesn't mean everyone is qualified to write that one, good story. In general, I would put my professional qualifications last in a query letter. In fiction, they are the element least likely to sell the manuscript, compared to the type of story, the current market demand, and how similar your work is to others. For example, if you write action-suspense novels, and you have experience in action sports or events, you might include a line like this: "The author's personal experience in scuba diving, shooting, and racing has helped to bring both excitement and realistic suspense to the action in this novel."

If I do include my qualifications, I would not use more than a single paragraph to describe them. If you have other published work, you might include a listing of those titles on an attached sheet, but I wouldn't include them in the body of the letter unless those titles were well known. Remember that you want your basic query letter to be short and easy to read. Putting a long list of other titles or a writing resume in an attachment gives the agent the option of reading additional details without distracting from your query.

Should You Include a Synopsis or Outline?

Not unless your initial information about the agent indicates that he wants a synopsis or outline submitted along with the query.

The query letter is just that—a query as to whether the agent is interested in representing a client who has written a work in a particular field, genre, or category. If the agent is interested in your work, he will tell you what he wants from you. For example, he will let you know whether he prefers the information about your work in an outline, as a synopsis, as sample chapters, or as the entire novel.

If you feel you must include an outline with your query, make sure the outline is on a separate page (or pages) from the one-page query letter. This allows the agent to read the entire query at a glance, and determine after that whether he wants to read the outline.

If you want to act professionally, then send the agent what he wants to receive—not what you want to show off. He wants only the information he needs in order to 1) determine whether or not he wants to represent your work, and 2) sell the book to an editor/publisher.

How Long Should You Wait for a Response from an Agent?

I'm tempted to say, "As long as it takes."

In general, agents say that they respond within three months to queries. However, remember that agents, like editors, are deluged with queries and manuscripts. It is not uncommon to see responses after six or even nine months. Some agents never respond to a query.

Should you follow up your query with a phone call? I'd say not at first. Follow up with another letter, and make sure the second letter is polite. Don't make accusations about the agent not bothering to respond, throwing out your query, etc. Instead, simply say something like: "This is a follow-up query regarding my completed manuscript, *Diseases of Little-Known Nematodes*. My previous query was sent to you on XX date, and I have not yet received a reply from you regarding the possibility of your agenting the manuscript." Then continue with the query as if it was a standard query letter, including the blurb, the brief description of why this novel is interesting, and so on. Most legitimate agents respond as soon as they can—they don't like piled-up paperwork any more than the rest of us.

If two queries have not elicited a response, it's time to make a phone call or try a different agent. However, if you make a phone call, make sure you continue to be courteous. Treat the call as if it is your first contact with the agent. The reality is that this call *is* your first contact. Be professional and be polite. You still have a chance to make an impression, and you want to make sure it's a good one.

How Not to Write Query Letters and Responses

Here's the actual text of part of a letter from someone who had just had a manuscript refused: "YOU F—ING LIAR, STAY OUT OF MY LIFE." As far as getting published goes, this person just got blacklisted. If you think editors won't remember you when you are rude, you're mistaken. There are too many decent writers who will behave professionally—or at least somewhat courteously—for an editor to waste time on an offensive idiot. If the idiot is that difficult to work with when he wants something (for an agent or editor to read the manuscript), imagine how horrid he will be when contracts are being negotiated, when changes are requested, and during any other normal business or publicity activities.

Regardless of how disappointed, humiliated, or otherwise unhappy you are about having your work rejected, do not take it out on the agent, editor, or publisher. If you want other professionals to respect you—in any field—you must create and maintain a reputation for professionalism. Curses, gratuitous insults, angry sarcasm—these things might be overlooked in a junior high student, but not in a professional. If you must, write out how you feel, but then burn that paper. Get it out of your system before trying to communicate again with the agent or editor. Don't sacrifice your future for a chance to prove how crass, immature, or offensive you really are.

17

Pitching to Agents at a Writing Conference

by Sue Fagalde Lick

Your heart pounds, your hands sweat, your knees shake on your way to what could be the most important meeting of your life: a 10-minute session with an agent or editor.

Is it worth the stress? Yes.

Many conferences allow writers to schedule short face-to-face meetings with agents and editors. It's a great opportunity to pitch one's book. It's also terribly nerve-wracking. After all, most of us are more effective on paper, and a bad meeting can ruin your chances with that person forever. But one successful meeting can make your book-publishing dreams come true. It can also save months of mailing queries and waiting for answers.[1]

Preparation is the key. David Hale Smith of DHS Literary, Inc., attends six to eight conferences a year looking for "that one diamond in the rough." Smith urges writers to prepare a three-minute pitch in which they boil their project down to three to five sentences. Practice that pitch until you can deliver it smoothly. The whole point of the meeting is to get your writing read. You're not there to chat, make a new friend, or list the problems you're having with your writing but to convince the agent to give it a look. "You're sitting there and the door's open."

Pitch sessions are obviously stressful. Smith admits he still gets nervous pitching books to editors, but he can handle his nerves because he is prepared. "Think of it as a business meeting," he says. "You're coming to a

---

[1] Editor's note: Keep in mind that you must register for the conference to be able to gain such an appointment (which means you may pay the conference registration fee), and you must generally book your appointment well in advance, as "pitch sessions" fill up quickly.

business meeting with a product." The writer must be able to describe his book clearly and briefly. If he can't, how is the agent going to describe it to an editor, who in turn has to pitch the book to his superiors and ultimately to the publisher's sales force, which has to pitch the book to the buyers?

Agent Jillian Manus, who spent several years as a development executive in the movie business, knows the importance of a pitch. She bought movie scripts solely on the basis of the writers' pitches, then turned around and pitched them to her production team. These days, the book publishing industry has also adopted the pitch as an essential sales tool. Writers who can't describe their work in four or five lines don't have a clear idea of what they are writing, Manus says.

For fiction, Manus suggests dividing the pitch into three points: the setup, hook, and resolution. For nonfiction, the title should convey the main concept of the book. Explain what the book is about, why you are qualified to write it, who will read it, and what you can do to promote it.

Be Prepared

Agents and editors are not usually willing or able to carry your manuscript home with them, but if they are interested, they will take a brief written summary. Don't expect an agent or editor to read your synopsis while you wait. "I hate to read in front of someone because I can't think and read it simultaneously or well in that situation," says Laurie Harper of the Sebastian Literary Agency. "If you hand me a synopsis, still be able to just tell me in three minutes what it is. I'll take the synopsis with me and reread it later, but at the moment, it's more constructive to get a conversation going and rapport. Sell me on you and then the book you're doing. It is much more helpful to convince me of your talent, vision, commitment and ability and then hopefully about the book itself. In a short meeting, if I'm taken with the author, I'll follow up on the phone later and we'll get into the book stuff. If I'm not sold on you, it doesn't matter about the book because I won't take it further."

Before the conference, it helps to do a little homework. Smith says he is impressed when a writer knows something about his agency and the writers it represents. At minimum, know whether the agent represents your kind of book. Don't pitch your adult thriller to an agent who handles only children's books. Know where your project falls in the marketplace. If it's fiction, is it a romance, a mystery, mainstream? Can you compare it to another published author's work? If it's nonfiction, who is the audience? What types of publishers are likely to buy it?

Harper says authors must know about similar books that have been published and why theirs will be different. What category does it fall into, who are the readers and how will it fit into the market?

If you don't have all of this information, perhaps you should wait until the next conference to pitch your book. If you're just starting to outline your nonfiction book or aren't sure how your novel will end, save the pitch until you know what you're pitching.

Conquer the Nerves

Nervous though you may be, don't tell the agent, "I'm so nervous. I'm not good at this."

"I don't want to hear that stuff," Smith says. "What do you have that I can sell, that's it."

Some writers can't bear the idea of pitching their work in person. They know they'll stutter and stumble. If you really can't do it, don't sign up for a pitch session. After all, as Smith says, "On paper's how we do most of our business."

It is possible to send your material to the agent before the conference, but allow plenty of time in advance. Smith says he receives 250 submissions a month and 200 to 300 query letters. He may not have time to get to your manuscript before the conference. It might boil down to taking it on the plane and hoping he has time to read it. It's better to wait for the conference, where he is expecting to hear your pitch.

You can certainly send a pitch to an agent after the conference instead of giving it in person, but sooner or later you'll have to do it verbally. Harper says, "I would encourage writers to try the verbal meeting, even if it doesn't go perfectly. Learn from it. Practice. Get comfortable talking to agents and get comfortable 'blurbing' your book."

Manus believes that writers must conquer the butterflies and learn to pitch. After the book is sold, the author will be expected to talk about the book with editors and marketing people and to help publicize it when it comes out. Fiction writers might be able to hide behind the written word, but nonfiction authors must learn to pitch in person, she says.

Anyone can memorize four lines, Manus adds. "You can blurt out those four lines and then that opens the door." Once the agent hears the basic idea, they can discuss it. "We're there to work as a team."

Accept Criticism

One of the things authors fear in meeting agents and editors is criticism of their work, but that's part of the deal. "Nerves should be left at home," Manus says. "Writers should bring confidence and a willingness to accept criticism." It's the agent's or editor's responsibility to help them figure out what might be wrong with their proposal. Not everyone takes criticism gracefully. "I've had people leap over the table."

Harper adds, "You have to want honest answers, even if it isn't what you want to hear. Professional feedback will help you get the book right for publication and success. If you act like you can't take the truth, the agent or editor will just give you an excuse and get away from you, and you'll be nowhere.

The more you ask for candid, honest advice or feedback and demonstrate you can handle it maturely, the better information and real help you'll get."

Malcolm Margolin, publisher of Heyday Books, says the thing he hates most at conferences is "neediness," writers who are looking to him to make all their dreams come true and can't take no for an answer. "I really don't like to be cornered or pushed. I'm particularly sensitive to someone who's practicing their assertiveness training on me."

Margolin urges writers to approach publishers and agents as "co-professionals" who can work together for mutual benefit. He appreciates finding writers who know about his publishing house and present appropriate ideas. Arrive with an open mind and if the project is not right for him, "Allow everybody room to back off with dignity."

Although a meeting may be scheduled for 10 minutes or longer, don't feel you have to fill the entire appointment time. The pitch has one purpose: to get your project read. "Once you've done that, you've done your job. You can feel a connection or not," Smith says. Don't stay after the meeting is over. Thank the agent and move on. Agents and editors at conferences often spend hours meeting with eager writers. A few quiet minutes to stretch, use the restroom, or get a cup of coffee are a real blessing.

They're Just People

Remember that the agents and editors attending conferences are working through the weekend instead of relaxing with their families. They may enjoy conferences, but respect that they get tired, just like you. Smith is not averse to accepting a beer or a cup of coffee in exchange for a few minutes of informal talk, but don't monopolize his entire weekend.

Manus, who attends an average of eight conferences a year, stresses that agents and editors go to conferences because they want to, even if they are not paid and have to give up their free time to do it. "They get as inspired by you as you do by them." She loves meeting new writers, seeing what they are writing, spotting trends. When talking to writers about their books, she hopes she can give the right advice. "We're as nervous as they are," she says.

One mistake authors make, says Harper, is wanting "any agent." "Agents are usually all good at what they do, but they're good at different things. A writer does not want any agent; he or she wants the right match of agent for their book and category." It's better to have no agent than the wrong agent. In meeting agents, it is perfectly okay to ask agents about their activities or interests in a given category of books, she adds.

"Authors tend to put agents on a pedestal, but the actual successful working relationship over the long haul is about the two of you working closely together as partners—business partners," Harper says. "Your agent offers the market and publisher savvy, together with contracts and money, and the author offers the talent, writing ability and audience savvy. It takes both."

Conference meetings are usually just a beginning, an in-person query. But they can lead to bigger things. If an agent or editor finds an author whose work matches what publishers are looking for, publication is almost guaranteed.

What you have at a conference pitch session, Margolin says, is an introduction. This is not the place where deals are closed but an opportunity to find out if both parties want to take the next step.

But it can be the beginning of something wonderful. If you don't speak up, you'll never know.

Approaching an Agent at a Conference
by Robin Catesby

How should you approach an agent at a conference?

Enthusiasm for your own work goes a long way. By that I don't mean saying "this is the best book you will read"—agents don't want to hear that—but rather, launch into your pitch with a great level of positive energy. Do what you need to do beforehand to get into this state of mind, whether it's a brisk energizing walk around the conference, or a relaxing cup of herb tea. You want to make sure your mind and body are ready and not all jittered out on caffeine or anything. I've seen people blow pitches simply because they haven't given any attention to being in the right state of mind. Also, don't schedule two pitches back to back. I did that once and discovered that I'd used up much of my energy on the first pitch, so the second wasn't nearly as good.

Another important point: You're not just presenting the agent with a verbal synopsis of your book, you are selling it to them, so you've got to think about what is going to make your book jump out from all the others they've heard about that day. Before even launching into the outline, have a hook—one or two sentences that sum up the theme, the lead character's dilemma, the tone...everything that makes your book a must-read. If it's a funny novel, don't be afraid to give them a funny pitch. If it's a mystery, build a little suspense. You don't need to turn it into a dramatic monologue, but a little of this kind of energy can be a huge help, especially if the agent has just gone through five monotone pitches in a row. Practice the pitch in front of a friend or two if you need to—it is, in a way, a theatrical experience, so a little rehearsal can't hurt.

The most you'll need to bring with you is a one-page synopsis. Very few agents are going to ask for sample chapters right then and there. If they are interested, they'll give you their card and ask you to mail them. Last time I pitched, I didn't have anything with me, and to be honest, I think it worked much better. If you have your synopsis in front of you, it can become a crutch, as with an actor who wants to glance at his script during performance. That reads as nerves to the agent, so if you bring one at all, keep it in a folder until the agent asks to see it.

Finally, remember that agents come to conferences to find clients, so unless they are just naturally grumpy, they aren't going to be brusque with you. The only exception would be if you didn't have an agent in mind already and you were to schedule an appointment with an agent who is entirely inappropriate for your novel. Do your homework. Get the conference brochure and study that guest list. Don't just grab the first agent's name out of a hat; make sure the agent actually represents your type of book!

Pitching can be scary, but if you're prepared, relaxed, and proud of what you've written, it can also be pretty great.

Agent Tips on Pitching at a Conference

Before pitching to an agent, put together a zippy two sentence description "a la *TV Guide*" about the book. Tell why it's different and new and better. Know what you're talking about—and don't be nervous. We're only human.

—Elizabeth Pomada
Michael Larsen/Elizabeth Pomada Literary Agents

When pitching to an agent or an editor at a writer's conference, don't read off of cue cards. This gives the impression that the writer doesn't know his/her own work. Don't exaggerate about your credentials and experience. Keep the pitch short and to the point. Answer any questions quickly and honestly. If they request your material, don't wait to send it out to them.

—Ginger Norton, Senior Editor
Sedgeband Literary Associates

Be succinct. Be able to sum up your book in a single sentence. Be professional, polished, and interesting—the agent looks at the writer the way an editor does: is the writer him/herself promotable? Would she play well on camera, in radio interviews? etc.

—Jeff Kleinman
Graybill & English

If you're going to pitch a book to agents/editors at a conference, you should be prepared to state concisely exactly what your book is about and who its audience is. And, be aware that most agents and editors are going to ask that you formally submit your material rather than giving it to them on the spot.

—Michael Psaltis
Ethan Ellenberg Literary Agency

18

The Novel Synopsis

by Rebecca Vinyard

I've attended many workshops on the topic of "how to write a novel synopsis" in the desperate hope I'd learn enough to compose a coherent synopsis. Sometimes, a speaker will attempt to whip up the audience's enthusiasm by saying things like "Repeat after me, the synopsis is your *friend*."

With friends like these, I don't need enemies.

However, certain elements are vital to any synopsis. Here are fourteen elements that can help keep your synopsis out of the trash bin. Afterwards, we'll look at a real synopsis—and then see how it incorporates those elements.

THE SETUP. This is the starting point of your story: premise, location, time frame, and main characters' backgrounds. Just as you want to hook your readers with the first page of your book, you also want to hook the editor on the first page of your synopsis. The sooner you can establish your set-up, the better. Choose your words with care to get the background information presented in a concise *and* entertaining way.

WHY? This is something you should consider throughout your synopsis. If you pose a question, answer it. A synopsis is *not* the time to tease a reader. Suppose your story begins with the heroine quitting her job. Explain *why* she quit it. Reactions, decisions... whatever your character does within the framework of your synopsis, the reasons behind the actions must be clear.

For example, you can't just say, "Something happens to make the heroine change her mind." Instead, you need to explain what that something is and *why* it made her change her mind. Clarity, clarity... make that your synopsis mantra.

CHARACTERIZATION. This includes background, personality, occupation—everything that makes up your character. It is *not*, however, a physical description of your hero and heroine. Usually, the less said about that, the better, unless the character's physique affects her/him emotionally. Example: She's extremely short and feels self-conscious about it.

Bear in mind you want the reader of your synopsis to feel a connection with your characters. Focus on the emotional elements. A deeply religious woman…A savvy businesswoman…An introverted professor…An agitated accountant. Phrases like these give emotional and background information in just a few words.

You should name only those characters who play major roles in your story. Often writers feel the need to include mention of secondary characters. Unless those characters' actions affect the main plot throughout the story, you shouldn't include them, because then you'll need to provide characterization and background for them as well (and in the process, inflate your synopsis!). If a necessary reference pops up once or twice, you can simply say something like "her best friend," "his sister," etc.

PLOT POINTS. These occur whenever your story departs from all that has gone before. Your character is forced to make a decision, or something unexpected and outside the experience of the character happens. You should include *all* the major plot points in your synopsis. However, do *not* include plot points for sub-plots. If it doesn't have anything to do with the main plot, forget it. Always concentrate on theme.

CONFLICT. Quick conflict lesson: Internal conflict comes from within the character, i.e., she has poor self-esteem. External conflict comes from without the character, i.e., a villain is blackmailing the hero.

For the purpose of the synopsis, you need to present your conflict clearly. This brings us back to the *why* element again: *why* is your heroine afraid of dogs? This is important if she refuses to go to the hero's house because he has a Doberman named Rex lurking about. Or perhaps your heroine refuses to go because she fears involvement and she uses the dog as an excuse. Why does she fear involvement? By the same token, how does your hero feel about being rejected like this? Is she rejecting Rex or him? Perhaps rejection makes him defensive because he seeks to be accepted. He resolves never to have anything to do with her again.

In other words, conflicts are the obstacles the main characters must overcome in order to achieve their goals. In a romance, the main goal is for the hero and heroine to fall in love and stay together. In a science fiction story, perhaps the goal is to overthrow an evil corporation dominating the planet. Whatever the goal, it can't be easy to achieve, or else you have no story. We need to know there's a problem and *why* this is a problem.

EMOTION. Actions cause reactions. He kisses her...how does she feel about it? How does he feel? Whenever you have the chance to put emotion into your synopsis, do it. It makes the difference between a dull summary and a lively recounting of your story.

ACTION. Action drives most stories and is probably the story element used the most. However, in your synopsis, you should only include those actions that have consequences. If your heroine takes trip to the store for some eggs, don't include that unless something happens to her along the way. If in doubt, leave it out.

DIALOGUE. Some folks say you should *never* include dialogue in a synopsis. Some feel a sprinkling of it here and there helps. My personal preference is the latter. If a specific line has more impact than a description of the same conversation, why not use it? However, I wouldn't advise more than a few lines of dialogue. Don't go crazy and start quoting all over the place.

BLACK MOMENT. When all is lost, when it appears your characters will never reach their goals...The odds are on the opposing forces' side and this is the moment when your characters realize it. In a romance, perhaps it's a conflict so overwhelming, it would appear that the hero and heroine will never be together. Whatever the genre, this moment of reckoning should not only be in your story, but also in your synopsis.

CLIMAX. Your story has been thundering along to this point. Everything that has gone before should lead up to it. Whether it's the bad guy getting what's coming to him, the hero finally getting over his lack of self-esteem or the heroine riding to the rescue, this is moment when it all happens. Naturally, this element must also be included in your synopsis.

RESOLUTION. All your loose ends get tied up here. Any questions posed in your synopsis should be answered by the time you reach here. Perhaps the goal is for the hero and heroine to live happily ever after. Or perhaps not, depending on your genre. Whatever the case, include the resolution to your story. This is not the time to play guess-the-ending!

THE BASICS. The number one essential is to write your synopsis in present tense. Think of it as telling a friend about your book. Avoid passive word usage. You want those words to flow evenly and keep the reader involved. Focus on the main story and avoid extraneous information.

FORMATTING. Most houses prefer a double-spaced format. However, there are exceptions, so *check the publisher's submission guidelines*. The majority of publishers prefer you to provide your contact information and word count on the upper left corner of the first page. On subsequent pages, include the title, your last name and the page number in your headers.

SUBMISSIONS. Check the guidelines. Am I making this point clearly enough? And for heaven's sake, make sure you have the editor's name spelled right. Always include a SASE with every submission. If you want to make sure your submission is received, include a stamped, self-addressed postcard that can be sent back to you.

And now let's see all this in action!

Sample Synopsis: Maggie's Wish
by Sharon Ihle

The sluggish days of summer are giving way to the crisper fall evenings of 1881 Prescott, Arizona Territory as MAGGIE THORNE glances out the kitchen window and sees her six-year-old daughter hoeing the pumpkin patch. Halloween is just two months away, which means that soon, Christmas will be upon them—again.

Just the mere thought of that most revered of holidays is enough to sink Maggie's spirits. Not that she has anything against Christmas itself. She has a lot to be thankful for when the sun rises each December 25. Her daughter HOLLY, whom she adores without reservation, came into the world at twenty minutes past eight on Christmas morning. A deeply religious woman, Maggie also thinks of the holiday as Christ's birthday, never failing to recognize it as such in a respectful manner.

As she is the bread baker and pastry chef in a small restaurant owned by her Aunt Lorna, the holiday season also keeps Maggie happily productive and fills her coffers well enough to see her and Holly though the winter. But something supersedes all the good the holiday brings, a dark and dreary cloud that obscures the yuletide lights and dulls the sparkle in Maggie's wide brown eyes. Lord help her, how much longer can she go on this way?

Maggie's first inkling that Christmas would become a time for sorrow struck nearly seven years ago on the very day Holly was born. Although the baby's father promised to show up in Prescott before the birth, he hadn't so much as written by the time their daughter pushed her way into the world. Maggie had an idea that he never would. So far and nearly seven years later, she is right.

She was a tall, plain-faced spinster of twenty-two with little hope of landing a man of her own the first time Maggie laid eyes on RAFE HOLLISTER. At the time, a hard Utah winter had settled over the family farm, bringing with it the kind of cold that bites hollows in the chubbiest cheeks and freezes nose hairs stiff as pokers—and that was if a body stayed indoors. Rafe was close to dead the morning Maggie found him huddled in a corner of her father's barn. He'd been shot clean through the shoulder, and while the wound itself isn't life-threatening, the loss of blood made him pitifully weak. When Maggie comes across him, he's also nearly frozen clear through. She should have run and got her pa the minute she saw him lying there. She should have taken the gun from Rafe's stiff fingers and finished him off right there on the spot, saving them all a ton of grief. Maggie could have done a lot of things, anything but what she settled on once Rafe turned those big calf eyes on her and grinned that devil grin. If she had, she wouldn't be sitting at her kitchen table now wondering how in hell she was going to explain one more time why Santa Claus hadn't brought Holly the only thing she'd ever asked for; her very own daddy.

It wasn't as if her first—and only—true love hadn't known the trouble Maggie was in. Spring thaw was late in coming that year. By the time Rafe had healed and Maggie had nursed him to his former robust self, she had a pretty good idea there would be a baby come Winter. She told him, of course, sure he'd do right and take her away with him, but excuses why not spilled out of his mouth faster than the teardrops from her eyes. He was on the run from the law, a thing she'd pretty well guessed on her own, and although he hadn't done a blasted thing wrong according to him, he had to get it set right before he could settle down and raise a family.

Maggie can hardly remember flying into hysterics that day, but she recalls flinging enough of a fit over what her future held once her father got wind of her "little" problem for Rafe to decide he ought to help her figure out what to do. After slapping her around a little, making damn sure she wouldn't alert her entire family to the fact that he was living in their barn, Rafe dipped into his overstuffed saddlebags, pulled out a wad of bills, and told Maggie to use the money to buy a train ticket. She chose the destination, Prescott, because her mother's sister lived there and would take her in until Rafe could join her.

On the morning Maggie runs away from home, Rafe tells her he loves her, shows her one more time exactly how much, and then promises to get square with the law and meet her in Prescott well before Christmas day. Six long years and six longer Christmases have gone by since then. And at each of the last four, a little red-haired girl cries fat teardrops all over her birthday cake at the close of that most celebrated day. This year, God willing, things will be different.

This year, Maggie has hired a retired Texas Ranger, a man just a few years older than she who has given up the badge and hard chases because of a bum leg. Her friend, the sheriff of Prescott, is also a friend of the ranger, a man he believes is perfect for the job because he's very, very good at tracking people who don't know they need tracking. People like Rafe Hollister who have lost their way.

Once she meets Ranger MATT WESTON, Maggie is suddenly at a loss to explain her circumstances and finds herself making up excuses for Rafe, not just for Holly's sake, but also for her own. After all, she'd once loved Rafe enough to bear him a child born in shame—how could she show herself as a woman who'd allowed that love to die? Wouldn't that make her time of sinning with Rafe somehow more depraved? Matt Weston would definitely think so—Maggie senses that in the man after one look in his silvery, no-nonsense eyes. For reasons she can't imagine, this near-stranger's opinion of her is extremely important. Evading the truth rather than lying to Matt, Maggie simply explains that her man ran out on his responsibilities and that she wants him brought back to her—alive and well. She believes that explanation will give the former lawman the impression that Rafe is her husband, and why shouldn't it? Her Prescott neighbors have long believed the very same thing.

At thirty-two years of age, Matt Weston hates his early retirement with a passion, and for what he sees as two good reasons: The first, and hardest to take, is his exclusion from the manhunts, the feel of his own blood thundering in his veins as he runs his quarry down. The second, and somehow more threatening than a cornered out-law with blazing guns, is his sudden vulnerability to the single ladies in town. For over thirty years Matt has easily avoided the perils, and he has to admit, the responsibilities of turning his life over to a member of the fairer sex. Now that he is almost desk-bound, he's practically tripping over available women, and even more alarming, rapidly running out of excuses for remaining a bachelor.

Funny how that final excuse—not to mention a man's mind—can vanish with the blink of a warm brown eye. A pair of them, to be exact, each rimmed by a lush bank of lashes the color of pitch. He has no business looking into those eyes or thinking thoughts that don't include ways of catching up to Maggie's wandering husband, but Matt can't seem to stop himself. He is an honorable, professional man, one who never lets his personal life get in the way of business, so why in hell can't he keep his mind on his work whenever she is around?

He supposes his lapse of ethics has something to do with Maggie's gentle ways and honest charms, the kind of beauty that fairly radiates the goodness in her heart. Not that he believes any of those things can excuse his utter fascination with the lady. He has a job to do, and sets out to do it with an almost personal vengeance.

It doesn't take Matt but two weeks to locate the bastard—the precise opinion he forms of Rafe Hollister within minutes of locating the man. The meeting takes place at a rundown saloon in El Paso when Matt stumbles over a drunken Rafe who is passed out on the floor. When Rafe finally comes to, Matt decides that Miss Maggie is in for a rude shock—and Miss Maggie is the way Matt thinks of her no matter how hard she hints that she's actually married to this stinking outlaw.

While Rafe is still unconscious, Matt takes him into his custody and discovers that he has been wounded—most of his left ear is blown to smithereens and a bullet fragment is lodged in his right wrist. Although Matt wishes whoever wounded the man had been a better shot, he tends to the injuries Miss Maggie's "lost" husband has suffered, then binds him hand and foot and tosses him in the back of his wagon.

When Rafe sobers up and awakens to find himself traveling west toward Arizona Territory, Matt informs the miserable bastard that his wife and child are looking for him, and that he's been hired to take him to Prescott. Far from being grateful, Rafe begins cursing Maggie, calling her a horse-faced spinster among other things and declaring that she was lucky to have gotten as much as she did from him—a good time and the only piece of "loving" she'd ever get from a sane man. He tries to go on raving about Maggie, assuring his captor that he wouldn't have touched her at all had he not been weak and crazy in the head from loss of blood.

When the ranger pulls the wagon to a halt and climbs down from the driver's seat, Rafe is certain that he is about to be set free. Instead he receives the worst beating of his miserable life. When he comes to again, Rafe quickly discovers that both of his eyes are swollen shut, his lips are split and caked with blood, and he is hanging by his wrists, including the injured one, from a rafter inside a darkened barn. Then through what is left of his ear, he hears the voice of the former ranger as he explains the terms of Rafe's "pardon."

You will submit yourself to a month of intensive training as a decent law-biding citizen and loving husband and father, he is told. This will take place in Prescott where Miss Maggie Thorne can follow your progress and make a final decision about whether she should or should not accept your marriage proposal—and yes, you will ask her to be your wife. You will then abide by Maggie's decision and do your level best to uphold it for the rest of your natural life.

If you chose not to do those few things, Matt informs Rafe, there's another option for you to consider: You can continue to hang by the wrists here in this abandoned barn which happens to be situated on the Mexican side of the Rio Grande. This will undoubtedly bring your life to a very unnatural end.

Rafe quickly accepts the original terms and keeps his complaints to himself during the rest of the journey to Prescott. Once they settle into Matt's cabin, Rafe is shackled to a chain hanging from an overhead beam, but otherwise free to move about the perimeters of the room. He also proves to be a surprisingly apt pupil, learning how to speak and behave like a gentleman in just a few weeks, and actually asks to see Maggie again in the hopes of meeting his young daughter.

For Matt, it is a time of raging conflict. Although he works hard to turn the outlaw into someone worthy of Maggie and Holly, from the basest part of his soul, Matt is praying that Rafe will fail. His visits to Maggie each day to report on Rafe's progress are taking a toll on his sanity, not to mention his body. He awakes in a sweat night after night, his dreams filled with images of the woman he has fallen in love with. Even worse, he has convinced himself that he sees his own frustrations and needs each time he looks into her expressive eyes.

It is as Thanksgiving draws near that Matt slips into the darkened coffee shop late one night to discuss Rafe's progress, and finds Maggie awash in tears. He takes her in his arms, comforting her, and asks her what is wrong. There is no way she can explain how much her feelings for Matt have grown or to let him know how badly she wants him—not after he's been working so hard to make her "almost" husband presentable enough for her to marry. Even Maggie can't understand how she can have such deep feelings for Matt when the man she thought she wanted is just up the street. In spite of her less-than high opinion of her lustful nature, Maggie's desire for Matt continues to build, turning her tears into sobs. When Matt's attempts to comfort her become passionate, Maggie does nothing to cool his ardor, allowing herself instead to linger over his forbidden touch. Unable to deny herself the man she so desperately yearns for, Maggie succumbs to temptation.

Although he wouldn't trade the night spent with Maggie for his own life, Matt is plagued with guilt and self-loathing the next day, taking the entire blame for what happened between them upon himself. He avoids Maggie as best he can while continuing to encourage perfection in this less than perfect clump of humanity known as Rafe Hollister, but it isn't easy. He punishes himself with thoughts of turning Maggie's perfect husband over to her once his job is done, and polishes the outlaw to perfection if for no other reason than just to see her smile, to witness for himself a sparkle of happiness in those sad brown eyes.

On December 15 and according to plan, Matt arranges the long-awaited reunion between Maggie and Rafe. She feels awkward in Matt's presence, certain that the coolness he exhibits toward her is due to her immoral behavior, but remains composed as he leads her into his cabin to visit her lost love. Although it's been almost seven years, Maggie notices immediately that Rafe still has those calf eyes and a devilish grin to match them. When he turns those consider-able charms on her, for a fleeting moment Maggie becomes that lonely, vulnerable farm girl again, grateful and smitten by what she'd once mistaken as true love.

Witnessing Maggie's rebirth, glimpsing the sweet hot luminance in her painfully honest eyes is more than Matt can tolerate. Without a word, he takes his broken heart and slips out of the room, leaving the pair of lovers with the only thing he has left to offer them—their privacy.

The click of the latch snaps Maggie out of yesterday and brings her back to the independent, self-reliant woman she is today, but by then, Matt is gone. Feeling in control of herself again and of Rafe for the first time ever, she sits him down, chews him up one side and down the other for his sins of the past, then queries him about his plans for the future. Where and how, she wants to know, will those plans affect Holly? What kind of a father does he expect to be and how long will he be there for her physically, emotionally, and financially? Exactly what does he expect in return?

This interrogation continues for nine days with Matt just outside the door of the cabin most times and generally listening in. No matter how far Maggie corners Rafe or how tough the questions, he always comes up smelling like a rose. All he wants out of this life, he swears, is to have Maggie as his wife and to be a father to his daughter at long last.

Throughout this period, Matt continues to instruct Rafe on the ways of gentlemen even though he hasn't behaved like one himself, fulfilling the task he was hired to do. When Christmas morning finally arrives, Maggie pleads with Matt to visit her home at sunup and share in the spoils of a job well done. Although he is reluctant, his heart heavy, the ex-lawman arrives just moments before Rafe does.

As Maggie carefully positions her former lover near the Christmas tree, then calls Holly to come downstairs and see what Santa has left for her, Matt can barely watch when the sleepy-eyed youngster drags into the room. Once she sees a stranger by the tree, and that stranger identifies himself as her father, Holly lets out a strangled cry and vaults into his arms. In moments the rest of them—Maggie, Matt, and even Rafe—are awash in tears.

Giving her daughter a few minutes alone with her father, not to mention time to pull herself together, Maggie tugs Matt into the kitchen and closes the door behind them. Remarking that she ought to be celebrating with the joyous pair under the tree, Matt thanks her for inviting him, then heads for the door, intending to let the newly reunited family enjoy their holiday in private. Maggie softly asks him to stay, even through Christmas dinner if he likes, but Matt can't understand why she'd want a used-up law-man hanging around on Christmas day, especially since his job is done. Maggie gently kisses Matt's weathered cheek and thanks him again for making Holly's wish come true. She then thanks him for the changes he made in Rafe Hollister, in particular the way Matt convinced Rafe to humble himself by begging her to marry him during each of the past nine days. It's done her heart good, she confesses, and also freed her enough to realize that she doesn't love Rafe and probably never did. Her answer for the past nine days, she says, has been an unequivocal, no, thanks to Matt Weston. With that, Maggie again kisses the man she really loves, this time square on the mouth.

Overwhelmed by her confession, unable to keep from touching her a minute longer, Matt takes Maggie into his arms, then asks her what she would do if he were to have an unfulfilled wish the way Holly did. Who could I hire to help me make my wish come true? he wonders aloud.

Maggie swears if there's anything she can do to help, she'll do it. Anything. Vowing to hold her to that promise, Matt pulls her even tighter into his embrace and whispers, "See if you can help me with this—I wish I could find a beautiful woman to marry who has laughing brown eyes, kissable lips, and is tall enough for me to kiss back without bending myself in half."

As tears of joy roll down Maggie's cheeks, Matt loosens her hair from the coil at her neck and fans it between his fingers. "Make sure the lady also has golden brown hair that smells of cinnamon and apples, and that she loves me at least half as much as I love her. When you find her, make sure to tell her that I promise to make her wishes come true for the rest of her life."

And so as Christmas of 1881 comes to a close, a daughter's wish for her very own father is fulfilled; an outlaw who thought he never wanted fatherhood or to know the true miracle of Christmas, finds both along with more joy than he's ever known; and a man and a woman find themselves free to love one another with everything they have to give, joining together as one to wish for a lifetime of happiness together.

19

Anatomy of a Synopsis

by Rebecca Vinyard

All right, remember those "essential elements" of a synopsis I listed in the previous chapter? Let's take a look at how Sharon Ihle put them to use in her synopsis for *Maggie's Wish*.

The Setup

Here's how Sharon's **setup** begins:

> The sluggish days of summer are giving way to the crisper fall evenings of 1881 Prescott, Arizona Territory as MAGGIE THORNE glances out the kitchen window and sees her six-year-old daughter hoeing the pumpkin patch. Halloween is just two months away, which means that soon, Christmas will be upon them—again.

Sharon packs a lot of information in two simple sentences. In the first sentence, she establishes setting, a home in 1881 Prescott, Arizona Territory. She establishes the heroine, Maggie Thorne and lets us know Maggie has a six-year-old daughter. We know the time of year, two months before Halloween. She also gives us an inkling of Maggie's mood, anxiety over Christmas. We read on, because we wonder, *why* is Maggie worried about Christmas?

That's what your setup should do: Establish location, character, and mood. But most of all, it should pique the readers interest. Just as your novel should hook the read on the first page, so should your synopsis. One of the best workshops I've ever attended on synopsis writing was done by Christina Dodd. She said you should be able to get the initial setup information across in one page or less.

To continue with Sharon's setup:

> Just the mere thought of that most revered of holidays is enough to sink Maggie's spirits. Not that she has anything against Christmas itself. She has a lot to be thankful for when the sun rises each December 25. Her daughter HOLLY, whom she adores without reservation, came into the world at twenty minutes past eight on Christmas morning. A deeply religious woman, Maggie also thinks of the holiday as Christ's birthday, never failing to recognize it as such in a respectful manner.
>
> As she is the bread baker and pastry chef in a small restaurant owned by her Aunt Lorna, the holiday season also keeps Maggie happily productive and fills her coffers well enough to see her and Holly though the winter. But something supersedes all the good the holiday brings, a dark and dreary cloud that obscures the yuletide lights and dulls the sparkle in Maggie's wide brown eyes. Lord help her, how much longer can she go on this way?

Here Sharon establishes **characterization**. We know now that Maggie adores her daughter and is a spiritual person, and we know her occupation. We also now know that Maggie is more than just anxious about Christmas, she dreads it. We can feel her emotions and again we ask, *why*?

In the next section of her synopsis, Sharon tells us why by providing Maggie's background:

> Maggie's first inkling that Christmas would become a time for sorrow struck nearly seven years ago on the very day Holly was born. Although the baby's father promised to show up in Prescott before the birth, he hadn't so much as written by the time their daughter pushed her way into the world. Maggie had an idea that he never would. So far and nearly seven years later, she is right.
>
> She was a tall, plain-faced spinster of twenty-two with little hope of landing a man of her own the first time Maggie laid eyes on RAFE HOLLISTER...
>
> ...On the morning Maggie runs away from home, Rafe tells her he loves her, shows her one more time exactly how much, and then promises to get square with the law and meet her in Prescott well before Christmas day. Six long years and six longer Christmases have gone by since then. And at each of the last four, a little red-haired girl

cries fat teardrops all over her birthday cake at the close of that most celebrated day. This year, God willing, things will be different.

This is only a few paragraphs from this section. All of the information Sharon included is important, though. We learn much about Maggie's character and Rafe's. We know how they met and how they parted. We know this relationship was the turning point of Maggie's life, causing her to move away from home to Prescott. Most importantly, we now know *why* Maggie dreads Christmas. It is because it is also her daughter Holly's birthday and her daughter wishes for her Daddy to come home every year.

Plot Points and Conflict

This year, Maggie has hired a retired Texas Ranger, a man just a few years older than she who has given up the badge and hard chases because of a bum leg. Her friend, the sheriff of Prescott, is also a friend of the ranger, a man he believes is perfect for the job because he's very, very good at tracking people who don't know they need tracking. People like Rafe Hollister who have lost their way.

Maggie has decided to do something about her daughter's unhappiness. This is the first **plot point**: the departure from all that has gone before. We understand her motivation for doing this because of the background information. It is also our first introduction to the hero. We know that he's a good tracker. In the next paragraph, Sharon tells us about Maggie's reaction to him as well as set up the **conflict** between them.

Once she meets Ranger MATT WESTON, Maggie is suddenly at a loss to explain her circumstances and finds herself making up excuses for Rafe, not just for Holly's sake, but also for her own. After all, she'd once loved Rafe enough to bear him a child born in shame—how could she show herself as a woman who'd allowed that love to die? Wouldn't that make her time of sinning with Rafe somehow more depraved? Matt Weston would definitely think so—Maggie senses that in the man after one look in his silvery, no-nonsense eyes. For reasons she can't imagine, this near-stranger's opinion of her is extremely important. Evading the truth rather than lying to Matt, Maggie simply explains that her man ran out on his responsibilities and that she wants him brought back to her—alive and well. She believes that explanation will give the former lawman the impression that Rafe is her husband, and why shouldn't it? Her Prescott neighbors have long believed the very same thing.

Maggie doesn't tell the whole truth about her relationship with Rafe because she's afraid if Matt knows she's an unwed mother, he won't help her—and because *his* opinion of her is extremely important. We can already sense that she is attracted to him. We understand her motivation and why she chooses not to reveal the truth.

In the next paragraph we are introduced to Matt's character from his point of view. You might call this the second *setup*. We get Matt's background and his current motivation:

> At thirty-two years of age, Matt Weston hates his early retirement with a passion, and for what he sees as two good reasons: The first, and hardest to take, is his exclusion from the manhunts, the feel of his own blood thundering in his veins as he runs his quarry down. The second, and somehow more threatening than a cornered outlaw with blazing guns, is his sudden vulnerability to the single ladies in town. For over thirty years Matt has easily avoided the perils, and he has to admit, the responsibilities of turning his life over to a member of the fairer sex. Now that he is almost desk-bound, he's practically tripping over available women, and even more alarming, rapidly running out of excuses for remaining a bachelor.

We know he's a man of action, forced into retirement. We also know he's not looking for a woman, that he prefers the bachelor life. Until ...

> Funny how that final excuse—not to mention a man's mind—can vanish with the blink of a warm brown eye. A pair of them, to be exact, each rimmed by a lush bank of lashes the color of pitch. He has no business looking into those eyes or thinking thoughts that don't include ways of catching up to Maggie's wandering husband, but Matt can't seem to stop himself. He is an honorable, professional man, one who never lets his personal life get in the way of business, so why in hell can't he keep his mind on his work whenever she is around?

> He supposes this lapse of ethics has something to do with Maggie's gentle ways and honest charms, the kind of beauty that fairly radiates the goodness in her heart. Not that he believes any of those things can excuse his utter fascination with the lady. He has a job to do, and sets out to do it with an almost personal vengeance.

Here we have Matt's initial *conflict*. He's determined to do his job, but his attraction to Maggie is getting in the way. And since he is an honorable man, he's disgusted with himself for having feelings for the "married" Maggie.

The Action

In the next section, we leave the second setup and begin the **action** of the story:

> It doesn't take Matt but two weeks to locate the bastard— the precise opinion he forms of Rafe Hollister within minutes of locating the man. The meeting takes place at a rundown saloon in El Paso when Matt stumbles over a drunken Rafe who is passed out on the floor. When Rafe finally comes to, Matt decides that Miss Maggie is in for a rude shock—and Miss Maggie is the way Matt thinks of her no matter how hard she hints that she's actually married to this stinking outlaw.

Again, we are shown Matt's conflict. He can't bear to think of Maggie as married woman. His feelings for her affect his dealings with Rafe. He always keeps Maggie's best interests in mind. In a romance synopsis, *emotion* is the most important element. You should convey what the characters are feeling as often as possible. A synopsis is *not* simply a summation of the story's action. If you just do that, you aren't doing enough.

> When Rafe sobers up and awakens to find himself traveling west toward Arizona Territory, Matt informs the miserable bastard that his wife and child are looking for him, and that he's been hired to take him to Prescott. Far from being grateful, Rafe begins cursing Maggie, calling her a horse-faced spinster among other things and declaring that she was lucky to have gotten as much as she did from him—a good time and the only piece of 'loving' she'd ever get from a sane man. He tries to go on raving about Maggie, assuring his captor that he wouldn't have touched her at all had he not been weak and crazy in the head from loss of blood.

Here we are introduced to the secondary character of Rafe. As a rule, the less secondary characters appear in a synopsis, the better, *unless* they are essential to the story. Rafe is. In the first *plot point* paragraph where Sharon mentions Maggie and Matt's mutual friend, the Sheriff of Prescott, we aren't given his name or background because his only major function is to get Maggie in touch with Matt. Rafe, on the other hand, is an important character. We want to know *why* this man would abandon his "wife" and child.

> When the ranger pulls the wagon to a halt and climbs down from the driver's seat, Rafe is certain that he is about to be set free. Instead he receives the worst beating of his miserable life. When he comes to again, Rafe quickly

discovers that both of his eyes are swollen shut, his lips are split and caked with blood, and he is hanging by his wrists, including the injured one, from a rafter inside a darkened barn. Then through what is left of his ear, he hears the voice of the former ranger as he explains the terms of Rafe's "pardon."

This section brings us to the second *plot point*. Matt has decided to depart from the simple plan of bringing Rafe to Prescott. He now want to reform him for Maggie's sake. *Plot points* are turning points in the story and here is Matt's first turning point. He gives Rafe an ultimatum and Rafe, seeing little choice, agrees to be reformed.

For Matt, it is a time of raging conflict. Although he works hard to turn the outlaw into someone worthy of Maggie and Holly, from the basest part of his soul, Matt is praying that Rafe will fail. His visits to Maggie each day to report on Rafe's progress are taking a toll on his sanity, not to mention his body. He awakes in a sweat night after night, his dreams filled with images of the woman he has fallen in love with. Even worse, he has convinced himself that he sees his own frustrations and needs each time he looks into her expressive eyes.

This paragraph describes the emotional consequences of Matt's decision. For every decision you describe in a synopsis, you should also show the consequence, not only in the action, but also in the *emotion*. We see here the internal conflict Matt is suffering. And notice the words Sharon uses here to convey... raging, basest, praying, frustration... all emotional adjectives. This is often the element new writers leave out of their synopsis... how the action makes the characters *feel*.

It is as Thanksgiving draws near that Matt slips into the darkened coffee shop late one night to discuss Rafe's progress, and finds Maggie awash in tears. He takes her in his arms, comforting her, and asks her what is wrong. There is no way she can explain how much her feelings for Matt have grown or to let him know how badly she wants him—not after he's been working so hard to make her "almost" husband presentable enough for her to marry. Even Maggie can't understand how she can have such deep feelings for Matt when the man she thought she wanted is just up the street. In spite of her less-than high opinion of her lustful nature, Maggie's desire for Matt continues to build, turning her tears into sobs. When Matt's attempts to comfort her become passionate, Maggie does nothing to cool his ardor, allowing herself instead to linger over his forbidden touch. Unable to deny herself the man she so desperately yearns for, Maggie succumbs to temptation.

This is *plot point* number three because here Maggie and Matt allow their feelings for each other to reach the physical level. It is another turning point, an *emotional* turning point, and as such will have consequences, which are described in the next paragraph. Cause and effect, folks. Show the reaction to every action. Am I stressing this enough?

Although he wouldn't trade the night spent with Maggie for his own life, Matt is plagued with guilt and self-loathing the next day, taking the entire blame for what happened between them upon himself. He avoids Maggie as best he can while continuing to encourage perfection in this less than perfect clump of humanity known as Rafe Hollister, but it isn't easy. He punishes himself with thoughts of turning Maggie's perfect husband over to her once his job is done, and polishes the outlaw to perfection if for no other reason than just to see her smile, to witness for himself a sparkle of happiness in those sad brown eyes.

Poor Matt. Being the honorable man he is, he blames himself completely for what happened. His guilt leads him to avoid Maggie and work harder on making Rafe a better man for her. This is the consequence of their succumbing to temptation.

On December 15 and according to plan, Matt arranges the long-awaited reunion between Maggie and Rafe. She feels awkward in Matt's presence, certain that the coolness he exhibits toward her is due to her immoral behavior, but remains composed as he leads her into his cabin to visit her lost love. Although it's been almost seven years, Maggie notices immediately that Rafe still has those calf eyes and a devilish grin to match them. When he turns those considerable charms on her, for a fleeting moment Maggie becomes that lonely, vulnerable farm girl again, grateful and smitten by what she'd once mistaken as true love.

And as we see here in the next paragraph, their tryst also had consequences for Maggie. She feels guilt over her behavior. But this doesn't stop her from being vulnerable to Rafe's charm.

Witnessing Maggie's rebirth, glimpsing the sweet hot luminance in her painfully honest eyes is more than Matt can tolerate. Without a word, he takes his broken heart and slips out of the room, leaving the pair of lovers with the only thing he has left to offer them—their privacy.

My heart just aches for Matt, doesn't yours? Again, as another consequence of his actions, he made Rafe into the perfect man, and now he has to live with how Rafe makes Maggie feel. Notice the emotional level of this simple paragraph. It has action, but it also makes the reader feel for Matt's pain. This is Matt's **black moment**. The Black Moment is when the character becomes certain he will not achieve his goal.

Climax and Resolution

Of course, Maggie is nobody's fool. She immediately gets hold of her emotions and for nine days, questions Rafe about his intentions. Then Christmas day arrives and we have the **climax** of the story.

> As Maggie carefully positions her former lover near the Christmas tree, then calls Holly to come downstairs and see what Santa has left for her, Matt can barely watch when the sleepy-eyed youngster drags into the room. Once she sees a stranger by the tree, and that stranger identifies himself as her father, Holly lets out a strangled cry and vaults into his arms. In moments the rest of them—Maggie, Matt, and even Rafe—are awash in tears.

This is the climax, the moment Sharon has been building towards since the first word. A happy Christmas morning. After the climax comes the **resolution**.

> Giving her daughter a few minutes alone with her father, not to mention time to pull herself together, Maggie tugs Matt into the kitchen and closes the door behind them. Remarking that she ought to be celebrating with the joyous pair under the tree, Matt thanks her for inviting him, then heads for the door, intending to let the newly reunited family enjoy their holiday in private. Maggie softly asks him to stay, even through Christmas dinner if he likes, but Matt can't understand why she'd want a used-up lawman hanging around on Christmas day, especially since his job is done. Maggie gently kisses Matt's weathered cheek and thanks him again for making Holly's wish come true. She then thanks him for the changes he made in Rafe Hollister, in particular the way Matt convinced Rafe to humble himself by begging her to marry him during each of the past nine days. It's done her heart good, she confesses, and also freed her enough to realize that she doesn't love Rafe and probably never did. Her answer for the past nine days, she says, has been an unequivocal, no, thanks to Matt Weston. With that, Maggie again kisses the man she really loves, this time square on the mouth.

Maggie's actions and emotions are resolved when she realizes Matt is the man she always wanted, not Rafe. This also resolves Matt's conflict, when he realizes he is now free to love Maggie. The moment carries the most emotion and Sharon emphasizes this by using **dialogue** in the next two paragraphs.

> Maggie swears if there's anything she can do to help, she'll do it. Anything. Vowing to hold her to that promise, Matt pulls her even tighter into his embrace and whispers, "See if you can help me with this—I wish I could find a beautiful woman to marry who has laughing brown eyes, kissable lips, and is tall enough for me to kiss back without bending myself in half."

> As tears of joy roll down Maggie's cheeks, Matt loosens her hair from the coil at her neck and fans it between his fingers. "Make sure the lady also has golden brown hair that smells of cinnamon and apples, and that she loves me at least half as much as I love her. When you find her, make sure to tell her that I promise to make her wishes come true for the rest of her life."

The dialogue and the action here precisely describe this emotional moment. Some folks say never to use dialogue in a synopsis, but when it can convey the feeling better than a summary, I'm all for it.

> And so as Christmas of 1881 comes to a close, a daughter's wish for her very own father is fulfilled; an outlaw who thought he never wanted fatherhood or to know the true miracle of Christmas, finds both along with more joy than he's ever known; and a man and a woman find themselves free to love one another with everything they have to give, joining together as one to wish for a lifetime of happiness together.

This is a final paragraph. It ties everything together, describing the changes this story has brought to each of the main characters lives.

20

The Complete Package: Sample Query and Synopsis

by Karen Weisner

Karen Wiesner
Street Address
City, State, Zip
Phone Number
E-mail Address
www.karenwiesner.com
www.falconsbend.com
www.firstdraftin30days.com
www.JewelsoftheQuill.com

March 19, 2009
publisher@whiskeycreekpress.com

Dear Ms. Womack:
A missing engagement ring leads to murder…

It's been a month since Denim McHart hung up his private investigating career after he ended up with a bullet in his leg. The injury has forced Den to re-evaluate future goals in his career, his love–life, and his spiritual life. To keep himself busy in early retirement, he's been attempting to restore an antique table and he's officially bored. He can't seem to keep his mind off his investigative partner, the lovely and complicated Sylvia Price with whom he's had an on-again, off-again romantic relationship in the past. When Sylvia calls him out of the blue, he doesn't waste time getting down to their office.

In this past month, Sylvia has been dealing with her own feelings for Den, her overwhelming guilt for the pivotal event that happened years ago and caused her mother to be mentally unstable, coinciding with her inability to forgive herself the way she knows the Lord has forgiven her.

Before the sparks can fly between Den and Sylvia in the direction he has his heart set, she says they've got company. Jilted bride Naomi Deva tells him that her groom—Mayor Thomas Julian—dumped her at the altar. Reluctantly, she admits he'd caught her in a compromising position with the best man only minutes before the ceremony. Naomi also reveals the reason why she's sought them: The local police department hasn't been able to turn up the 6.1 carat diamond engagement ring Thomas gave her...and the groom wants it back. Immediately.

Retired and on the Rocks is an approximately 62,000 word inspirational romantic mystery. The novel is complete. My original intention with this book was to have it as part of a trilogy I'm calling Denim Blues Mysteries. Attached, you'll find the full manuscript with a synopsis and trilogy overview.

I look forward to discussing this project with you.

Sincerely,
Karen Wiesner

Attachments:
Retired and on the Rocks Synopsis/Denim Blues Mysteries Trilogy Overview
Retired and on the Rocks Manuscript

About the Author:
Karen Wiesner is an accomplished author with 70 books published in the past 11 years, which have been nominated for and/or won 95 awards, and 12 more titles under contract. Karen's books cover such genres as women's fiction, romance, mystery/police procedural/cozy, suspense, paranormal, futuristic, gothic, inspirational, thriller, horror, and action/adventure. She also writes children's books, poetry, and writing reference titles such as her bestseller, *First Draft in 30 Days*, available from Writer's Digest Books. Karen's second release from Writer's Digest Books is *From First Draft to Finished Novel: A Writer's Guide to Cohesive Story Building*, available now. Her previous writing reference titles focused on non-subsidy, royalty-paying electronic publishing, author promotion, and setting up a promotional group like her own, the award-winning Jewels of the Quill, which she founded in 2003. The group publishes two award-winning anthologies

together, edited by Karen and others, per year. Karen is also a member of Sisters in Crime Internet Chapter, BooksWeLove.net, Infinite Worlds of Fantasy Authors, and World Romance Writers. In addition to her writing, Karen enjoys designing Web sites, graphics, and cover art.

For more information about Karen and her work, visit her Web sites at *www.karenwiesner.com, www.firstdraftin30days.com, www.falconsbend.com,* and *www.JewelsoftheQuill.com.* If you would like to receive Karen's free e-mail newsletter, *Karen's Quill,* and become eligible to win her monthly book giveaways, send a blank e-mail to *KarensQuill-subscribe@yahoogroups.com.*

Retired and on the Rocks
Book 1: Denim Blues Mysteries
by Karen Wiesner

Synopsis

A missing engagement ring leads to murder...
Thirty-year-old Sylvia Price can't keep her mind off her partner, Denim "Den" McHart. In the month since he decided to retire from their private investigation business, everything seems to have gone wrong. Her mentally unstable mother is being ousted from yet another private nursing home because they can't handle her frequent suicide attempts. Sylvia has to find a place to care for her. Before she ran out of options with nursing homes close by, she'd refused to consider a psychiatric hospital. Now she wonders if she has any choice about that. To add to it, Sylvia's former partner when she'd been a cop and the man who'd led her to the Lord, Orlando Bateman, had confessed just the night before to being in love with her and proposed to her.

Den and Orlando couldn't be more opposite. Den's charm makes everyone fall instantly in love with him. Sylvia is no exception. She'd gone from stranger to besotted within ten minutes of meeting Den, and the years of knowing it could never work out for them hasn't made her any less enamored with him. With no defenses against him, she overcompensates just to keep him at an uncomfortable distance he breaches time and time again. Orlando is shy, sweet, awkward, overprotective, and steady through and through. He'd love her exclusively and be there for her whenever she needed him. His traits are those she'd longed for all her life, longed for in Den. Absence has made her heart grow even fonder of her partner.

She opens the morning newspaper, eager to hear how the wedding between Cinderella-turned-princess Naomi Deva and Mayor Thomas Julian, Jr. went off the day before only to find out that the bride had been jilted at the altar. When Sylvia gets to work, she finds Naomi Deva waiting there for her and realizes that this is the perfect case to make Den come back to work full-time. She's just not sure how she'll juggle her mother's situation with the case.

It's been a month since Den hung up his sleuthing skills after a case that put a bullet in his leg and forced him to use a cane, possibly for life. To keep himself busy in early retirement, he's been attempting to restore an antique table and he's officially bored. He can't seem to keep his mind off his part-ner at McHart and Price Investigations, the lovely Sylvia Price with whom he's had an on-again, off-again personal relationship for years. They've been officially off for some time now, and, at the ripe old age of 32, Den won-ders if he's ready to hang up more than investigation. His father visits and naturally brings up the subject of whether or not Sylvia has called yet. Den's large, Christian family had fallen for Sylvia from the first time they met her. His father reminds him that it doesn't make Den less of a detective or a man because he wasn't armed when he was shot and couldn't protect Sylvia, the person who means the most to him in the world. No, Sylvia had protected *him*. Advising him to contact Sylvia himself, to invite her to Sunday dinner and pick up where he left off with her, his father leaves him to his misery.

When Sylvia calls him only minutes later, Den assumes her mind is in the same place his has been. He doesn't waste time getting down to the office. As heartsick as he'd been when he made his decision to give up sleuthing, he can't deny how much he feels at home again when he gets inside the building. And when has Sylvia ever looked better to him? He can't imag-ine how he ever let the dark, exotic beauty go. Before the sparks can fly between them in the direction he has his heart set on, she tells him they've got a case. Den insists he's done with P.I. work.

Jilted bride Naomi Deva has blond hair and green eyes that would put any man in a frenzy. She tells Den and Sylvia that her groom dumped her quite literally on the altar at the eleventh hour. They'd been minutes from becoming legally hitched when he called it off. Reluctantly, she admits that the groom caught her with the best man just prior to the ceremony. When she mentions the name of the groom, Briar's Point Mayor Thomas Julian, Jr., Den suspects she may have been marrying him for his money.

At his question of what she needs them for, Naomi says the 6.1 carat diamond engagement ring Julian had given her is missing, and the groom wants it back without delay. She last saw it the Friday before the wedding at the bakery where she works, but she doesn't know where it might have gone since then. She'd taken it off at work, and that's the last place she remembers seeing it. Unbelievably, she claims to have gone home after work and completely forgotten about it again due to pre-wedding jitters until Julian asked for it back on the orders of his mother. Den promises her they'll find it.

After Naomi leaves, Den and Sylvia argue about whether the bride or groom is entitled to keep the ring, then she tells him he's on his own for the searches at least. She won't tell him why, outside of that she has an appointment she can't reschedule. Sylvia runs out for the interview with the new nursing home only to find Orlando waiting for her in the parking lot. He's taken the day off to go with her as a supportive friend. It's no surprise that Orlando is always there for her, but his jealousy at finding out Den is back makes Sylvia uncomfortable.

Grimacing at her refusal to confide the nature of her secret errand to him, Den gets to work searching the bride's apartment, the church and the bakery. The ring is nowhere in sight. Someone must have stolen it. According to Naomi's boss at the bakery, two people visited Naomi at the bakery that day—Abby Watson and Wesley Ruch, the respective best friends of the bride and groom.

Following a fruitless effort to place her mother in a new nursing home, Sylvia has Orlando drop her off with Den so they can interview the mayor. A visibly infuriated Julian tells Den and Sylvia that he hadn't seen Naomi since the Thursday before their wedding day, when he'd told her in no uncertain terms that if she ever betrayed him, he'd leave her with absolutely nothing. He has no idea whether or not she had the diamond prior to that time as it's bad luck for the bride and groom to see each other before the ceremony. On his way to the altar that morning, he'd heard a noise coming from the broom closet and opened it to get the surprise of his life. He hadn't known whether to be angrier at Naomi or Ruch, his oldest friend who'd admittedly had a thing for his fiancée throughout their whirlwind courtship. He was so furious that his constantly interfering mother had been right that Naomi would turn out to be just like the other money-grubbing wenches he's had to deal with all his life, he demanded she give back the engagement ring there and then, only it hadn't been on her finger. Den realizes getting the rock back is Julian's equivalent to getting his pride back. At the very least, it's what the guy deserves for the humiliation his bride and friend put him through.

Wesley Ruch freely admits that he went to the bakery to talk Naomi out of marrying his old friend. He and Naomi had been seeing each other on the sly practically since she started dating Julian. As bad as Ruch implies he feels about betraying his pal, he'd obviously been too infatuated with Naomi to care. Mixed in with Ruch's obsession with Naomi is anger at how she'd dumped him after they'd been caught.

Den and Sylvia wonder if the ring had come off in the closet and Ruch had been the first to see, and pocket, it. Did he hope to blackmail Naomi with it, or does it have something to do with how fiercely competitive Ruch has reputedly always been with Julian? His motive for stealing the ring is weak, but his motive for trying to steal the *bride* is strong enough to consider he might have taken the ring.

Next, they interview Abby Watson, who turns out to be Naomi's Maid of Honor and closest friend. The more Abby talks about the groom, the more obvious it becomes to Den and Sylvia that the wires got crossed somewhere. Abby is in love with Thomas Julian, Jr., whom she'd been dating before she foolishly introduced him to her best friend Naomi. It's no stretch to wonder what her motive in taking the ring could be—she obviously believes she—the woman Julian's mother approves of—should have been the one wearing it in the first place. Yet she genuinely seems to consider Naomi a dear friend. As Ruch had, she submits to having them search her home. The odds are slim that either of them would hide it so close if they had stolen it, and Den and Sylvia suspect neither of them have it. As for why Abby had visited Naomi at the bakery on Friday, her claim that they each needed last minute alterations on their dresses proves to be valid.

All through the interviews, Sylvia has tried to hide from Den how her confrontation with the nursing home her mother is being ousted from and the possibility that she may have to put her in a psychiatric hospital has upset her. Den seems genuinely interested in the case, yet she can't help sensing there's more to his interest in coming back to work than he's letting on. He's been trying to get her to tell her what's happening in her personal life since she joined him for the interviews. Den implies she might be losing confidence in him, and that confuses her more. She hasn't been sure if that bullet he took a month ago made him face his own mortality, or if he'd faced for the first time that they've chosen a dangerous profession.

Back at the office, they talk about the case. Den speculates that Naomi is a girl who's worked hard to get ends to meet and, after having viewed the good life, has no intention of losing it completely despite her indiscretion. Sylvia counters that Naomi has spent her life trying to rise above her humble roots.

When Sylvia had asked Naomi about her family, she coldly claimed they were all dead. Later, Abby says her friend hates to talk about her past. She remembers only once Naomi telling her where her mother lives and works.

Den and Sylvia interview Naomi's mother, who ascribes greedy ambition and sheer stupidity to Naomi's motives and reveals that Naomi changed her name after she left home at nineteen.

Den and Sylvia discover that Naomi has a police record, but it's been sealed. Added to that is the fact that Abby has had jewels and cash missing over the past few years. Den and Sylvia wonder if Naomi's been stealing from Abby and Ruch has blackmailed Naomi to keep the secret and to keep her from dumping him.

Abby's mother doesn't seem sure what to think about her daughter's best friend beyond that her daughter had spent years trying to help someone who genuinely didn't want help. Sylvia finds it unimaginable that Naomi would throw away all the progress she's made for a silly indiscretion, unless she really loves Ruch. Ruch had probably dragged her into the broom closet to try to change her mind again the morning of the wedding. Den says maybe she has feelings for the guy, but she clearly has more for Julian's fat finances. They know they need to find out more about why Naomi has a record—for stealing?—and they enlist Sylvia's former partner to help them.

Why did Naomi work the day before her wedding, mere hours before she became the richest woman in the county? They return to the bakery where Naomi works to find out. Her boss confirms that she'd quit the previous Monday, but she'd been adamant about coming in on Friday. When Den asks what she did there, her boss says she finished making the top tier of the wedding cake. Naomi had made her own wedding cake, which she'd destroyed in a jilted rage after Julian called off the wedding. The case seems to have run into a dead end, and Den and Sylvia return to the office once more.

With very little recourse since the current nursing home Sylvia's mother is in has required she be out by six o'clock, Sylvia quickly ducks into her office. By phone, she arranges to have an in-home nurse stay with her mother at her apartment tonight, and Orlando has agreed to help pack her mother's things and bring her there.

When she comes out, she finds Den in the research room, trying to come up with new angles on the case. He steals a kiss that nearly shatters her. Sylvia is feeling more vulnerable than ever and inadvertently gives Den the impression that she's seeing someone else. That brings back the memory she'd tried to ignore as much as possible today, and her guilt about Orlando's marriage proposal. She's selfishly avoided him all day, only contacting him when she needs help. She loves Orlando like a brother, and he's the only person who knows the truth of her past. He'd been there for her at her lowest point.

After Sylvia became a police officer, she went home to find her father beating her mother again. When Sylvia tried to stop him, he'd punched her and then thrown her across the room. The way she'd only dreamed of protecting her mother as a child, Sylvia had pulled out her service revolver and killed him. Her father was, in every sense of the word, a Dr. Jekyll and Mr. Hyde. To the world, no one could have been more good looking and charming than he was. But at home he'd turned into a monster. Sylvia spent her childhood faltering between loving the charming side and hating the cruel counterpart. Her mother had been too fragile to defend herself then and, after his death, she'd altered between long periods of withdrawal and then lucid periods of attempting suicide.

While Sylvia has accepted Christ and knows in her soul she's forgiven for defending her mother and herself the way she did, her guilt has manifested itself in other ways. Like her inability to trust Den enough to even tell him that he sometimes reminds her of her sometimes-charming father when he was alive. But Den doesn't have a violent bone in his body. He refuses to even own a gun.

She knows now that Den believes he almost got her killed because he's so adamant against carrying a piece. She doesn't care about that, and she certainly doesn't think he failed her in the situation where he got shot. It'd simply been a case that went down bad. She doesn't blame him for that. Her fear has been that he'll be as unfaithful to her as her father had been to her mother. That she'll become desperate for him, like her mother did for her father, and will accept pain as a condition of love. Rather than taking a risk, she's pushed Den away each and every time he started asking to know her better—to know her past—and she hasn't seen the connection between this event and his sudden interest in other women. Den makes her see it this night, and it shocks her.

Before they go home to their separate abodes, Den asks her if she'll come to dinner with his parents on Sunday. Sylvia loves his family and they've always made her feel a vital part of them, but she'd promised Orlando she'd given him an answer about his proposal that day. She finds Orlando still there when she gets home, sitting with her mother, and she knows she can't wait until Sunday to tell him the truth. She knows he'd be everything she needs in a man, but she accepts now that she's been to blame for Den's withdrawal from their relationship. He'd been searching for deep intimacy with her each time in the past, but she'd pushed him away because she was afraid to admit her past to him—afraid to see disgust in his eyes.

Whether or not her reasons for doing it were justified, she'd murdered her own father and put her mother on the suicidal course she's now on. Orlando says she needs to learn to forgive herself—not to simply accept grudgingly that the Lord has forgiven her already. Sylvia concedes he's right. The first step in forgiving herself will be in telling Den the truth—taking the risk she couldn't let herself before.

Den is deeply disturbed by Sylvia's unwillingness to talk to him about the problems that so upset her this day. Between her constant need to push him away, his jealousy over her relationship with another man, and, of course, his failure to solve the case that day, Den has a hard time sleeping that night. He spends most of it praying for illumination and guidance in the situation.

At the crack of dawn the next morning, he gets a call from Sylvia saying Abby Watson is dead. Her car went over a bridge railing and into the gully below only a few miles from Julian's house. The police suspect foul play. Phone records show a call had been placed from Julian's home at eleven o'clock the previous night to the Watson home. Abby's mother had picked up the phone when it rang only to hear her daughter's greeting followed by an urgent Julian, saying he needed to see her right away. When Den and Sylvia later question Abby's mother, she tells him Julian sounded far away, as if he'd been calling from a cell phone.

Julian insists that he did make one call at ten-thirty last night—to Naomi from his office. And, yes, he'd risked his mother's wrath by telling Naomi he needed to see her because he couldn't live without her. The night watchmen and videotapes confirm his presence at the government building.

Naomi and Ruch provide alibis for each other, claiming they were together all night. Naomi admits to Sylvia and Den that Ruch was there when the call from Julian came in. She'd let her answering machine pick it up. While Sylvia and Den believe Naomi's grief over the death of Abby is authentic, they know she's hiding something, especially when they find that the cassette in her answering machine is missing.

Later, Naomi confesses Ruch flew into a rage after Julian's phone call came in, then left her apartment for several hours. When he returned she knew he'd done something horrible, especially at his threat that if she didn't give herself to him and corroborate his alibi in order to make Julian look guilty of killing Abby, he'd make sure the police found her answering machine tape in a suspicious place that would connect her to Julian's alleged crime. Naomi also admits that Ruch was stalking her and Abby came up with the idea of engagement to the mayor to protect her. She refuses to confess that she stole anything from Abby, nor that Ruch was blackmailing her because of it.

Den and Sylvia set the police on the trail they've found, and their suspicions are proved true. Ruch took the recording of Julian's call from

Naomi's answering machine, stole a car in her neighbor and drove to Julian's house. After letting himself into Julian's house, he called Abby and played the message Julian left on Naomi's machine in order to get her to come to him. He then ran her vehicle off the bridge with the stolen car, plunging Abby to her death, before abandoning the stolen car in a public parking lot and returning to Naomi. The idea of losing the woman he loved to his always-successful pal was more than the obsessive, fiercely competitive Ruch could bear. Abby had sympathized with her friend because of Ruch's violent tendencies and had thought marriage to Julian would protect her. As has been the case as long as the two have known each other, Ruch's plan to get his old friend out of the way by having a murder pinned on him has failed.

As gratitude for their help in catching Abby's murderer, Orlando tells them that Naomi robbed the restaurant her mother worked at when she was sixteen, taking multiple deposits that added up to almost ten thousand dollars. Naomi's mother talked her boss into dropping the charges against her if she'd give the money back. Naomi refused to admit she had it, even though everyone knew she took it. Later, Jan Smothers got the DA she was dating to seal her daughter's police record. Naomi hasn't had any legal trouble since then. However, Den and Sylvia had faxed the insurance photos of Abby's missing jewels to every pawn shop in a two hour radius. One confirmed that he'd gotten both Abby's necklace and earrings years apart. He remembered the woman who brought them in each time and confirmed Naomi was the one when he saw a picture of her. Ruch somehow found out about the things she'd lifted from her best friend, and he was blackmailing her to get what he wanted with her.

With one mystery solved, Sylvia and Den are left with the original puzzle of who took Naomi's wedding ring and where someone would hide a diamond that big. They know for a fact that Naomi Deva is at dead-center of both cases.

The next day, Sylvia and Den hear the front door of Naomi's apartment open. Without breaking stride, Den continues eating. The look on Naomi face when she sees him greatly enjoying the top tier of her wedding cake is priceless. Even if he hadn't already found the bling of the century inside it, her expression would have given away her attempt to steal the ring, hiding it where no one would ever think to look in her own freezer, until either Julian took her back or sufficient time had passed and she could pawn it and live like a queen. When she glares at then for figuring out her plan, Den says not to bother asking them to give it back to her. She may be paying the bills, but she also has a debt to satisfy. Julian will arrive in a moment to take back what rightly belongs to him.

Sylvia has spent the day doing what she rebelled against doing for years, because she hadn't been ready to forgive herself. She's found a psychiatric hospital that she feels will take the best care of her mother. She goes to work afterward, and Den comes in to tell her he found the ring in the cake and Julian got it back. Sylvia says some women expect to keep the ring when a man breaks the engagement. Den reminds her that Naomi shouldn't have expected to have her cake and eat it, too. Den asks her if that's why she's currently off the market for him now—if she's serious about Orlando. Even as he takes a step closer, way too close for comfort, she's slipping away, calling back over her shoulder to ask when she can expect him to come in for work on Monday. Den concedes his retirement had apparently been more of a vacation. But he's nowhere near ready to give up this chance to woo Sylvia back into his arms.

When she asks him if he wants to meet her mother, he goes in a heartbeat. He asks her why she's so afraid of getting involved with him. He knows he didn't protect her like he should have when he got shot. Sylvia realizes then that part of his retirement had been because he didn't feel qualified to protect *her* on dangerous cases. She reminds him that he went out of his way to get the attacker to point the gun at him—which gave her the chance to save them both. But she can see he's been torn up about those few moments that the attacker's gun had been trained on her. When she asks him why, he tells her because he'd realized how close he came to losing her. He never wants that to happen again. While it's true he enjoys the female species immensely, only one woman holds his heart. But he wants every part of her, not just the 'safe' parts she's willing to part with. He wants it all or nothing. It's up to her to decide what she wants; whether she can trust him enough to spend her lifetime with him. She tells Den the truth about her past, surprised that he takes her in his arms and holds her instead of looking at her like the cold blooded murderer she's considered herself all these years.

On Sunday, Sylvia comes to his parents' house the way she promised she would. Den introduces her to their new security guard—a former police dog. Den admits he missed not having her next to him every step of the way while they solved this last case. They're both capable of doing it solo, but he's got his heart set on a lifelong partnership. When he proposes to her, Sylvia says she's ready for that. He reminds her that Orlando Bateman wanted to marry her, too. She admits she let him down easy and he wishes them well. Incidentally, Julian and Naomi's wedding is back on. Den isn't surprised. He understands best that the heart won't be denied.

Love is Blind... and it Don't Pay the Bills Either
(Denim Blues Mysteries, Book 2)
Genre: Inspirational Romantic Mystery
Word count: 55,000–60,000 words

Briar's Point Police Department Detective Orlando Bateman and his partner Tyler Shaw attempt to solve a missing person case. Keeya Nilsen, blind since birth, comes to them and has a justifiably bad attitude about love, since all the men she's ever loved have cheated on her and robbed her blind... including the last one, who absconded with some of her most prized possessions—her grandfather's unpublished blues songs—when he flew the coop. As together they search for her last boyfriend, Orlando reminds Keeya about her childhood faith and makes her see love as God intends.

Souls on (B)Oring Street
(Denim Blues Mysteries, Book 3)
Genre: Inspirational Romantic Mystery
Word count: 55,000–60,000 words

Erin Shanley, a hospice nurse, becomes an amateur sleuth when she realizes some of her patients are being swindled out of their life savings by the new 'psychic' fortuneteller in Briar's Point. Erin's neighbor, Detective Tyler Shaw, whom she went to school with, is someone she's always had a bit of a crush on. But this shy, sweet guy has been burned in love and isn't sure he's the right material for any woman, even someone as amazing as Erin.

SECTION 5
Other Opportunities

21

Speaking and Teaching

Whether or not you subscribe to the adage, "Write what you know," sooner or later you're probably going to know quite a lot about *writing*. At that point, you have a new option for marketing your "writing" skills: Becoming a speaker and/or instructor on writing-related topics.

While public speaking is rarely high on a writer's list of favorite activities, it is often a wise step. If you've published a book, you may find that the best way to promote it (and yourself) is to offer talks and workshops. At conferences where I've given talks, for example, my books have flown off the book-table. This makes my publisher happy, and adds a few dollars to my royalty check. Add to that the honorarium you're likely to receive just for talking about your favorite subject for an hour or two (and the fact that your travel expenses and hotel room are—or should be—paid for by the conference, which may well take place in an exotic locale such as Maui), and you might just view the prospect of speaking in public in a new light.

Speaking opportunities abound for writers. Writing conferences and workshops are always looking for speakers. Local clubs and organizations (including bookstores and libraries) are delighted to "book" authors for talks and will generally let you set up a book table. (This enables you to buy copies of your book from your publisher at the typical author's discount of 40 percent and sell them at full price, or at a minor discount). Local colleges welcome writers who can offer classes on their area of expertise. And finally, if the thought of speaking to a group is still too horrifying to contemplate, you can offer a class online, and "speak" to your audience by e-mail.

Why Speak?

Writers typically branch out into speaking and teaching for one (or all) of the following reasons:

1. To earn additional income;
2. To promote their books (or themselves);
3. To pass on what they have learned to others.

SHOW ME THE MONEY

If income is your goal, you'll want to limit your engagements to those that actually pay. Not all conferences offer honorariums, and many do not cover travel expenses. Before pitching a talk, therefore, make sure you'll be paid for your trouble, and that the cost of getting there won't eat up your profits.

Smaller conferences usually can't pay much for speakers. Some offer as little as $100 per workshop, and no travel expenses. High-end conferences, on the other hand, may offer $1000 or more for a well-known speaker and cover your expenses. Almost all conferences offer free registration to speakers, which enables you to attend all the other talks and events. As many conferences are in attractive locations (and nice hotels), getting a speaking engagement can be a way to get a paid vacation!

Most conferences will also order copies of your books—not only those that relate directly to your talk, but any other books that you've published. If your books are commercially published, this will add a few extra dollars to your royalty statement, but it won't make you rich. If, however, you're self-published, those book-table revenues can add up.

Local clubs and organizations rarely offer a large fee ($50 to $100 is typical), but most will let you set up a book table (again, ideal for self-published authors). Since you won't have travel costs, these engagements are well worth an hour or so of your time.

Payment for a continuing education course can vary widely. Some give instructors a percentage of registration fees—e.g., $25 per student. Others pay a flat rate, but insist on a minimum number of attendees (which means your class will be cancelled if not enough students sign up). Some schools also deduct taxes from your check.

When offering a class, be sure to consider all the hours involved: not just those in the classroom, but also those you'll spend in preparation and reviewing student assignments. A fee of $300 may sound impressive, until you realize that it covers six nights of instruction at two hours per night, plus the time required to write lectures and reading homework. Classes also offer fewer opportunities to sell books; while most private continuing education programs don't mind if authors hawk their books, most colleges frown on this.

MAKE ME FAMOUS

If your goal is to become better known as a writer, conferences are a tremendous way to boost recognition. This is your opportunity not only to speak to fans but also to hobnob with other writers, agents, and editors as a peer. Once you've been invited to one conference, you're likely to be invited to others, because you're now recognized as a speaker.

If you want to become better known in your community for your particular area of expertise, seek out speaking engagements with civic and community groups. Don't just market yourself as a "writer"; consider other topics on which you're qualified to speak (such as the subjects you write *about*). If you're a business writer, for example, consider giving talks on business; if you write about travel, consider offering talks about some of your favorite destinations, or on how to travel on a budget. Don't limit yourself to adult audiences; you'll also find speaking opportunities with youth organizations and schools.

Internet "chats" are another way to gain publicity (and, perhaps, to sell more books). All you need to "chat" is the ability to type quickly and accurately; it's a great "speaking" venue for anyone who gets butterflies at the thought of facing a crowd.

LET ME HELP
Finally, any of the opportunities described in this chapter will give you a chance to "give something back"—to pass one what you've learned as a writer, to help the next generation of writers, and to share tips on a subject you love. Sometimes, that by itself is ample reward!

Writers' Conferences

Writers' conferences are always looking for interesting speakers who have a sufficient reputation to draw attendees. The first question to ask yourself, therefore, is whether you have the credentials to interest a conference—or its participants.

To win an invitation to speak at a conference, you will need to be a published writer. Having a published *book* is often helpful, but not absolutely necessary; my first conference invitation was based on articles I'd published online. If you write fiction, having a few stories published with reputable publications may be all you need.

It also helps to have a certain amount of "name" recognition. If no one has ever heard of you, your name isn't going to be a draw, and conference organizers look for writers who will attract attendees. However, "fame" is difficult to define; chances are, you won't have heard of half the speakers at any conference you attend, so don't assume you don't have a chance just because your publications have been limited to obscure literary magazines.

You also need to have something to *say*. If you're already known for a particular subject or write in a particular field or genre, this will probably be the best topic to pitch. For example, if you write mystery fiction, you should probably offer to talk about how to write mystery fiction. Such a topic offers many possibilities: perhaps you could pitch a workshop about forensics, or police procedures, or incorporating "true crime" into one's stories. Or, you could discuss how to create suspense, how to plant clues and red herrings, or—the perennial favorite—how to get published.

MAKING CONTACT

One of the best places to find writers' conferences online is The Shaw Guide to Writers Conferences & Workshops (*writing.shawguides.com*). This site lists conferences by date and by location—thus, if you only want to apply to conferences in your area, you can look for listings in your state (or nearby states).

Each listing gives you the date of the conference, the general subject matter, the location, and a contact person and address. Look for titles like "conference organizer," "conference coordinator," or "conference chair" (or "co-chair"). You'll find these names toward the bottom of the listing.

Conferences (especially the larger ones) often plan their schedules as much as a year in advance, so don't expect to get an engagement in the actual conferences listed in the Guide. Your goal is to find conferences that may be willing to add you to *next* year's speaker's list. (If you can attend the conference this year and get a better idea of its focus, so much the better!)

Make a list of conferences that interest you—conferences in your area, conferences that focus on your subject, etc. Make sure that the dates fit into your schedule and that you're actually willing to travel to wherever the conference is held.

Now it's time for the initial pitch. Your first contact with the conference organizer should be a basic query letter, stating your interest in offering a workshop, and your credentials. Offer two or three ideas for workshops, along with a brief (one paragraph) outline of each. Include a copy of your resume or writer's bio and publications list, and a few relevant clips. Be sure to include a SASE. And be prepared to wait; conferences are planned by committee, so you won't hear anything until the committee has met and reviewed your proposal.

MAKING YOUR PITCH

If the response to your initial query is favorable, you will be asked to submit a more complete workshop proposal. You may be asked to submit a proposal for just one of your topics, or for all of them—or even for completely different topics.

These proposals should be far more detailed than your original query. A good proposal length is about half a page; anything longer, and you are either giving too much detail, or your topic will be too long to cover adequately in the time available. Keep in mind that you will have somewhere between 45 and 90 minutes to speak, and you will be expected to leave time for questions at the end of your talk. Don't try to squeeze "Twenty ways writers can benefit from the Internet" into 30 minutes of speaking time!

Your proposal should include the following information:

- The title of the talk.
- A general overview of what you plan to cover (giving an idea of what participants will learn from your workshop).
- Any interactive elements you'd like to include (such as exercises).

- Any special equipment you'll need (such as a slide projector, an overhead projector, or an electrical outlet).
- The proposed length of the talk (you can often wangle a longer time-slot, if you want it, by indicating the need for more time in your proposal). If you don't care, you can omit this section.
- Whether you are offering handouts or other materials (find out first whether the conference will copy handouts for you).

Following are two sample proposals. One offers considerable detail; the other is shorter and punchier. Both were successful.

How to Write Effective Query Letters

One question I often hear as a writing instructor is, "Why bother to write a query when I could write the complete article?" This seminar will offer the answer to that question, along with tips on how to develop effective, successful queries. Some of the topics addressed in the seminar will include:

Why query letters are so important

- Because many publications don't accept unsolicited articles
- Because queries can save a writer valuable time
- Because some publications pay more for assigned articles

How to develop an effective query letter

- How to write an attention-grabbing "hook" or lead paragraph
- How to demonstrate the topic's relevance to the audience
- How to summarize the article's content
- How to present your credentials (even if you have never been published)
- How to solicit a response

What happens next

- Understanding assignments vs. "on-speculation"
- Understanding the editorial process (and mind-set)

E-mail queries and other "netiquette" issues

- When (and how) to submit an e-mail query
- When (and how) to follow up by e-mail

When to write a query—and when to write the article instead

Proposed length: 1 hr. 15 minutes
Handouts to be provided

Conducting Research Online: Beyond Basic Searching

When you're looking for the answer to a complex question, basic search techniques often aren't enough. This workshop offers tips on locating information quickly and effectively. It will cover advanced searching techniques, how to select effective keywords and phrases, how to use alternative search engines, and where to find information outside of search engines (including newsgroups, e-mail, experts, databases, and international information sources). Participants are invited to bring their own "challenging research questions" to the workshop so that we can explore how to find the answers online.

Once your proposal is accepted, you'll be asked to provide a bio and a photo. At this time, you might also want to write a condensed version of your proposal for use in the conference bulletin. Otherwise, you may be surprised by the way your workshop is actually described. For example, the bit about bringing "challenging research questions" in the second sample never made it into the final description, which meant that the interactive portion of the workshop had to be dropped.

Keep your presentation flexible. Rather than writing out a talk that you plan to deliver word-for-word, write an outline of the points you want to cover. This enables you to drop material if you run out of time (e.g., if you have to answer lots of questions or you find that your audience already knows the material and is starting to look bored), or to add in material if you find that your audience has less background in the subject than you expected (or no one asks any questions). Be sure to bring flyers for your book, business cards, and any other materials that you'd like to distribute; conference participants love handouts and "freebies."

Once you've completed your workshop, shaken hands with everyone, and gone home, sit down at your computer and work up a proposal for next year. Send it to the conference organizers while they're still basking in the success of the last conference, and you're that much more likely to get a new engagement!

Speaking Locally

Conferences aren't the only place to give talks about writing—or about subjects related to your writing. Local organizations—clubs, associations, youth groups, writers' groups, libraries, and bookstores—are all in need of speakers and are delighted to work with local authors.

Your telephone directory is the best place to start your search for local speaking opportunities. Look in the yellow pages under listings like:

• Clubs
• Associations

- Foundations
- Organizations (including political organizations, religious organizations, social service organizations, and youth organizations and centers)

These headings will provide you with an ample list of local civic and community groups, local branches of national organizations, and a host of special interest groups (such as boater's clubs, gardening clubs, cooking clubs, etc.). Don't overlook the latter, especially if you happen to write about a specialized subject area!

Your local Chamber of Commerce is also likely to have a list of local clubs and organizations. For groups that don't tend to be listed in the yellow pages (such as writers' groups and book clubs), check with your local libraries and bookstores. Many Barnes & Noble branches, for example, offer a bulletin board (usually near the restrooms) where such groups can post meeting announcements, and many also announce regular writing group meetings in their in-store newsletter. While you're there, be sure to ask the library or bookstore if they would be interested in a talk or book signing from *you*, as a local author.

Before approaching a group, it's a good idea to find out something about them. Call and ask for an information packet. Find out if the group has a Web site. Once you know what the group is "about," you'll be better able to pitch a talk that matches their needs and interests.

Then, call the organization and ask to speak to the person who handles event scheduling. Explain that you are a local author and would be interested in speaking at a luncheon, dinner or special event. Mention a few appropriate topics (based on your research). At libraries or book clubs, a "how I got started" or "how I got published" talk is often a good draw, especially if you're a well-known author. If you have any prior speaking experience, mention that as well.

With clubs and organizations, your telephone conversation may be the only "pitch" you need; you may not be asked to write up an actual proposal. In many cases, your talk may be scheduled and confirmed before you even hang up the phone. In others, you may be asked to send along some biographical information and clips. If you have a Web site, mention it—and, at an appropriate point in the conversation, ask if you can bring copies of your books to sell. Then, just show up, give a good talk, have a good time—and be sure to ask if you can use the organization as a reference for your next pitch!

Teaching a Class

Adult education programs offer excellent opportunities for writers. These go by many names: community education, continuing education, etc. Some are managed by local colleges and universities; others are offered by private organizations, such as The Learning Annex. Civic centers sometimes offer classes; so do many parks and recreation departments.

Many offer classes in creative and professional writing (including business and technical writing). Since such classes are usually not offered for academic credit, you don't need the same credentials that are often required for regular courses (such as a specific degree). Instead, most programs are looking for instructors who have actual experience in the field. If you're going to pitch a course on writing a novel, for example, you should have actually written (and published) a novel. If you're going to talk about freelance writing, you should have some magazine sales under your belt. In short, if you can prove that you have *done* it, you can probably make a case for your ability to *teach* it.

MAKING CONTACT

The first place to search for teaching opportunities is your local yellow pages. Try looking under the following headings:

- Schools: Business and Secretarial
- Schools: Technical and Trade
- Schools: Universities and Colleges (Academic)

If you'd like to explore opportunities outside your immediate city or county, you can find listings of colleges and universities by state at several Web sites. To locate independent programs, look for flyers at your local library, bookstore, or community center.

Your directory may not actually list the number for a continuing education department. To find the right person to contact, simply call the college or university and ask for that department. (Usually, the operator will know what you mean, even if the department uses another name.) Be sure to ask for the actual extension and a contact name if you can get it, so that you can call back directly if you don't make a connection the first time.

Once you're connected with the right department, ask to talk to the person in charge of hiring instructors. Tell that person (often the director of the program) that you are interested in teaching a class through that program, and ask about the application procedure. Usually, you'll be asked to give a little information about yourself and the type of class you'd like to teach. If your initial telephone pitch interests the director, you'll be given more detailed instructions about how to actually apply. Sometimes this involves filling out an application package; sometimes it's as simple as submitting a class proposal and a cover letter. You'll also need to provide a curriculum vitae (a resume, to non-academics!).

PROPOSING YOUR CLASS

Continuing education programs can be remarkably flexible about the structure of a course. Often, they'll leave it up to you to decide how many nights a week you wish to teach, and how many hours per night. You may also have the option of offering day-long (or half-day) courses on weekends.

After you've decided *what* you want to teach, therefore, you'll need to decide how much time you need to teach it effectively. If you don't plan to offer actual writing assignments, you might want to consider teaching a single-day course (usually six hours with a break for lunch). If you want to give homework, or give students a chance to review handouts between sessions, it's better to schedule several classes over a period of days or weeks. For evening classes, a schedule of four class sessions of two hours each usually works well (though some instructors opt for six or even eight classes).

You'll also want to find out whether the department will pay for photocopying handouts. Some continuing education departments have very small budgets, and expect you to pay for your own copying. Others may allow you to order a textbook, which students will pay for as part of the course. (You may also be able to assemble your handouts into a single "reading package" that can be copied by the department and sold to the students at cost.) If you want to provide extra materials, be sure to discuss this with the program director. Similarly, make sure the director knows whether you'll need special equipment (such as a slide projector) or an electrical hookup.

Finally, you'll need to provide a detailed overview of the course you want to teach. Your overview should provide:

- A class title
- A description of the course (including the expected "outcome" of the course, i.e., what students will learn or achieve during the course)
- A schedule (the number of sessions and the topic of each session; for a one-day course, include topics for "morning" and "afternoon").
- Special needs, such as photocopying, electrical outlet, projector, etc.
- A minimum/maximum number of students, if appropriate. (If, for example, you're planning lots of one-on-one interaction or homework, you may want to limit enrollment.)

Here's an example:

SUCCESSFUL FREELANCING: WRITING FOR THE MAGAZINE ARTICLE MARKET

Instructor: Moira Anderson Allen, M.Ed.
Length: 8 weeks/3 hours per class

Participants who have basic writing skills and an interest in writing professionally will find this the perfect opportunity to develop their freelance potential. The instructor, who has worked as both a freelance writer and a magazine editor, will guide students through the process of developing articles tailored specifically for an appropriate market.

Students will learn how to explore and familiarize themselves with markets, how to work with editors, and how to make their work stand out from the competition. By the end of the class, students will have written a complete, marketable article, and have begun the process of submitting that article to a magazine.

Session 1: You are an expert. Discover your area(s) of expertise, and learn how to "mine" it for article topics. In this session, students will identify areas of interest and knowledge, and develop potential article topics from those areas. The session will also include an introduction to the magazine market: its potential, how to break in, and what to expect from the market.

Session 2: Focus, focus. Students will learn how to turn an idea into a topic, a topic into an outline, and an outline into a rough draft. Exercises include "focusing" (narrowing down a subject) and "brainstorming" (building up a topic).

Session 3: Who's your audience? Before one begins to write an article, one must identify whom one is writing for. This session teaches students how to locate markets, how to identify the needs of a particular market (magazine) just by looking at it, and how to approach that market with an idea.

Session 4: Putting meat on the bones. Now that participants have defined a working topic and identified the audience for that topic, it's time to start building a rough draft. This session explores different approaches to articles, sources of information, interview techniques, and decisions that must be made before and during the development of the article.

Session 5: Playing editor. By now, students should have an actual working draft of an article. Guided by the instructor's editorial expertise, students will now learn to look at their article the way an editor would. In this session, participants will learn about expanding, cutting, slanting, using quotes and interviews effectively, and tailoring information to the target audience.

Session 6: Making it irresistible... As participants move closer to having a completed, saleable article, they will learn how to add "bonuses" that save editors work—and enhance sales. Students will learn how to use artwork, photos, stylistic techniques, and other tools to "rejection-proof" their material.

Session 7: Taking the plunge. This session focuses on how to sell one's work. It will explore query letters, working with editors, and presenting manuscripts properly. Students will be asked to "query" the instructor, and receive feedback on how to target their queries to actual magazines.

Session 8: What next? The final class provides an in-depth exploration of the freelance marketplace. It discusses editorial procedures, building relationships with editors, understanding contracts, payment schedules, different types of magazines, rights and sales, and professional standards. It answers the questions, "What happens to my article when it is submitted/ accepted/published?" The session will also explore book markets and contracts.

Each session will include approximately 10 pages of handouts.

Include a separate proposal, on a separate piece of paper, for each class that you want to teach. Provide a cover letter that summarizes the classes you're offering (and keep in mind that those summaries may be used as the official catalog course descriptions).

TEACHING ONLINE

The process for obtaining online teaching jobs is much the same as for obtaining "real-world" positions. The difference is that you're no longer limited by geography: You can offer your services to any of dozens of sites that offer online writing courses, no matter where you live. You also don't have to worry about scheduling "convenient" hours, hiking up lots of steps to a dingy classroom, or making your way through a dark parking lot when the class is over.

There are many sites that offer online writing courses; try simply typing appropriate search terms into your favorite search engine. Try several different terms, such as:

- Writing classes
- Online writing classes
- Writing courses
- Internet writing courses

Before pitching your class, visit the site first, and determine whether (a) you like the presentation and content of the site, and (b) you have something to offer that isn't already being taught. If you're not sure about a site's reputation, run a search on the name of the site. Search newsgroups as well to see whether the site has been discussed (positively or negatively). Review the site thoroughly to determine whether it has received good reviews, and whether it seems to be a "class act." (A site that purports to teach "writing" but is riddled with typos and grammatical errors, for example, would not give you much of a career boost.)

If the site doesn't offer an obvious link for potential instructors, search for contact information. Send a basic e-mail query describing the type of course you'd like to teach, and your credentials. If you receive no response after two to three weeks, follow up; if you still don't get a response, move on.

Internet courses can be a good alternative for a writer who isn't quite comfortable with the idea of "speaking" in public. Most courses are conducted primarily by e-mail, which means that you'll need to be able to write weekly lectures and respond to student questions. If you give assignments, those will also be submitted and reviewed by e-mail. What you won't have is the interaction of discussion and question-and-answer sessions (though some courses do include chat meetings). Instructors are usually paid a percentage of each enrollment.

Chances are that you became a writer because you felt that you had something to share. As you become more proficient in the writing field, you may discover that you have even more to share: Your love of writing, your expertise as a writer, and your desire to "mentor" the next generation of writers. By stepping up to the podium—whether at a writing conference, a civic club meeting, or in a classroom—you can give back some of the lessons you've learned along the way, promote your career, and earn some extra income at the same time.

22

Pitching to the Greeting Card Market

by Sandra Miller-Louden

Submitting and pitching greeting card ideas to existing companies is truly an art—and one that many people handle poorly and unprofessionally. It is also a topic on which one can find a lot of misinformation and dated information, which can make your ideas seem dated and you (to paraphrase Humphrey Bogart in *Casablanca)* seem woefully misinformed.

The good news is that this lack of information on the actual submission process is one of the main reasons this genre remains a virtually untapped, low-competition field compared with other writing areas. People simply do not know how to submit their work. Intertwined with this is another strong misconception: that you must be able to draw or submit artwork in order to submit your writing. Thus, many would-be greeting card writers never get to swing at the first pitch, because they believe that greeting card editors want the entire package—art and verse. In fact, just the opposite is true. Editors only want verses from writers, and artwork and photography from artists and photographers. Knowing this one all-important detail can open an entire creative world to the writer willing to enter.

So, let's turn our attention to submitting greeting card ideas to existing companies. We'll start with the traditional way, since many companies still accept work sent in that manner. We'll soon see, however, that once writers begin submitting—and editors begin receiving—work in what I term "the new millennium way," not only do both parties become quickly accustomed to it, they become positively addicted to it. However, it's important to understand the traditional method first, even if it may seem to be on its way out, because the essentials of that method—idea coding, formatting of ideas, mixing of ideas, etc.—apply equally to any method of submission.

First, a definition of terms. When I talk about a **batch** of work, I mean a group of between 10 and 20 *regular* ideas sent at one time. **Regular** ideas are those that rely solely on the words, or simple artwork (a visual), to get the message across. The card (or idea) does not depend upon any sort of mechanical feature—such as pop-ups, puzzle spinners, springs, music, etc.—to function.

The Traditional Approach: Surface-Mail Submissions

Here are the important factors in sending in your work the traditional— or snail-mail—way:

In their guidelines, companies may ask for up to twenty ideas sent in a single envelope (which always means a #10, business-size envelope). Although most companies will ask for between ten and twenty ideas sent in a single envelope, **eleven** ideas plus your SASE (always use a return #10 business-size envelope as well) will get you the most for your stamp. (Your major cost at this time will be postage, so look for every way possible to conserve in that area!) Sending out eleven ideas instead of the more conventional ten gives you a free batch every tenth submission. Often it is the final idea you throw in at the last second that sells!

Give the editor a treat… *be neat!* I always hesitate to add this most fundamental of points, because it just seems so basic. However, in talking with editors over the past 24 years, they tell me a whopping 25 percent of all submissions come scrawled in pencil on the backs of envelopes or loose scraps of paper, misspelled, smudged, soiled by coffee cup rings, or decorated by breakfast jelly stains. Many arrive without a name or address, or worse, with no SASE. Most editors will simply pitch this sort of haphazard presentation into the nearest trash bin. So, please, just as you would never go to a job interview in cut-offs and sandals, don't approach this job with a sloppy mailing.

Let's do a quick definition of neatness. It really isn't difficult to achieve. For greeting card submissions, neatness is defined as typewritten copy, or at the very least, hand-printed submissions in block letters, *in blue or black ink.* (For printer-generated copy, such straightforward fonts as Bookman Old Style, Arial, Times New Roman, Tahoma, Book Antiqua, or Courier New will do the trick.) And dot each "i" with a real dot, not a little heart. (I don't make this stuff up. Editors really do have some incredible stories to tell.)

The generally accepted format to submit *regular* greeting card ideas is as follows: Write each idea on a 3 x 5-inch index card—**one idea, no matter how short, per index card.** (Do not use 3x5" slips of paper. These are too flimsy.) Your index cards should be *unlined,* white or cream-colored. Companies do *not* want eyeball-popping purple or tangy tangerine index cards. In other words, don't use gimmicks to sell your ideas. Allow your creativity to shine in your *writing!*

The information on the card should be typed horizontally, not vertically (unless the company's guidelines state differently). An example of a submitted idea would look like this:

ABC-074 (Graduation–General)

O: You can't have graduated already…
I:…you just learned your locker combination.
Congratulations!
Your Name
Address
Phone # With Area Code
Fax # With Area Code (if applicable)
E-mail address

Let's look at each of the above components:

- **ABC-074:** This is the code that you have assigned to this specific idea. Greeting card companies expect every idea to have a code, which will be used if and when the idea is purchased and you are paid. Every idea should have its own code. Different ideas may have more than one code (see more on this in the sidebar on "Codes"), but no code should be applied to more than one idea. The code will be of your own making; there are several systems, discussed in the sidebar, that you can use.

- **(Graduation–General)**: This defines the main "occasion" for which you are submitting the idea, followed by the subset for that occasion. For example, if you are writing verses for Mother's Day, your occasion might be "Mother's Day—Mother-in-Law," or "Mother's Day—Like a Mother to Me." If you are writing for an alternate product, such as a mug or t-shirt, you would head your index card "Mug—Office Humor," or "Post-It Note—Generic Humor." The second sidebar to this chapter describes common "occasions" in more detail.

- **O:** This is short for Outside. If your verse is like the one above where the words are self-evident, you begin immediately with the verse itself. No visual description is required, because the words do not depend upon the artwork. Ideas depending on a visual would lead off with a short description of the suggested visual (no more than two sentences—one sentence is better) and then the outside verse.

- **I:** This is short for Inside and specifies the portion of the verse or sentiment for the inside text of the card. Some cards today also have a visual on the inside; if your idea incorporates this, this is the place where you would describe it. These two designations—O and I—are the crux of the card, the actual verse.

- **Personal Information.** Your name, address, phone, and e-mail address are vital. A fax number is optional (faxing ideas, while extremely popular a decade ago, is rapidly becoming obsolete). Your Social Security number is also optional at this stage (you'll be required to supply it later if the company accepts an idea and pays you). I highly recommend having a rubber stamp made with this information on it. Or, if you run the cards through your printer, create a template with the information. You do not want to have to hand-print or retype this information constantly (for one thing, this creates too much opportunity for errors). Nor do you wish to affix mailing labels to the cards, as this will cause the cards to bulk up at that spot; having a lump in the envelope will ruin an otherwise streamlined, professional presentation.

This information should always be presented on one side of the card only, unless the company's guidelines instruct you differently.

This is the *standard procedure* for submitting ideas, and should be followed unless the company's guidelines go into detail about how they want ideas sent in. If a company wants a different format for submissions, here are some of the variables they may ask for:

- Information typed vertically (i.e., with the card positioned on the vertical rather than horizontal axis)
- 4x6 index cards rather than 3x5
- All ideas typed on 8.5x11 sheets of paper
- Card verses only typed on the front of the index card; other information (name, address, occasion, code) typed on the back

You'll note that I have been referring to "typing" throughout most of this discussion. I first began writing verses in 1986, when home computers were still years away. I started typing 3x5 cards on a Smith Corona SD700 and felt that cutting-edge technology had arrived! I could type a line of copy and the typewriter would store it into memory; no more carbon paper! It had the sheer luxury of a self-correcting key; no more white, flaky pieces of plastic to insert whenever I needed to fix a line.

I still use that Smith Corona for snail-mail submissions—when I actually make snail-mail submissions, which is rare. While it may seem archaic, typing index cards is actually fast and efficient (and I've gotten some excellent verses from the act of retyping or even from making typos). This doesn't mean that you have to go out and buy a typewriter to submit greeting cards. However, if you plan to print them from your computer, here are some things to consider:

- Index cards designed for a computer printer come ten to a sheet, perforated much like print-your-own business cards—and of course these are much more expensive than a stack of individual index cards.
- Printer-ready index cards are a heavier stock than normal paper and often must be hand-fed individually through the printer.

- You will need to develop a template (one may be included with the card stock or with your printer) to enable you to print out ten cards at once. It can take quite awhile to fiddle with the template and get it just right (be sure to test-print it on regular paper before printing it on your card stock)—and in the time spent fiddling with designing your cards on the computer, you could easily have them all typed and ready to go on a typewriter!
- Given the complexities of a template (and the variance of the length of your verses), you may still need to hand-stamp your personal information on each card (especially if company guidelines require you to put some of this information on the back).
- You may also be able to print individual 3x5 cards on your printer, if your tray allows for different paper sizes (or if you can run them through a top-feed), but again, you will often need to hand-feed them because of the size and paper thickness. You will also need to develop a template for individual 3x5 cards if you use this approach.

The first time you send a batch of ideas, you may wish to include a short cover note stating that you've reviewed the company's guidelines and feel you've come up with appropriate material. (Even better, if you've seen a retail display of the company's cards, be sure and mention that, even quoting one you particularly liked). Thank the editor for her time and that's all. The rest is up to her. *Remember, include a No. 10 SASE!*

Once you begin a regular working relationship with a company, no note of explanation is needed when sending your ideas. It's not rude to simply put your ideas (along with your SASE) in an envelope and send them. If you have something short to say (for example, if you've just received samples of a card you've written and want to thank the editor), use a sticky note attached to the first card of the batch. Editors appreciate economy of paper more than you can imagine.

Learn patience! The longer you wait, the better your chances become for a sale. My fastest sale came in a week; my longest took six years! The best thing about this business is that you never know what the day's mail will bring. And when those inevitable rejected ideas come back, *immediately* resubmit them to another company. (Always retype the idea on a new card when resubmitting it to a different company.) I've had ideas rejected as many as fifteen times before they sold *for more money* than I would have received from the companies that originally rejected them. In fact, I estimate that 40 percent of all my sales have been ideas that were previously rejected. I've even had the same company reject an idea, only to buy it the second time I submitted it. Often times a simple rewrite will turn a failed idea into a sale.

The "New Millennium" Approach to Submissions

Okay, now we've looked at the traditional way to submit material. But, surprise, surprise, the advent of home computers, cyberspace, and Web sites has also updated and changed the way we submit our greeting card ideas. While it's still important to be familiar with the traditional way of submitting ideas (a few companies *only* accept that method), in many cases, you will be asked—or even required—to submit your work electronically. It's vital that you be aware of these electronic methods—how they are similar to and how they differ from the 3x5" index cards we've looked at previously. In addition, you'll need to know which methods are more cost effective and which are more convenient.

There are three main ways of submitting work electronically:

- via fax
- via e-mail
- directly on a company's Web site

SUBMITTING BY FAX

Faxing greeting card verses is basically like any other fax you send. First, you need a cover page, telling how many pages (including the cover page) are sent. Your submission itself begins on Page 2 (the one after the cover sheet), which should contain your personal information. You should not only number each page, but also create a header for your entire submission in case the sheets get separated. This header should include your name, and possibly your e-mail. Always type END OF TRANSMISSION after the very last verse sent on the last page.

When faxing ideas, *please note that you should not put a single verse per page!* This is just the opposite of the one-idea-per-index-card method. Instead, type your verses, in the same format as described above for index cards, one after another on 8.5x11 paper. Each "pitch" should include the code number, occasion/subset, O/I verses, and information about artwork if any. One sheet of paper will usually hold from seven to eight verses. Even though you can obviously send more than eleven verses by fax, you should still *not* send more than twenty verses at a time. The only exception is if you are faxing an assignment, especially an image-based assignment. Then, of course, you'll send verses to as many drawings or photos as the editor has provided.

If you're working on assignment or from a specific Needs List provided by the company, you'll want to note that on the cover sheet. Also, if you have a job number (again, because you are working on an assignment), this should be included on the cover sheet and in the header on the subsequent pages of your transmission.

For larger companies, send your copy to an editor *by name*. You may also be requested to phone first to alert the editor that the fax is coming. In companies of all sizes, many people share the same fax, which means that your work could end up on the wrong person's desk.

SUBMITTING BY E-MAIL

During the mid- to late '90s, the majority of my verses were faxed. Today, my fax is basically idle; with so many digital-mailing programs available, such as WinRAR, editors can easily embed images into e-mails or attach them to files as JPGs when sending out assignments. If you aren't familiar with these programs already, it's a good idea to become familiar with them so you'll be prepared if an assignment comes your way.

Submitting verses by e-mail has now become the much more commonly accepted approach. However, you must first be sure that an editor *will* accept e-mail submissions. Some welcome them; others do not. Some require *all* submissions to be sent by e-mail.

When using e-mail, you'll follow the same rules as with faxing your work, except that you don't need a cover page. Again, don't forget to include your personal information. It's a good idea to make sure that your full, real name is included in your "sending" address; screen names or cute e-mail addresses (like "*cardwizard@myisp.com*) give an editor no idea of the identity of the sender. Be sure to include a relevant subject line as well. Don't use a "cute" subject line like "Hello" or "Greetings from…"—such subjects can look too much like spam and cause your submission to be routed directly to the trash bin.

Just as with a fax, *all verses should be sent in one, single e-mail.* No editor wants twenty separate e-mails, each containing a single verse. And be sure to note "End of Transmission" on your e-mail as well; things can and do get cut off.

Make sure you save a copy of any e-mail submission you send; printing a hard copy is also a good idea. Also, request a confirmation of receipt. If you don't receive one within three to four days, e-mail again. (Don't wait that long if there's a deadline involved and you've waited until the virtual last minute to send in your verses; in that case, you might want to call the editor to let her know that your work is sitting on her hard drive.)

If you have high security settings on your e-mail (such as one of those programs that requires people to type in a jumbled code word to reach you), make sure that your settings will allow the editor to respond to you. Nothing is more annoying than having to wade through several levels of security just to respond to a submission. Also, as with faxed ideas, don't get carried away and send more than twenty ideas, unless it's for a specific assignment. Editors will consider an idea-crammed e-mail as overkill, and if the first few ideas don't grab an editor, trust me, she'll never read Idea #74.

The format for submitting ideas by e-mails is the same as in faxing. You'll want to include the code number, the occasion heading and subset (e.g., Birthday—Belated), Outside/Inside line, and any visual components. Sandwich your verses between your personal information—i.e., begin and end your complete set of verses with your contact information. Again, the very last line should read "END OF TRANSMISSION."

SUBMITTING ON A COMPANY WEB SITE

The third way of submitting work—directly upon a company Web site—is convenient, challenging, and a whole lot of fun. Although you may not have as many opportunities to use this approach as a beginner, you may be asked at times to "verse" to artwork or photographs that have been placed on the company's Web site. You'll be directed to a secure Web site with a username and password, which the editor will supply to you.

You will then go directly to the images. Underneath each image will be a box where you'll type your verses. Before sending them to the editor (you will not get a copy of this e-mail once it has been sent), be sure to highlight your work, copy it, and paste it into another document, which you should save on your computer. Then, click on the "submit" or "send" button and your verses will be received by the editor.

There is no question that faxing or e-mailing copy can be much more convenient than typing and mailing 3x5 index cards. It's also far less expensive, assuming you already have an Internet connection and an e-mail account; the cost of sending a regular batch of index cards by mail is now nearly $1.00, plus the cost of the envelopes and cards themselves.

No matter what format you use, however, remember never, *never* to send the only copy of your work. Always back up, print out, or make a duplicate!

And finally, please remember that no matter what method you use, you still need the basics: a consistent, easy-to-understand coding system; an order to your submissions that enables an editor to read your work without skipping back and forth between occasions (or being bored to tears with twenty "Thinking of You" verses); clearly defined Outside/Inside lines, with any visuals described succinctly and accurately; and, of course, your complete personal contact information.

Sooner than you may think, the mechanics behind the submission process will become second nature and take a back seat to what most writers consider "the fun stuff," i.e. being creative and coming up with those memorable, sendable greetings that commemorate, commiserate and congratulate.

Coding

Every greeting card idea that you pitch should have its own unique code. This is your system for tracking ideas, sales, etc. Your editor doesn't care what code you use, but does expect you to provide a code for ease of reference in invoicing.

One idea can have many different code numbers throughout its life; however, an individual code number can only be attributed to *one* idea. Put another way, every code is distinct and refers to only *one* idea, even though one idea can have many codes.

For example, a verse that is sent to five different companies might be coded ABC-001, DEF-015, GHI-059, JKL-074, and

MNO-507—i.e., a different code on each trip out your door. However, the code ABC-001 will *only* refer to that specific verse, and no other. (Remember, you cannot resell an idea—so once you've sold this particular verse, the code under which it is sold is now "out of circulation" forever, though you could then, in theory, recycle the code numbers that were applied to the verse in submissions when it *didn't* sell.)

Though your codes are of your own making, they should be grounded in some form of reality. Choose a method of coding that gives you certain information quickly. There are three main coding methods; choose the one that best suits how you process information:

- **By Company.** This is the method I use. Coding by company means that you choose two or three initials from the company's name that allow you to immediately identify where the idea was sent. A card idea sent to Oatmeal Studios in Vermont, for example, might be coded "OAT" or "OTM," followed by the number. The number should always be chronological, so if you see the code OAT-017, you'll know that this is the 17th verse you've sent to Oatmeal Studios.
- **By Occasion.** Some writers prefer to code by occasion, meaning that all birthday ideas, for example, might be coded "BIR" or "BRT," followed again by the number of the idea. To reflect a specific subset in your code, you might use a code like "BIR DIL" for "Birthday—Daughter-in-Law," or "GW HOS" for "Get Well in Hospital," again followed by the number of the idea. Thus, BIR DIL 018 would be the 18th "Birthday—Daughter-in-Law" idea that you've sent out.
- **By Date.** I use a form of this method when working from a specific assignment. Actually, I combine company and date. For example, if I receive an assignment from Gallant Greetings, I would code my ideas "GAL010210-005," which is the company, a six-digit date, and the number of the idea.

When a company buys one or more ideas, it will refer to them by the code numbers on its purchase order, check stub or correspondence. Be sure to keep a master sheet of what you've submitted, with the correct code number!

What's the Occasion?

What constitutes a solid "pitch"? Your best pitch lies in your choice of material. Don't just pitch ten, or eleven, or twenty ideas for "Birthday—Mother." Remember, you're dealing with companies that use many different ideas for many different occasions, so use what I call the "inverted triangle" method. This method starts with the most commonly published occasions, and works down toward the narrowest (i.e., occasions that will be relevant to the most tightly focused audience).

- For an everyday submission, include
    - Birthday (General, Specific Family Member, Specific Age/Year [e.g., Happy 50th, Happy 6th], Belated, Across the Miles)
    - Friendship (General, Woman-to-Woman)
    - Get Well (General, Hospital, From All in Workplace)
    - Anniversary (To the Couple, To Wife, to Husband, to Parents, to In-Laws)
    - New Baby (General, Son, Daughter)
    - Sympathy (General)
    - Lesser Occasions (Retirement, Coping, Miss You, Death of a Pet)
- For spring seasonals:
    - Valentine's Day (To Sweetheart, to Spouse, to Parents, to Child)
    - Mother's Day (Mom, Grandmother, Mother-in-Law, Like a Mom)
    - Easter (General Wish, Religious, Cute: Bunny, Decorated Eggs, etc.)
    - Father's Day (Dad, Grandfather, Father-in-Law)
    - St. Patrick's Day (General Wish)
    - For winter seasonals:
- Christmas (General, Family, Acquaintance, Across the Miles, Workplace)
    - Hanukkah (General Wish, For Family, Across the Miles)
    - Kwanzaa (General Wish, Family Heritage & Pride, Across the Miles)
    - Halloween (Funny, Risqué, Scary)
    - Thanksgiving (Across the Miles, General Wish, Gratitude)
    - Patriot Day (General Wish, To Someone in Service, In Remembrance)

Always have variety in your ideas, yet proceed in a logical order, beginning with the most popular, widest occasion and funneling down to the narrower occasions. With this method, an editor is not forced to skip back and forth between occasions, but follows a logical sequence. Provide her with order, yet provide an assortment. Your creativity is not only in your writing, but your choice in grouping—and effectively pitching—your greeting card verse ideas.

23

Writing for the Business World

For a writer accustomed to the world of query letters and manuscript submissions, writing for the business world may seem like a huge leap. For many, this was the world we were trying to escape by becoming freelance writers; what could possibly induce us to return?

The answer might be "good pay and lots of opportunities." While business writing is rarely as glamorous as writing for magazines (you probably won't want to pass around copies of your latest sales letter to family and friends), it can offer a steady, reliable income. Often, it can fill the gaps left by more unreliable types of markets—and give you more freedom to write what you really want to write.

Understanding the Market

Business writing is often referred to as "corporate freelancing," but don't be fooled by that term. There is more to the business world than corporations. You can find opportunities with big businesses, small businesses, nonprofit organizations, academic institutions, research centers, and even home-based and "Mom and Pop" companies. For example, I've edited research reports for a nonprofit "think tank," written computer documentation for a government office, developed an internal newsletter for a private corporation, and edited a book manuscript for a lawyer. All of these qualify as "business writing."

Peter Bowerman, author of *The Well-Fed Writer*, divides business customers into two categories: "end users" and "middlemen." End users are those businesses that are the direct users of your product: The company for whom that brochure, report, or press release is written and distributed. "Middlemen" are agencies—such as graphic design firms, advertising agencies, PR firms, and writing brokers—that offer a range of services to end users. You can work directly for end users, or market your services to and through "middlemen" agencies.

CHOOSING THE WORK

Business writing doesn't have to be boring (though some of it undeniably is). While you may want to take any work you can get in the beginning, you'll soon determine what types of projects interest you most. Some options include:

- Press releases
- Brochures and handouts
- Product documentation and literature
- Employee instructional materials
- Sales literature (including direct mail promotions)
- Speeches
- Annual, company, and sales reports
- Research reports
- Web site development and content
- Audio-visual materials (including promotional videos)
- Company newsletters (internal)
- Company newsletters/magazines for external distribution
- Grant/fundraising proposals
- Company biographies and "histories"
- PR material for publication in magazines and newspapers

Each of these categories offers a variety of opportunities for free-lancing. You may offer your services as a writer (developing original material, often through interviews and research), or as a copyeditor or proofreader. If you have other skills, such as graphic design, desktop publishing, photography, Web site development, or translation abilities, you can make yourself even more marketable by offering a "package" deal—such as the ability to write, edit, design, and produce a company brochure from the ground up.

FINDING CLIENTS

If you're accustomed to hunting for traditional writing markets, the prospect of seeking corporate clients may seem intimidating. It doesn't have to be, however. Information on potential clients is everywhere; once you start looking, you'll be amazed at how many sources are available.

Start with the yellow pages. If you'd like to work for a particular type of company (e.g., law firms, nonprofit organizations, public relations agencies), check your telephone directory under that category. Make a list of likely prospects.

Next, review your local paper. The Writers-Editors Network suggests scanning the Sunday "help wanted" pages for ads for writers, editors, copyeditors/writers, advertising, public relations, proofreading, technical writing, and anything else that might relate to the type of services you offer.[1] A company that is seeking to hire a full- or part-time writer might be open to the suggestion of contracting out those same tasks to a freelancer, who can offer the same services as a regular employee without the added costs of benefits, insurance, vacation pay, etc. A scan of the want ads will also give you an idea of the types of businesses in your area.

Your town may have a business-related newspaper; check office-supply stores, and business printers, or ask your local chamber of commerce (COC). Or, check the yellow pages under "publishers: newspaper."

Your local COC is also a good place to look for potential clients. Many will have display racks that offer flyers and cards from local businesses. Ask for a list of businesses that are members of the COC. Find out whether the COC sponsors any sort of networking functions.

Do an online search on the name of your city. The official "city Web page" will usually pop up among the first ten results. Look for links such as "businesses" or "community" to find direct links to many local firms.

Visit online job sites, such as Craigslist. You can usually set search criteria to select companies in your area. You might also consider joining a writing or editing guild or organization that offers job listings to members.

Finally, corporate freelance writer Tina Scott notes that it's a good idea to spread the word that you're looking for this type of work. "I try to tell everyone I know—including people I'm interviewing for articles for the newspaper and for magazine and e-zine articles—that I also do business writing, ghostwriting, Web content, etc. I've got several irons in the fire right now as a result of that."

Making Contact

THE BUSINESS "QUERY"

There are two ways to approach a potential client: by mail, or by phone. Tina Scott uses the first approach: "Believe it or not, I have never yet made a cold call." She recommends that your mail package include a "brief, professional cover letter, a marketing brochure outlining your services, your business card, and possibly a list of your previous and existing clients. If desired, you may wish to include a few clips or samples of your work, depending on the type of projects you're trying to land."

Your cover letter should include a brief overview of the services you would like to offer—proofreading, newsletter development, ad copy, audio-visual scriptwriting, etc. Focus on two or three services at most; even if you can offer more, listing too many services can make you look like a "jack of all trades, master of none." Emphasize any supporting skills you can offer, such as graphics or Web site design.

---

[1] The Writers-Editors Network, *www.writers-editors.com/Writers/Free_Tips/Marketing/marketing.htm*

What if you have no previous business-writing background? One option is to determine how your other writing credentials may "fit" into the business world. "If you've written anything similar before, use that as a sample and emphasize the parallels," says Scott. For example, if you've written magazine articles, you can apply those skills to writing corporate bios, profiles, and similar PR pieces for local and national publications.

Another option is to emphasize your subject background. "If you're familiar with the particular industry and its unique jargon, that may be a plus even if you haven't actually written for that industry before," notes Scott. "It may increase the client's comfort level if you 'speak' their 'language.'" If all else fails, Scott suggests getting samples by "volunteering to write for a local effort you believe in."

The Cold Call
by Peter Bowerman

Peter Bowerman prefers to approach clients by telephone. "If people aren't expecting your correspondence, chances are excellent it'll go into the trash unopened. You really need to establish that connection with someone so that they know what your package is when it shows up on their desk," he notes. Here's his approach to the cold call:

Your Script. Know exactly what you're going to say when your prospect answers the phone. Write it out word-for-word on a 3x5 card and keep it in front of you. Always say it, and never say anything but. In my opinion, this is a critical secret to staying focused during prospecting, while removing one potential source of anxiety from the process. Keep it brief (15 seconds or less), simple, and to the point.

My basic version goes like this: "Good morning, my name is Peter Bowerman, and I'm a freelance writer, making contact with local banks [for instance], to determine whether you have any ongoing or occasional needs for a good freelance writer to help create marketing collateral material: brochures, newsletters, ads, etc. Who might be the best person to talk with?" The word "collateral" is industry standard. Use it and you'll fit in.

Ideally, you'll have a name, but if not, this'll do and it's always enough to get some reaction, which then drives the rest of the call. Hopefully, you know what to say if they respond, "Great! Your timing couldn't be better." It happens.

How To Talk. Slowly, clearly and evenly. When you get someone on the phone, don't just chat away like you normally would.

Adjust to accommodate people who don't know you and weren't expecting your call. Make it easy for them to switch gears.

What Not to Say. Refrain from cuteness like an ultra-cheerful, "How are you today!?" unless they ask you first. Coming from you, it fairly screams "Salesman Butter-Up Line!!" If they ask, it can be like a cool drink of water. Simply reply politely, "Very well, thank you. Yourself?" Resist the urge to jump all over them with dirty paws like a golden retriever greeting its master after a two-week absence.

THE MEETING
Whether your initial approach is by telephone or letter, you will usually need to arrange a face-to-face meeting with potential clients. This is one of the key differences between business writing and magazine freelancing. In the latter case, you never have to leave your desk (or change out of your fuzzy bunny slippers). When dealing with businesses, however, you'll need to present a businesslike image not only on your letterhead, but also in person.

Don't make the mistake of treating a client meeting like a job interview, however. You are a professional, not an applicant, and you should dress and act the part. Display confidence in your skills, and in your ability to handle the type of work you're trying to solicit. Don't convey the impression that you will be humbly grateful for whatever crumbs the client cares to toss your way—at whatever salary they might choose to offer!

Create a portfolio to bring to your meetings. Invest in a good-quality binder (preferably leather) and plastic sheet-protectors. Include copies of any clips or materials that are relevant to the services you're trying to pitch. If you don't have any "real" clips yet, consider dummying up a sample brochure or newsletter to show the type of service you can provide. Include a few writing samples from magazines if that's all you have, but don't expect a client to be impressed; "business" samples will be much more useful.

You'll also want to prepare a package to leave behind. Bowerman recommends the following: "I take a regular manila file folder (or better yet, a colored one to stand out) and on the tab, affix a printed label with four lines: your name, 'Freelance Copywriter' in big letters, your company name, and phone number. Into the folder go a resume/client list, three business cards, and appropriate samples. Now they have your stuff all in one place, in a folder that's ready for easy accommodation into their system. And, you'll instantly impress them with your organizational skills."

Bidding on a Job

Making contact is only half the battle. Once you've convinced a potential client that you can offer a useful service, you must still convince that client to hire you.

Usually, you won't be invited to a meeting unless the client has a specific project in mind and believes that you might be a likely candidate to handle it. The client may be considering several freelancers—or, you may be the only one. Either way, you will still have to convince the client that you can handle the project in a reasonable amount of time, at a reasonable price. This means preparing a "bid."

A bid should present your client with the following information:

- What you will do
- How long it will take
- What you will charge

On the surface, that all sounds simple enough! In practice, however, developing an effective bid can be quite a challenge—especially if you're not accustomed to setting your own rates or estimating how long a project will take. The most common "beginner" mistakes are failing to clearly define the project, underestimating the time factor, and setting rates too low. Here are some ways to avoid those mistakes.

DEFINING THE PROJECT

The first step in submitting a bid (or in determining whether to bid in the first place) is to determine exactly what the project involves. This means finding out what the client wants. If, for example, the client wants a brochure, find out how much information will be provided, how much you'll have to dig up on your own, how it should be presented, and whether you are expected to provide a finished product or just written copy. Determine the goal of the brochure, including its audience and the "image" the company wishes to project.

Similarly, if you're asked to edit a document, review the material first. Find out what level of editing is desired: proofreading for typos, copy-editing for grammar and style, or content editing for readability and accuracy? Does the copy need a lot of work, or is it fairly clean?

Don't settle for statements like, "I want you to make this report sing," or, "I want a brochure that will generate more sales." Don't play mind-reader; ask questions until you're sure that both you and the client have the same idea as to what constitutes "singing copy." If necessary, use your "interview" training as a writer to draw out more information: "What would make *you* want to buy this product?"

Once you've determined what is expected of you, spell that out in your bid, in writing. In other words, tell the client what the client has told you. This is your only protection against unexpected demands, changes, or requests for endless revisions.

DETERMINING A TIMELINE

Once you have defined what a project entails, you'll need to determine when it can be delivered. In many cases, the client will set the deadline, whereupon you'll have to determine whether you can meet it. In other cases, however, the client will ask you how long the project will take. You may be required to offer a completion date, an estimated number of hours, or both, depending on how you will be billing the client (see below).

Think carefully before you answer this question! It is easy, especially in the beginning, to underestimate how many hours a project will require. Be sure to leave room for unexpected delays, difficulties, changes in direction, and people who don't deliver their part of the work (such as instructions, information, or reviews) on schedule. If you have to submit the project for corporate approval at various stages before completion, remember that this can also add significant delays.

Also consider any other projects you have (or hope to have). Can you fit this project into your existing schedule? Will you have to drop or postpone other projects or clients? Will you be able to take on new projects? Again, budget extra time for the unexpected: If problems arise in another project, will they delay this project?

Resist the temptation to underestimate the amount of time required in an effort to "impress" the client with your speed and efficiency. Often, this can backfire: Too short an estimate can convey the impression that your work is hasty and slipshod. Though clients value speed, they also want to know that you are giving their work your full attention.

As a writer, you may be accustomed to thinking only about "writing" time. As a business writer, however, you'll be billing for all the time you spend on that project—including telephone time, meetings, research, errands, revisions, more revisions, etc. Be sure to include all those hours in your estimate.

SETTING FEES

Many writers find this the most difficult aspect of business freelancing. We're used to being told what we can hope to receive—and not a penny more! We're *not* used to determining what our time is worth, or what to charge for a particular task.

One place to check for "going rates" is the current *Writers Market*, which lists fees for a wide range of writing services such as copy-editing, copy writing, speech writing, brochures, and so forth. In some cases, these fees are listed by hour; in others, they're listed by project.

Most of these listings offer a range of fees—usually somewhere between $20 and $100 per hour. Where you should place yourself on that range depends on a variety of factors, including your experience *and* your geographic location. Freelancers based in New York City, Los Angeles, or Silicon Valley will be able to charge higher rates than freelancers doing the exact same work in Kansas or Nebraska.

Don't assume that you have to start at the bottom of the rate scale. Instead, call around and try to determine the "going rate" in your area. Look for editors online (run a search on "business editors" and refine it by including criteria such as your city and/or state), and contact them to determine their rates. (If you're not comfortable admitting that you want to know how much the competition charges, pretend you're a potential customer.)

Another way to determine your fee is to determine how much you need to earn. First, determine how much income you'll need in a year. Then, determine how much of that income will come from other sources, such as freelance articles. Divide the remainder by the number of *billable* hours you believe you'll be able to devote to business freelancing. (Keep in mind that you'll be spending a fair amount of time on non-billable tasks, such as prospecting for clients.) If the resulting number is in line with general and local rates for the type of service you're offering, use it!

Just as you shouldn't underbid on hours, you should also avoid underbidding on price. It's tempting to bid low, on the assumption that a client will prefer to hire the cheapest contractor available. In reality, clients tend to avoid contractors who price themselves too cheaply; just as you might wonder why something is "marked down" to a bargain price, your client may also wonder why you charge so much less than your competitors. Also, avoid the temptation to "underbid" the competition. It's wiser to build good relationships with other business freelancers, who may then refer clients to you when they're overloaded.

Once you've determined your hourly rate, you can calculate how much a project is worth. Your final decision, as you prepare your bid, is whether to price the project on an hourly basis, a flat rate, or some other rate scale. Each has advantages and disadvantages.

If you are concerned that a client will think your hourly rate is too high, a flat rate may work best. The advantage of a flat rate (i.e., "$300 per brochure") is that you get the same fee even if you put in fewer hours than you originally estimated—more profit to you! The disadvantage, obviously, is if the reverse occurs: If the project runs longer than you anticipated, you won't get more money. (You will, however, get an education on how to price future projects, which is worthwhile.) Some clients like flat rates; others don't. Often, this is something you'll need to determine by working with the client.

An hourly rate has the advantage of being more open-ended. If the client wants revisions, makes changes, or adds extra tasks, you just add extra billing hours. The disadvantage of billing by the hour is that some clients have no understanding of how long things really take and may assume that you're "padding" your bill. Again, it may not be possible to determine the best approach until you've actually discussed the project with the client.

A third approach is to bill by some other measure, such as "per page" (which is a good way to charge for editorial services). The way to determine this type of rate is to simply estimate how many pages you can edit in an hour, and then divide your hourly rate by that number! The advantage of this approach is that it is easy to calculate: The client only has to count the number of pages in the project to determine the final cost. Another advantage is that, like the flat rate, you'll get paid the same amount even if the work goes more quickly than expected. The disadvantage, of course, is also the same: If the work goes more slowly than you expected, you get paid less.

The final element you'll need to calculate into the billing portion of your bid is expenses, if any. If you will need to purchase special software to handle the job, or subcontract portions of the job to others (such as artists or designers), be sure to include an estimate of those amounts in your bid. Make sure that these are listed separately from your own billing hours. Try to determine exactly what those costs will be, so that you don't surprise the client at the end of the job with an unexpected list of outside expenses.

GET IT IN WRITING

When you bid on a project, submit your bid in writing. E-mail is often acceptable. Don't be surprised if you have to negotiate before your final bid is accepted. Don't start the project until the client has accepted your bid in writing.

Here's a sample bid letter from British writer Dawn Copeman, who is offering a variety of copy-writing services to a single client. Note that each section of the bid includes detailed specifications of the services that will be covered for that portion of the project, including planning meetings, revisions, and sample designs.

> Dear [Client]:
>
> Thank you for inviting me to your offices yesterday to discuss your copywriting needs.
>
> As per our discussions yesterday I understand that you would like me to come up with a new look for your Web site for your Web site builder to install. You would also like me to write new copy for your Web site, including any additional pages that we decide you need following our meeting to discuss and approve a Web design. Finally, you need content for a new, 16-page A4-sized glossy brochure.
>
> Here is my bid for providing these copywriting services.
>
> Web Site Design Advice
>
> I will provide you with five different suggestions and mock layouts of your Web site within two weeks of your go-ahead. My fee for this service will be $400 to include all conceptualization, research and one planning meeting.
>
> Web Content Writing
>
> My fee for writing the content of the Web site will be $1400. This will include two revisions and two planning

meetings. The copy will be delivered to you within one week of approval of final Web design and agreement of page content. Following our first planning meeting, I shall return any redrafts to you within 48 hours, and following our second meeting, the final copy shall be with you within 24 hours.

Brochure Content

To write copy for a new 16-page, A4-sized brochure, my fee will be $500. This is to cover an initial planning meeting with you at which we shall discuss photos to be used and the focus of the brochure, all conceptualization, research, and two sets of revisions. As I understand it, you wish to have the new Web site up and running before commencing work on the brochure.

Before commencing on the Web design conceptualizing and the Web content writing, I would require half my fee to be paid in advance, with the remainder to be paid within 30 days of delivery of final approved copy and design. Before commencing work on the brochure I would likewise require half my fee to be paid in advance with the remainder within 30 days of delivery of final approved copy.

If these terms are acceptable to you, please sign and date the agreement below and keep a copy for yourself, returning a copy to me via post or e-mail.

I look forward to working with you,

Sincerely,
Dawn Copeman

I have read and agree to the above terms and payment conditions.

Name:_____

Print Name: _____

Date: _____

And here's a sample "letter of agreement" to provide a newsletter for a business Web site, also from Dawn Copeman:

Letter of Agreement

Dear

Following our recent e-mail conversations, I have agreed to write and edit the newsletter for your site. I will produce one 400 to 500 word article per month on the topic you provide to me. In addition to this I will format and edit the newsletter, inserting links and advertiser promotions and ensuring that all content is grammatically correct and reads well.

My fee for this service is \$XX per newsletter, with half the amount to be paid in advance and the remaining half within 15 days of completion of the project. This fee includes one rewrite per newsletter. Payment is to be made via PayPal to my e-mail address.

I hereby confirm that you will own all rights to the articles and the newsletters as this is a work-for-hire agreement.

We have both agreed that this agreement is a temporary one valid only for the next three issues of the newsletter. We will both review the situation after delivery of January's newsletter.

I will provide you with the first article by Friday November 10th 200-, with the second article by December 5th and the third article by January 5th.

If this agreement is acceptable to you, please sign below, keep a copy for yourself and return this copy to me. (I will accept confirmation via e-mail stating you understand and agree to these terms.)

I look forward to working with you,

Sincerely,

Dawn Copeman

Understood and Agreed_____

Date: _____

You also need to determine exactly when and how you will get paid. If you're undertaking a large job (e.g., worth more than $500 or $1000), you may wish to ask for payment in installments. Some writers ask for payment in thirds: one third when the bid is accepted or the contract is signed, one third halfway through the project, and one third on completion. Others ask for half down and half at the end. If you have to buy materials or software to complete the project, ask for payment for those items in advance. If you need to subcontract part of the work, you'll usually ask for reimbursement of those expenses after the work has been completed.

Business clients expect to be invoiced. Accounting departments are more likely to respect a professional-looking invoice; it's worth going to the office supply store and buying a pack of preprinted forms. Find out whether you need to provide a purchase order number to get paid.

FOLLOW UP!

Once you've completed a job, follow up! Find out whether the work was considered satisfactory, and remind the client that you would welcome other projects. Ask the client to refer you to other companies, and ask whether the client is willing to be used as a referral when you contact other prospects.

A word of warning, however: Not every corporate client is easy to work with. A bad customer can waste your time—and in the business of corporate freelancing, time is money. Don't spend time dealing with clients who don't know what they want and are never satisfied with what you give them. Don't let such clients deter you; just finish the job and move on. There are lots of other prospects available; use your newly gained clips and go after them!

Finding Business Clients Worldwide
by Dawn Copeman

I live in a small town in England, a town that doesn't generate much work for copywriters, yet I still work as a copywriter. How? I get work outside my local area.

I have written a monthly customer newsletter for a gift company in the United States, and written press releases for American cake decorations, for balsamic vinegar from Italy, and for countless clients based in London. And I got all this work simply by having a Web presence.

My Web site works for me twenty-four hours a day, seven days a week. Through it I gained the job of writing and editing the monthly newsletter for the gift company in the U.S.

It also came in handy when I responded to a call for freelance writers from a newly established food public relations agency. The manager could see samples of my writing immediately, and as a result I got plenty of freelance copywriting work for a wide variety of companies. These are clients I have never met in person and speak to only occasionally by phone; almost all our contact is via e-mail. In fact, in all the time I've been copywriting, I've only done one job locally! Most of my work has been via the Internet and I expect it to continue to be so.

As a first step to find clients outside your local area, you need to set up a Web site. You can get hosting deals from as little as $20 a year. Ensure that your site shows you and your copywriting skills to your advantage. Double-check, no, triple-check to ensure it reads well and contains no spelling or grammatical errors. Use it to state who you are, any relevant experience you have and what services you offer. Also use it to showcase your copywriting skills. Use any real samples you have, or make up samples of press releases, brochures and letters. A better option if you have no samples is to offer to do some copywriting on a no-fee basis for a local charity, church, or nonprofit organization. Then at least you have some real-life examples to show potential clients.

Then you need to join any online writers' organizations you can and state in your online portfolio that you are a copywriter and put in a link to your site. Once you've done this, e-mail any public relations agencies that you find online and see if they require any extra freelance help. Also keep an eye out on job boards for copywriters. Remember, unless the client specifically demands a local writer, you don't need to be in the same state or even the same country.

Finally, consider joining in the Social Networking revolution. Many of my fellow copywriters are now getting a high proportion of their work via sites such as LinkedIn, Plaxo, Bixnik, Facebook, and MySpace. Some are better for finding work than others, with LinkedIn and Plaxo being the top runners at the moment. Whichever social network you decide to join, ensure you update your profile regularly and that you check your profile at least daily for any messages from potential clients. If you are tempted to play games on Facebook, then set up a different account for your copywriting work. Remember, you are participating in the networks to gain work, so you must appear professional at all times.

Even if your clients live halfway around the world and will never see you!

24

Grants for Writers

by Kelleen Zubick and Maryo Ewell

Many opportunities are available for writers of fiction, poetry, drama, journalism, nonfiction, children's book, and screenwriting that offer cash stipends of $500 or more. These opportunities generally fall into two (imprecise) categories: *Awards* and *grants*.

- **Awards** are cash prizes given to writers in recognition of outstanding promise or accomplishment. Fellowships and scholarships for writers should also be considered awards, because these are also often cash stipends given in recognition of talent, as is the case with fellowships awarded by the National Endowment for the Arts. (In cases like this, "fellowship" is often used interchangeably with "award.") However, sometimes this type of award is restricted. For example, most fellowships and scholarships awarded by academic institutions and artists colonies are meant to recognize talent *and* to be used for a specific purpose, such as a course of study or residency expenses at a particular colony.
- **Grants** differ from awards in that they are usually funds given to writers to accomplish a particular project described in a proposal. Many arts agencies and organizations offer grant funding categories that are open to individual writers. Sometimes individual writers are funded directly, but more often they are funded as part of a team proposal in which an organizational partner is the actual applicant. Limited opportunities exist for "emergency grants," which are short-term funds available to writers experiencing hardship, and which require a statement of need rather than a proposal.

Grants and awards are usually offered by publishers, foundations, arts organizations, and academic institutions. They provide an invaluable source of both income and recognition for writers. Nearly all have an application process involving the submission of an application and an excellent manuscript. This chapter will emphasize how to develop a successful application.

Resources

The best sources to consult for information on awards and grants to writers are the annual editions of the PEN American Center's *Grants and Awards*, the F&W Publications' directories such as *Poet's Market*, *Writer's Market*, and *Children's Writer's Market*, and the Theater Communications Group's *Dramatists Sourcebook*. Monthly or bimonthly publications such as *Poets and Writers Magazine*, *The Writer*, *The Writer's Chronicle* (published by the Association of Writers and Writing Programs), and *Writers Digest* are good professional resources, containing updated information on opportunities for writers as well as application deadlines. Other good resources are the publications of writers' associations such as The American Society of Journalists and Authors, The Modern Language Association, and the Editorial Freelancers Association.

State arts councils or commissions, which can be found in every state or territory, usually sponsor grants, fellowships, or residencies for writers residing within their states. These state agencies can also provide writers with leads for additional resources, both locally and nationally.

Types of Support

AWARDS

Awards are generally made to writers in recognition of outstanding promise or accomplishment. Many of the awards for accomplishment, such as the Heinz Awards or the American Academy of Arts and Letters Awards, are determined by internal nomination only. However, publishers often hold contests and give awards as a means of acquiring new material, and organizations often give awards as a means of raising the visibility of particular groups of writers or genres or the mission of the organization.

For emerging writers, first-book awards such as those offered by Bantam Doubleday Dell (Books for Young Readers), the National Poetry Series, or the Academy of American Poets, provide new talent with remuneration, publication, distribution, and lots of visibility. Even magazine contests like the River City Writing Awards in Fiction or the *Highlights for Children* Fiction Contest offer a chance to get published with more visibility and remuneration than sending a query and work directly to an editor at the same publications.[1]

---

[1] Many such contests can be found in Moira Allen's *Writing to Win: The Colossal Guide to Writing Contests*, updated annually and available from Amazon.com.

FELLOWSHIPS

Fellowships are often just another label for awards of recognition. The National Endowment for the Arts and many state arts councils/commissions award individual fellowships in recognition of exceptional talent. These awards include cash amounts to be used for general career advancement. Other significant recognition fellowships include Princeton University's Alfred Hodder Fellowship, which is given to those (usually) from outside academia and in early stages of their careers for independent work in the humanities, and the Pope Foundation's Journalism Awards, an open-ended working fellowship given to mid-career investigative journalists or social commentators. (For an extensive listing of journalism scholarships and fellowships, visit the Dow Jones Newspaper Fund at *www.newspaperfund.org*, click on "Programs," then on "Scholarships.")

Some fellowships and/or scholarships are restricted in terms of use, but they can still be wonderful opportunities for writers, furthering both careers and finances. For writers of fiction, nonfiction, poetry, and play/screenwriting, many residency opportunities offer space and a literary community within which to create. In addition to room and board, a small number of residency fellowships also include modest living stipends.

For writers who have the ability to live away from home "in residence" from two weeks to two years, these are wonderful opportunities to build relationships with other writers and to produce work in a supportive environment. Some fellowships, such as those to colonies such as Yaddo or the Fine Arts Work Center in Provincetown, make no other demands on the writer's time. Others, like the Jerome Playwright-in-Residence at the Playwrights' Center in Minneapolis or the Wallace Stegner Fellowships at Stanford University, require fellows to participate in some institutional activity.

Other examples of restricted awards are scholarships offered by many institutions to writers to produce works of particular institutional foci. For example, the Schomburg Center for Research in Black Culture offers stipends of up to $30,000 for scholars studying black history and culture, and the American Institute of Physics gives Writing Awards in Physics and Astronomy to writing (including journalism and children's) that improves public understanding of physics and astronomy.

GRANTS

Project grants are different from fellowships/awards in that they require a proposal for work to be completed in the future (often within a specific time period), while awards are based on the perceived excellence of past work. Here again, it is important to ask the staff for clarification. Generally, by "project grant," an agency means "community-oriented project," which lets you know that you need to be collaborating with others, putting your literary skills to work in the service of some community end. (While many agencies do offer grants to individuals, in most cases grants are offered to teams that have an organizational sponsor as the actual applicant.)

For example, a community project might involve offering writing workshops for underserved kids in a particular housing project. In this case, you would want to write a proposal that demonstrates that you and the housing authority people have been collaborating to make this happen—that this isn't just a brainstorm of yours that doesn't already have the approval of the housing authority. Or, a community project might involve a series of readings commemorating special occasions, or a first-ever literary series within an ongoing performing arts festival.

Since the term "grant" typically refers to funds received for an event that you have projected for the future, your idea cannot be judged simply on the merit of work you have already done. Instead, it will be judged on the degree of careful, detailed planning evident in your proposal. What, precisely, will happen, and when? Who will be involved in each phase, as artists, participants, and audience members? What will be the impact on the artists, the participants, and the audience, and how will you know if that impact has happened? How, in short, will you evaluate the project? What is your project timeline for the grant period? Who will be your partners, and how will each partner be involved? It's important to demonstrate up-front that these partners are working with you.

Many grants require "matching funds," meaning that for every dollar you hope to receive, you must raise a certain number of dollars elsewhere. It is important to be specific about your sources of matching funds. Even if you don't have them in hand yet, you can show that you have done your homework by saying that you will receive "$500 from the XYZ trust, to be applied for on December 15" or income from "400 chapbooks to be sold at $5" or "freewill donations averaging $100 per reading." Never say just that your funds will come from unspecified "local businesses" or "individual donors," because reviewers will dismiss this as wishful thinking. Find out if the match needs to be cash, or if it can include donated ("in-kind") goods and services.

Most arts agencies that fund projects in which writers are involved will want to see work samples as described below (the same kind of work samples you'll need to prepare for fellowship applications). They will also want to see evidence of collaboration with your community partners and evidence of community need. Ask the staff of the funding organization what kind of support materials are most appropriate.

EMERGENCY FUNDS

These are the rarest of grants for writers, but foundations do exist that provide *professional* writers with short-term grants to help in situations of hardship caused by medical conditions, disability, advanced age, or professional crisis. Among those organizations accepting applications for this type of assistance are the American Society of Journalists, the Authors Charitable Trust, and The Actors Fund of America.

A WORD ABOUT ENTRY FEES

Many awards, including contests and fellowships, require entry fees. This is becoming standard practice for organizations trying to cover hefty reading fees and in-house processing costs. At $15 to $25, these entry fees can add up, so it is important to research the organizations giving the awards and be familiar with their past winners' work. Paying entry fees is nothing to be worried about once:

1. You are sure you've found an appropriate market for your work—i.e., you have a reasonable chance at receiving the award, and

2. The potential benefits (significant prize money, publication by a well-known press, or honor conferred by a venerable institution) exceed the cost.

Note that the presence or absence of an entry fee is *not* an indication of an awarding agency's credibility or merit. It is important to research any organization thoroughly before applying for an award or fellowship.

Crafting Successful Applications

Not all grants and awards applications require the same materials. However, the requirements are often similar, and eventually you'll need some basic application materials on hand so that when a sudden opportunity arises that's just right for you, your application materials are ready. These include a writing sample, a curriculum vitae (CV), and letters of recommendation/support. These core materials take time to develop, and consequently tend to be of better quality when prepared well in advance.

WORK SAMPLES

Regardless of the kind of award or grant for which you are applying, having an excellent work sample of between ten and thirty pages will be crucial to your success. But how do you know when your work sample is excellent? If your work is being published regularly in standard journals and magazines, chances are your writing is consistently well received. If you're not seeking publication in journals and magazines, start doing so, because in addition to giving you feedback on the "readability" of your work, this will also help you develop a track record as a writer that you can cite in your CV. Since few editors have the time or inclination to comment on submissions, and those that do don't necessarily do so *quickly*, this is obviously something that you'll need to begin well in advance. Getting feedback from publication is an important but long-term strategy for developing a critical sense of your work.

In the short-term, joining a writers group can be a way of receiving immediate reaction to new work. Just make sure that the members of your group can offer constructive criticism in addition to being supportive and nurturing. If your group is not doing this for you, or if your group members are not seasoned writers, it may be time to attend a writer's conference or festival that offers manuscript review by established writers, agents, or editors.

By following these strategies for determining what others perceive as good examples of your work, you should be able to identify at least three to five work samples for your application file. Pick and choose from these on the basis of the guidelines of specific applications. Having published as well as unpublished strong work (for publication awards) is also important.

When your work samples are excerpts of longer pieces, try to include sections in which characters are introduced (as in novel excerpts) or that include the thesis of the piece (for nonfiction). Sections of longer work that include a limited number of characters or ideas are often more successful, because readers don't have to rely on context to follow the narrative. Including one brief paragraph of context for the reader—a precis—with the work sample or manuscript is also acceptable and helpful for panelists evaluating your application.

THE WRITER'S CURRICULUM VITAE

For both grants and awards, but especially for fellowship and scholarship applications, conveying your professionalism and commitment as a writer is critical to your success. Every writer's CV should have a section for publications; a section for literary activities, including readings and public appearances, coursework or workshops attended or given, and teaching or volunteer activities; and a section listing honors. Beyond your talent as a writer, the people evaluating your applications are often trying to discern the appropriateness and the benefit of an award to a writer. If you're applying for a fellowship appropriate to someone in mid-career, your CV should reflect five to ten years of steady publishing and literary activity. If you're an emerging writer, the prominence of your honors or publication and presentation venues won't be as important, but you'll still be expected to demonstrate that you're actively seeking to participate in your literary community. If you're just starting out, attend local readings and writing workshops, share your work and knowledge with the organizers, and let them know you'd like to participate. There should also be room on your CV for professional experience and education information, but these should generally be included at the end of the CV rather than at the beginning.

LETTERS OF RECOMMENDATION AND/OR SUPPORT

Hopefully you will have met a few other writers or editors (a teacher at the very least!) who've had great things to say about your work. Stay in touch with these people, because sooner or later you'll need letters of recommendation for some of your applications. When that time comes, and as far ahead of the application deadline as possible, ask your recommender for a letter. Be sure to explain what you're applying for and why you're asking for his or her recommendation. Go ahead and remind that person what he or she found so attractive about your work: the more specific the praise, the more convincing the letter.

Similarly, if you're writing a project proposal for a grant, you might benefit from having three to five potential "letters of support" sources in mind. Ideal sources are prominent individuals and key organizations relevant to your project who can write a letter of support for your proposal that demonstrates knowledge of and enthusiasm for your project. For grant proposals where such testimonies are permitted, letters of support can move the judges' perception of a project from possibility to actuality—a subtle but powerful edge in the competitive grants arena. Just be sure to give your sources as much advance notice as possible (once you've established that including support letters with your proposal is permissible). You might also want to share a rough draft of your proposal with the source, and then look over the letter to make sure there are no errors or inconsistencies with your proposal *before* the letter gets signed.

Preparing Application-Specific Materials

MAKE SURE GUIDELINES ARE CURRENT

After obtaining general information on an award or grant and deciding that your work is a good match for the opportunity, contact the granting organization for current guidelines. Send a brief note of request along with a SASE. Current guidelines may also be available on organizational Web sites, but always check posting dates to be sure you're not looking at last year's forms. Call or send an e-mail with any questions or concerns about the application, and always use an organization's official application form, if required.

Make several copies of the form and complete a practice copy to make sure your information can be concisely and clearly presented. When you're satisfied with your answers, type them neatly onto the original. The staff— especially in public agencies—is responsible for assisting you to the best of its ability; don't be shy about asking questions on anything you want clarified.

Here are a few questions that are worth asking, for they will guide you in providing information:

- What is the ideal formatting? Very often, the guidelines won't give you details like spacing, margins, minimum type size or binding, so don't hesitate to ask.
- Who will be reviewing the proposals (e.g., staff, publishers, fellow writers etc.)?
- What types of support materials would be helpful to include with the application?
- Can you expect feedback on your work samples?
- How many submissions are anticipated by the organization, and how many awards will be made?

Once you've determined exactly what is required for a particular application, you're ready to write any application-specific materials necessary, such as the creative purpose statement, the needs statement, or the grant proposal. The key to all of these materials is keeping them brief, accurate, specific, and relevant to the particular opportunity for which you are applying. Add these to your impressive core materials and your impeccable application forms, and you've got a winning combination for success in the grants and awards arena.

THE CREATIVE PURPOSE STATEMENT

Creative Purpose Statements or Artist Statements are often required for fellowship and scholarship award applications. Outstanding creative purpose statements are concise and specific statements focused on the anticipated outcomes for a writer receiving a particular grant. In less than two pages, try and capture your development as a writer to date. Briefly include your achievements and then describe the benefits that would be afforded to you as writer-in-development as a result of receiving the award for which you are applying.

For example, an emerging fiction writer who has published three stories and has six others finished and who is applying for a fellowship for a residency at the Atlantic Center for the Arts, could emphasize the benefit of working closely with a "master" fiction writer. (The Atlantic Center for the Arts has a mentoring program that pairs emerging and established writers.) The applicant might propose that working with a "master" writer would allow him/her to learn how to develop and organize a book of short stories, and include his/her vision for what that book might be. The applicant could also compare and contrast his/her work with the "master" writer's and offer an explanation as to how both writers would benefit from working together. Lastly, the applicant, knowing from the guidelines that financial need should be established along with artistic merit, could explain his/her specific financial obligations or limited annual income that prevents him/her from taking advantage of the residency opportunity to advance his/her development as a writer without the assistance of a fellowship.

STATEMENT OF NEED

Foundations and associations providing emergency funds for writers in need will scan an applicant's statement of need for two main qualities: evidence that the applicant is a professional writer, and evidence that the applicant is indeed experiencing hardship for which he/she has no other recourse. To establish yourself as a professional writer, you should describe the span of your career, and back this description up with your CV. You may even want to include a tax return on which "writer" or "author" is listed for occupation. You want to make a clear connection between writing and your livelihood in order to motivate the reviewer to read on about your case.

The best case for hardship is built with a specific detailing of events in chronological order, ending with your current circumstance and documented need. Do you have medical bills that exceed your ability to pay for them? Including a tax return, annual budget, and copies of the bills and a documented medical diagnosis will establish this case.

TIPS FOR GRANT PROPOSALS

The acronym "PLEASE" is an organizing principle and "secret recipe" for a successful grant proposal:

P is for Passion—don't be afraid to let it show

We're often asked about using a professional grant writer, and we recommend against it. No one can tell your story with the same passion that you can, and in your own words. Use a forceful tone (you *know* you're going to do that project, right?)

L is for Literally Follow Every Direction

One state arts agency estimates that over a third of the proposals they receive don't follow the guidelines. Common mistakes include: exceeding the page limit, using a typeface that's too small, or submitting one big essay instead of answers to each question. There's a reason for every requirement. If you don't follow all instructions to the letter, it can really hurt you. Take the example of one grant writer who called the National Endowment for the Arts to see whether "no more than ten pages" meant ten single-sided or double-sided pages—and was glad she did. Half of her proposal would have been thrown out.

E is for Easy to Understand

What, exactly, will you spend the money on? It's amazing how many proposals go on for many pages and never say, exactly, what's going to happen or how the money will be used. Find someone on your team who can write a good freshman composition. This includes a topic sentence, active verbs, and paragraphs that relate. Use action verbs and the active voice. Make sure your proposal tells your story in a way that anyone will understand it, including someone who doesn't know you at all. There's no need to write a proposal that resembles a government document—the reviewers will probably be writers like you.

A is for Accuracy in All, from Assertions to Arithmetic

Make sure that your assertions of what will happen and how many people will be involved are grounded in reality—and that your budget figures are, too. Make sure that your claims relate to your budget. For instance, if you say that your total attendance will be 5,000, and your organization sells tickets to events, then income should reflect 5,000 times a reasonable ticket price. The reviewers are likely to know what is realistic. Budget-padding is too easy to spot. By the same token, don't undervalue your work, hoping that if it's cheap it will be funded.

S is for Show Me with Specifics and Examples

We're talking about arts proposals that will probably be reviewed by artists. Assuming that the guidelines allow you to provide sample work, it's more powerful to give people sounds rather than a description of sounds. An image of a painter's personal work can help the reviewers imagine the mural she would create with kids. Many a grant writing error has been forgiven if the art is inspired.

Consider these examples: Instead of this...

Music of great quality and diversity will be performed for underserved audiences in locations convenient for them.

...try saying it this way:

A chamber group from the Big Apple Symphony will perform short selections from contemporary composers on Sunday afternoons for 300 senior citizens gathered in the dining room of their nursing home. (See Attachments 1 and 2 for a tape of the chamber group and three possible programs).

The second version provides a mental picture that a reviewer can see, and music that a reviewer can hear.

E is for Easy to Read—margins, typeface and white space

Think about it. The reviewers may be reading fifty proposals, skimming them again at the last minute to refresh their memories. The agency may limit each review to a very few minutes. So make it easy for the reviewers—use white space, bullets, a clear organizational scheme, a typeface that's large and clean, good margins, and underline key points.

When to Give Up

As long as you find satisfaction in your work, the answer is *never*. Ultimately, grants and awards are only a means to spur and sustain writers, and not a measure of the value of a writer's work. Competition for grants and awards is fierce, and the subjective nature of evaluating "excellence," "talent," and "merit" means that an application that "fails" with one jury may find success with the next. Walt Whitman published his own work (and wrote his own favorable reviews) for lack of patronage. Recognition is not a requirement for excellent work.

25

A Final Word: Capitalizing on Success

Much of this book has focused on how to prepare a pitch or proposal in such a way as to minimize your chances of rejection. But what happens when you succeed? What comes next?

Don't let success take you by surprise. While it's unwise to "count your chickens before they're hatched"—or spend your advance before your proposal has been accepted—you should have some ideas about what you will do when you get that letter you've been hoping for. Here are some tips on what to do after the celebration:

- **Read the acceptance letter carefully**. Make sure you understand what is expected of you. Has an editor made any changes to your proposal? Are you being asked to make changes to your work or idea? If so, are those changes acceptable?

- **Review any terms that have been offered with care**. Don't be so overcome with joy at the thought of getting published that you throw caution to the winds. Book contracts, in particular, tend to be written in dense legalese (though I have also seen four-page magazine contracts). If you have any doubts about the rights you're being asked to grant, or the compensation you will receive, have your contract reviewed by a qualified contract or copyright lawyer.

- **Make sure you can provide what you have promised** (or what is being asked of you) by the specified deadline. If you've promised to hand in a complete novel in one month, and you really *haven't* finished the final draft, it's time to get writing.

- **Make sure that you deliver exactly what the editor, publisher, or agent expects.** Don't do a "bait and switch." Fulfill your end of the agreement to the letter, and then some.

- **If you have any doubts about anything, call the editor or agent for clarification**. Get all important terms and agreements in writing.

Finally, perhaps the most important step of all is to *follow up!* You will never be as "hot" as you are right now. Follow up that magazine query with another query. Follow up your book proposal with another idea. Go back to that editor or agent *now,* while s/he remembers you and is impressed with your work. Keep the queries and proposals flowing. Establish yourself as a regular, reliable, high-quality contributor. If you're writing for a business client, go back for more business, or ask for referrals.

That's the way to keep work—and checks—flowing across your desk. By following up immediately on a positive response, you'll not only land more assignments, but you're also likely to find that, before too long, editors start calling *you* with ideas. And then you'll be in the ideal position to decide whether to accept—or to write a rejection letter of your own!

Contributor Bios

Peter Bowerman (quoted in chapter 23) is a veteran commercial freelancer and business coach, and the author of the award-winning self-published Well-Fed Writer titles, the how-to "standards" on lucrative commercial freelancing writing for businesses (*www.wellfedwriter.com*). He chronicled his self-publishing success (52,000 copies of his first two books in print and a full-time living for seven-plus years) in the award-winning 2007 release, *The Well-Fed Self-Publisher: How to Turn One Book into a Full-Time Living* (*www.wellfedsp.com*).

Denene Brox ("Approaching Trade Magazines with Letters of Introduction") is a professional freelance writer and author of the e-book, *The Weekend Writer: Launch Your Freelance Writing Career (Part-Time)*. Her work has appeared in more than twenty publications and Web sites including *Heart & Soul, Minority Nurse, Community Banker, MyBusiness, QSR*, and Yahoo! HotJobs. Visit her online at *www.WeekendWriter.net*

Robin Catesby ("Approaching an Agent at a Conference," sidebar, chapter 17) is a short-story writer, novelist, and author of ten plays, including three highly successful children's musicals. She is a member of Willamette Writers and assists in the agent/editor pitch area during their annual conference.

Amy Chavez ("Newspaper Queries," "How to become a Syndicated Columnist") writes a humor column for *The Japan Times*. Her work has appeared in humor magazines, inflight magazines, anthologies, and newspapers around the world. She is the author of *Guidebook to Japan: What the Other Guidebooks Won't Tell You*. Visit her Web site at *www.amychavez.com*, where you can subscribe to her weekly *Japan Times* column.

Dawn Copeman ("Finding Business Clients Worldwide," sidebar, chapter 23) is a freelance and commercial writer who has published more than 100 articles on travel, history, cookery, health, and writing. As a copywriter Dawn has written press releases, Web content, brochures, newsletters, company reports, articles for trade journals and newspapers and has devised recipes for clients to use in press releases. She is the editor of the Newbie

Writers Web site (*www.newbiewriters.com*) and also edits the Writing World newsletter (*www.writing-world.com/newsletter/index.shtml*).

Maryo Ewell ("Grants for Writers") is the Community Arts and Grants Consultant for the Colorado Council on the Arts; she has been at the CCA since 1982. Prior to that, she worked for the Illinois Arts Council and for two community arts councils in Connecticut. In 1995, she was awarded the Selina Roberts Ottum Award by Americans for the Arts, acknowledging leadership in the community arts field.

Debbie Farmer ("How I Became a Syndicated Columnist," sidebar, chapter 8) is a contributor to *Chicken Soup for the Soul*. Her family humor essays have been published in over 500 publications throughout the United States, Canada, and Australia. Her award-winning weekly family humor column "Family Daze" has been internationally syndicated to newspapers, magazines and newsletters and Web sites.

Lynn Flewelling ("The Fiction Query Letter," sidebar, chapter 15) is the author of the internationally acclaimed Nightrunner Series and the Tamír Triad. She also writes the occasional short story, works as a freelance editor, and serves as adjunct faculty at the University of Redlands, Redlands, California. For more information, visit her Web site at *www.sff.net/people/Lynn.Flewelling*.

Huw Francis ("Pitching to International Book Publishers") has worked in the United Kingdom, Hong Kong, Turkey, and France as an engineer, communications consultant, international business consultant, and business manager, and also as a freelance writer and author. His work has been published in many countries and also translated into French, Spanish and Korean. He is the co-author of *Live and Work Abroad: A Guide for Modern Nomads* and author of *Live and Work in Turkey*.

Tara K. Harper ("Writing the Agent Query," sidebar, chapter 16) is the author of nine science-fiction novels, including the best-selling and critically acclaimed Wolfwalker series and Cat Scratch series, as well as other stories. Her work is available internationally in a variety of languages and as books on tape. Two of her novels, *Cat Scratch Fever* and *Wolf's Bane*, were nominated for the Oregon Book Awards. She has also received numerous awards for science writing, has been Guest of Honor at several conventions, and was nominated in 1999 to a University of Oregon inaugural Hall of Achievement. Visit her Web site at *www.tarakharper.com*.

Sharon Ihle ("Sample Novel Synopsis," chapter 19) is a best-selling and award-winning of author of western historical romances, including *Maggie's Wish, The Marrying Kind, The Bride Wore Spurs*, and *Untamed*.

Sue Fagalde Lick ("Pitching to Agents at a Writing Conference") is the author of *Freelancing for Newspapers*, published by Quill Driver Books. In addition to many years as a staff reporter and editor, she has published countless freelance articles and three books on Portuguese Americans, including *Stories Grandma Never Told.* Her articles, short stories and poetry have appeared in many magazines and newspapers, as well as two Cup of Comfort anthologies. She lives with her dog Annie on the Oregon Coast. Visit her Web site at *www.suelick.com.*

Sandra Miller–Louden has written greeting cards since 1986. In addition to teaching online and speaking at conferences, Sandra has been interviewed in various venues, including NBC-TV, the BBC, Voice of America, *National Examiner, Christian Science Monitor, 801* (Columbia School of Journalism), *Washington Post,* and *The Philadelphia Inquirer,* as well as making the cover of Parade Magazine. Her book on greeting card writing, *Write Well & Sell: Greeting Cards,* has become a well-known, coveted classic and Sandra herself is known for being personally accessible for aspiring writers in this unique genre. Visit her Web site, *www.greetingcardwriting.com,* for more information.

Tina L. Scott (formerly Miller; quoted in chapter 24) has been a freelance writer, editor, corporate writer, instructor and motivational speaker since 1999. In addition, she is a professional photographer and operates her own studio in Merrill, Wisconsin (*www.photographybytina.com/*).

Amy D. Shojai, CABC (quoted in chapter 10) is a nationally known authority on pets, radio host, and author of 23 nonfiction books and more than 1,000 articles and columns. Amy is a certified animal behavior consultant, a founder/past president of Cat Writers' Association, Inc., past president of Oklahoma Writers Federation, Inc., and frequently answers questions about pets—and about writing—during Animal Planet television appearances, in-person lectures, and "virtual" chats. She can be reached via her Web site at *www.shojai.com.*

Diana Lynn Tibert ("A Successful Proposal," sidebar, chapter 8) is a writer and professional photographer based in mainland Nova Scotia, Canada. She specializes in genealogy, gardening, and history. Her self-syndicated genealogy column, "Roots to the Past," appears in ten newspapers in Atlantic Canada. She is found on the Web at *www.thefamilyattic.info/Tibert.html.*

Rebecca Vinyard ("The Novel Synopsis," "Anatomy of a Synopsis"), a former journalism major and e-zine editor, is published in poetry, fiction, and nonfiction. Her novels include *Diva,* a historical romance, and *Deadly Light,* a romantic suspense. She is the author of *The Romance Writer's Handbook: How to Write Romantic Fiction and Get It Published.* Ms. Vinyard is a member of the Dallas chapter of the Romance Writers of America.

Kelleen Zubick ("Grants for Writers") is principal consultant of Outcome Solutions, a management support organization based in Colorado. Previously she has worked as Director of Consulting for the Community Resource Center, Denver, and was Associate Director of the Colorado Council on the Arts. Kelleen was awarded a creative residency at the Anderson Center for Interdisciplinary Studies in 2009, and her recent poetry has appeared or is forthcoming in *Agni Online, Barrow Street, Dogwood,* and the *Great River Review.*

Appendix

Additional Resources

Links to a wide range of online resources relating to the topics discussed in the preceding chapters can be found at the author's Web site, Writing-World.com (*www.writing-world.com/links/index.shtml*). This site offers links to writers' guidelines, publications for writers, column and syndication services, directories of book and magazine publishers, market guides, and much more. It is updated annually.

Index

Books from Allworth Press

Allworth Press is an imprint of Allworth Communications, Inc. Selected titles are listed below.

Starting Your Career as a Freelance Writer, Second Edition
by Moira Anderson Allen (6 × 9, 304 pages, paperback, $24.95)

The Author's Toolkit: A Step-by-Step Guide to Writing and Publishing Your Own Book, Third Edition
by Mary Embree (5 ½ × 8 ½, 224 pages, paperback, $19.95)

The Birds and the Bees of Words: A Guide to the Most Common Errors in Usage, Spelling, and Grammar
by Mary Embree (5 ½ × 8 ½, 208 pages, paperback, $14.95)

Marketing Strategies for Writers
by Michael Sedge (6 × 9, 224 pages, paperback, $24.95)

Business and Legal Forms for Authors and Self-Publishers, Third Edition
by Tad Crawford (8 3/8 × 10 7/8, 304 pages, paperback, $29.95)

The Writer's Legal Guide: An Authors Guild Desk Reference
by Tad Crawford and Kay Murray (6 × 9, 320 pages, paperback, $19.95)

The Complete Guide to Book Marketing, Revised Edition
by David Cole (6 × 9, 256 pages, paperback, $19.95)

The Complete Guide to Book Publicity, Second Edition
by Jodee Blanco (6 × 9, 304 pages, paperback, $19.95)

Writing the Great American Romance Novel
by Catherine Lanigan (6 × 9, 224 pages, paperback, $19.95)

Making Crime Pay: An Author's Guide to Criminal Law, Evidence, and Procedure
by Andrea Campbell (6 × 9, 320 pages, paperback, $27.50)

The Elements of Internet Style: New Rules of Creating Valuable Content for Today's Readers
by Tad Crawford (6 × 9, 192 pages, paperback, $24.95)

Successful Syndication: A Guide for Writers and Cartoonists
by Michael Sedge (6 × 9, 176 pages, paperback, $16.95)

The Perfect Screenplay: Writing It and Selling It
by Katherine Atwell Herbert (6 × 9, 224 pages, paperback, $16.95)

The Journalist's Craft: A Guide to Writing Better Stories
by Dennis Jackson and John Sweeney (6 × 9, 256 pages, paperback, $19.95)

To request a free catalog or order books by credit card, call 1-800-491-2808. To see our complete catalog on the World Wide Web, or to order online, please visit ***www.allworth.com***.